Critical Muslim 38

Humour

T0322511

Editor: Ziauddin Sardar

Deputy Editors: Samia Rahman, C Scott Jordan, Ebrahim Moosa

Senior Editors: Aamer Hussein, Hassan Mahamdallie, Ehsan Masood

Publisher: Michael Dwyer

Managing Editor (Hurst Publishers): Daisy Leitch

Cover Design: Rob Pinney based on an original design by Fatima Jamadar

Associate Editors: Tahir Abbas, Alev Adil, Abdelwahab El-Affendi, Naomi Foyle, Marilyn Hacker, Nader Hashemi, Jeremy Henzell-Thomas, Leyla Jagiella, Vinay Lal, Iftikhar Malik, Peter Mandaville, Shanon Shah, Boyd Tonkin, Medina Tenour Whiteman

International Advisory Board: Karen Armstrong, Christopher de Bellaigue, William Dalrymple, Syed Nomanul Haq, Anwar Ibrahim, Robert Irwin, Bruce Lawrence, Ebrahim Moosa, Ashis Nandy, Ruth Padel, Bhikhu Parekh, Barnaby Rogerson, Malise Ruthven

Critical Muslim is published quarterly by C. Hurst & Co. (Publishers) Ltd. on behalf of and in conjunction with Critical Muslim Ltd. and the Muslim Institute, London.

All editorial correspondence to Muslim Institute, CAN Mezzanine, 49–51 East Road, London N1 6AH, United Kingdom.
E-mail: editorial@criticalmuslim.com

The editors do not necessarily agree with the opinions expressed by the contributors. We reserve the right to make such editorial changes as may be necessary to make submissions to *Critical Muslim* suitable for publication.

© Copyright 2021 *Critical Muslim* and the individual contributors.

All rights reserved.

C. Hurst & Co (Publishers) Ltd., 83 Torbay Road, London, NW6 7DT

ISBN: 978-1-78738-487-3 ISSN: 2048-8475

To subscribe or place an order by credit/debit card or cheque (pounds sterling only) please contact Kathleen May at the Hurst address above or e-mail kathleen@hurstpub.co.uk

Tel: 020 7255 2201

A one-year subscription, inclusive of postage (four issues), costs £50 (UK), £65 (Europe) and £75 (rest of the world), this includes full access to the *Critical Muslim* series and archive online. Digital only subscription is £3.30 per month.

The right of Ziauddin Sardar and the Contributors to be identified as the authors of this publication is asserted by them in accordance with the Copyright, Designs and Patents Act, 1988.

A Cataloguing-in-Publication data record for this book is available from the British Library

IIIT BOOKS-IN-BRIEF

Concise Summaries of Key IIIT Publications

The IIIT Books-in-Brief Series is a collection of the Institute's key publications produced as short, easy-to-read, time-saving editions, to act as companion synopses to the original.

Books-in-Brief Boxed Set

Contains 24 of IIIT's recent and most popular publications as condensed book summaries.

ISBN 978-1-56564-993-4

Contact:
Marketing Manager IIIT (USA)
500 Grove Street, Herndon,
VA 20170-4735, USA
Tel: 703 471 1133 ext. 108
• E-mail: sales@iiit.org
• Website: www.iiit.org

Critical Muslim

Subscribe to Critical Muslim

Now in its tenth year in print, *Critical Muslim* is also available online. Users can access the site for just £3.30 per month – or for those with a print subscription it is included as part of the package. In return, you'll get access to everything in the series (including our entire archive), and a clean, accessible reading experience for desktop computers and handheld devices — entirely free of advertising.

Full subscription

The print edition of *Critical Muslim* is published quarterly in January, April, July and October. As a subscriber to the print edition, you'll receive new issues directly to your door, as well as full access to our digital archive.

United Kingdom £50/year
Europe £65/year
Rest of the World £75/year

Digital Only

Immediate online access to *Critical Muslim*

Browse the full *Critical Muslim* archive

Cancel any time

£3.30 per month

CM38

SPRING 2021

CONTENTS

HUMOUR

ARTS AND LETTERS

REVIEWS

ET CETERA

HUMOUR

INTRODUCTION:
WE HAVE NO HUMOUR

Hassan Mahamdallie

I start with an admission. I have no idea how comedy and humour work. Sure, there are rules to writing comedy that one can follow – clash of context, tension and release, the ridiculously inappropriate response, and such like. But they don't really explain the magic of comedy. I am with Shazia Mirza, who declares, 'laughter is a beautiful thing. So, why ruin it by talking about it?'

I can tell you very little about the mechanics of making people laugh, despite having acted in theatre comedies, and having toured a few cabaret shows in the working men's clubs of the north of England, packed with hard-drinking rowdy audiences that have historically been the baptism of fire for aspiring comics. There is no worse feeling than to watch helplessly from the stage as pot-bellied men and their wives desert their tables, turn their backs on you, and walk to the bar at the back of the club in a show of contemptuous disinterest in your flailing antics.

What I can tell you is that when you get it right (in my case more by accident than design), and you have to stop while the audience roars with laughter, you do feel for a split second like you have harnessed some magical force. You can read as many learned intellectual treatises on comedy as you like, but trust me mate, that ain't going to help you when you're out there dying in front of a heckling audience in a sticky-carpeted club somewhere off the M62 motorway. Comedy must be a serious business, because when you have failed to elicit laughter from a group of strangers you are said to have died.

There are many claims made for comedy, some or all of which may be true: that it talks truth to power, it brings people together, that it's an essential element of the human condition, that it's as old as humanity, that it is transgressive and taboo-busting, it can heal (laughter is a medicine), it's universal, timeless, and so forth. All this is claimed for comedy, and yet the world is still full of miserable people.

Go figure, mate!

And true life has a tendency to outstrip even the most wildly imagined invented humour. One of the supremely grimly funny things I remember seeing is the diminutive comedian Norman Wisdom, who had a famous slapstick routine where his limbs would go rubbery and he would collapse to the ground, so completely drunk at the Epsom Derby race day that his legs failed under him and he collapsed to the ground. In his later years, Wisdom would become a national celebrity in communist Albania, hailed by murderous dictator Enver Hoxha, who was apparently his biggest fan.

When I was growing up in the UK in the 1970s, comedy rarely spoke truth to power. Instead of punching up, the comedy I saw nearly always punched down. I assumed that comedy and humour was just another cruel reminder of a hostile, bigoted society. The stand-up comedians you saw on the variety shows that were popular on a Saturday night after 9pm were almost exclusively males of a certain kind, and incredibly racist and misogynist when you look back on it. Les Dawson's mother-in-law jokes were keenly anticipated by his audiences:

> Actually, despite the things I say about the mother-in-law, I'm very fond of her. When she was ill last year, I said to the wife 'Don't worry – if she's at deaths-door, I'll pull her through'. (Audience laughter). I hadn't seen her for a fortnight. I was in a public house of dubious distinction and there she was lying on the floor of the bar, in a pool of spilt Britvic and cashew nuts. Six men from an oil-rig were hitting her with bar stools. One of my neighbour's said "So, are you going to help?". (Pause). I said no – six of them should be enough'. (Roars of laughter).

And then there was Bernard Manning. His stand-up set was simply a stream of homophobic, sexist and racist insults. He was as racist as you could get and clearly in sympathy with the far right. He had his own venue in north Manchester, the self-styled World Famous Embassy Club. Famous for what exactly – verbal slurry? In the early mid-1980s, the club burnt down. I was living nearby at the time. Me and my mates drove by it a few times cheering out of the car windows. Our celebrations were only slightly tempered by the rumour that Manning had it torched to collect on the insurance money.

Les Dawson and Bernard Manning were born into poverty in Manchester, both leaving school at the age of fourteen to go to work. They were Northern comedians of the old school, talented but toxic. They were an aspect of working-class culture – loud-mouthed and sweary- but they did not represent all of it. You were supposed to identify with them because they were working class – but interestingly enough it was the middle-class intellectuals and television programmers who stuck up for them and gave them TV and radio airtime. When Manning died in 2007, *Guardian* columnist John Moore wrote a glowing obituary that started: 'Yes, I know he was offensive, homophobic and racist – a self-confessed unpleasant man with few, if any, redeeming features – but there was something about Bernard Manning that I greatly admired. And I suspect many other readers of this blog will agree. Before you accuse me of being a narrow-minded bigot for finding him funny, I should point out that Manning, however distasteful to some, was only a teller of jokes, but had – in my 'umble opinion – the greatest delivery of any comedian I have ever seen. Humour is necessarily cruel; there has to be a victim.' Easy for you to say pal. And what's with the Dickensian 'umble' – do you think that's how the hoi polloi actually speak?

This defence of the monster that was Bernard Manning reminds me of the British establishment's undying love affair with the 1960s race-baiting patrician Tory Enoch Powell and their endless attempts to rehabilitate him. Racist comedians and TV sitcoms were so ubiquitous and mainstream when I was growing up, they generated a whole branch of left-leaning media-studies and academic careers. The racist core of British humour was so strong that talented Black comedians were forced to bend to its will and humiliate themselves and be humiliated.

Take the case of 1960-70s British Black comedian Charlie Williams. Born in the mining town of Barnsley in West Yorkshire, son of a local white woman and a coal miner originally from Barbados, Williams became a professional footballer before turning to comedy, hardened through performances in the northern club circuit. He had a broad Yorkshire accent, his catchphrase being *'me old flower'*. His speciality was to tell funny stories and he had great timing. But he would pepper his routines with racist cracks at himself:

It was so sunny today I thought I'd been deported.

If you don't laugh, I'll bring my tribe in and we'll eat the lot of you.

I invited a fellow round to dinner last night. Half-way through the meal he says, 'I don't like your mother-in-law.' So, I said, 'Leave her on the side of the plate and just eat the chips and peas'.

If he was heckled Williams would shoot back: 'If you don't shut up I'll come and move in next door to you', which would be met with roars of laughter, but actually wasn't that funny when you considered that during those times white 'residents associations' would organise to oppose or chase out Black families who moved into their neighbourhood and estate agents would have covert racist policies of not selling properties in certain areas to anyone who was not white. When I was young the man opposite us was so enraged by a brown family moving in to the house facing him, that my (white) mother told me he had never spoken a single word to her fifty years later.

You gotta laff!

Williams would throw in racist epithets 'Paki' and 'Coon' to great comic effect. How satisfying and affirming that must have been for racists in the audience to see a Black man, talking like a white man with a broad Yorkshire accent and constant toothy grin, reinforce their prejudices. However, some of what Williams was trying to do was slip a little bit of irony in here and there: 'During the power cuts I had no trouble at all because all I had to do was roll my eyes.' But I reckon that was lost on most people, who took his self-debasement as a mark of their superiority, very much like they took the fascistic character Alf Garnett from the highly successful 1960s–70s BBC sitcom *Till Death Us Do Part* at face value. The sitcom was supposed to lampoon the character's bigoted behaviour, instead he became a cult hero for far-right supporters, for saying on prime-time TV what they dare not say out loud as often as they'd like to.

Charlie Williams would appear on TV comedy shows with Bernard Manning, thereby giving cover for Manning and his ilk to really push the boat out. Here's one of Manning's classics:

> Who wants to work? You slog your guts out, come home and the Paki in your road hasn't had to work, he's on social security.

So much to admire.

Eventually Charlie Williams 'the man' seems to have merged with his on-stage persona. He toured white supremacist Southern Rhodesia, which was the subject of an international boycott at the time. He ended his life defending the indefensible – the Golliwog label on Robertson's jam.

But even in those days there were oases in this desert. When I was young, I was transfixed by Saturday night TV appearances by Dublin comedian Dave Allen. There he was, sharp mod-style black suit and tie, black shoes, white shirt, gelled-down collar-length jet black hair parted on one side, perched on a bar stool in front of the camera, cigarette dangling between his fingers and glass of whiskey in reach. Unlike the legion of working class comedians, Dave Allen was middle-class with a pleasing Irish brogue. As he told the long, witty shaggy-dog stories, comic sketches and observational comedy he was famous for, he would scratch his cheek, revealing a stunted left forefinger, the top of which had been lost in a machine accident.

Unlike almost all the others, Dave Allen was always for switching the tables, and putting the underdog on top:

> The English have always considered the Irish a very strange nation. An Irishman applies at a building site in London for a job. The cockney foreman says 'Well, we're going to have to give you an intelligence test, aren't we?' And the Irishman goes 'Yes, of course'. The foreman says, 'What's the difference between a girder and a joist?' And the Irishman goes 'Well, that's simple, Goethe wrote Faust and Joyce wrote Ulysses'.

In contrast to Manning and the others, who seemed to get a free pass from the TV controllers, Allen would get into hot water. He had a gimlet eye for whatever political goings-on were current; and it was Allen and the likes of him who started the unpleasant but overdue task of dragging British comedy out of the gutter. I believe that many of the left-wing comedians in the UK who emerged during the Thatcher years of the 1980s, owe a debt to Dave Allen. I'm thinking of those who came to be known as alternative comedians, who I saw perform at benefit gigs during the Miners' Strike of 1984–85 and other political gigs, including Linda Smith, Mark Steel, Jeremy Hardy, Stewart Lee and Jo Brand.

Dave Allen was a religious sceptic, and a lot of his jokes took a pot shot at religion. This one, paraphrased by me, provides a taste. A priest and an atheist get into an argument. Frustrated by the atheist's position, the priest says: 'you are like a man in a dark room, looking for a black cat that isn't there'. The atheist replies: 'in that case, there is only one difference between you and me. You claim to have found it'. When he finished his set, Allen would sign off every week with the same farewell: 'Goodnight, thank you, and may your God go with you'.

Allen, and his (non-existent) God, would have enjoyed the company of Muslim humorists of the classical period – such as Ashab the Greedy (d. 771), Ibn al-Muqaffa (d. 756/757), and al-Jahiz, (796–869). According to the noted Iraqi satirist Khalid Kishtainy, Ashab was 'the first professional wit and comedian in Arab history'. He was Caliph Uthman's jester and worked as an entertainer in Medina. 'With blue eyes, dark skin and peculiar face amenable to freakish distortions and grimaces, he could not fail to amuse his clients with his singing, dancing and tomfoolery'. 'Your father had a respectable beard', someone said to him, 'but you have a flimsy one. Who are you taking after?'. 'After my mother', Ashab replied. The sting in the joke is that Ashab was, it is said, illegitimate. Ashab's countless original, irreverent anecdotes would fill many volumes of Arabic works – and, indeed, they can be found in various volumes of *Kitab Al-Ghani* ('The Book of Songs'), the twenty or so volumes of encyclopaedic collections of poems, songs, and anecdotes that took Abu al-Faraj al-Isfahani (897–967), some fifty years to compile. Ibn al-Muqaffa, like Allen, was a sceptic; a Persian, he disliked Arabs as much as Allen disliked nuns and priests who beat him mercilessly during his school days. Known for *Kalila wa Dimna*, a translation from Persian of a series of maxims and anecdotes put into the mouths of animals and widely regarded as a model of elegant style, Ibn al-Muqaffa's satire and humour was largely directed at the rich and powerful. A regular target was the governor of Basra, Sufyān bin Mu'aviya, who happened to have a rather large nose. Ibn al-Muqaffa would greet him with *asslamo alaikum*ā (peace be upon both of you). Al-Jahiz was not only a humorist but wrote extensively on humour. Indeed, the sheer number of books he produced on humour is quite astounding: *Kitab al Nawadir* (Book of Jokes), *Kitab Nawadar al Hasan* (Book of Hasan's jokes), *Kitab al Mulahi wa Alturaf* (Book of funny stories and cosmic anecdotes), *Kitab ul Muzahik* (Book of laughing stock), *Kitab al Muzāh wa al Jidd* (Book of humour and fun), and the most famous of all, *Kitab al Bukhalā* (Book of Misers), which is still widely read today.

Al-Jahiz's take on humour is elegantly dissected by Hussein Abdulsater in his article, 'Humouring the Humourless'. Another famous humorist, atheist and lover of wine, Abu Nawas, himself lampooned by Ibn al-Muqaffa, is discussed by Samia Rahman in her review of a new translation of his poetry. As Abdulsater points out, a common assertion is that Muslims cannot take a joke. This contemporary assertion has a historic precedent. A number of Western scholars and writers, most notably colonial administrator and translator, Edward W Lane (1801-1876), English Orientalist David Samuel Margoliouth (1858-1940), and the Victorian novelist and poet, George Meredith (1828-1909), argued that Arabs had no sense of humour, and by logical extension, no civilisation: 'there never will be civilisation where comedy is not possible', wrote Meredith. We can dismiss such assertions with the contempt that they deserve.

However, one does need to understand the context to really appreciate Muslim humour. As Bruce B Lawrence's essay on Sufi Satire and Robert Irwin's excavation of 'Old Arab Jokes' (Well You Had to Be There Then) show, without context the punchline has little significance. Even the famous, universal anecdotes of Nasreddin Hodja, lovingly retold by Mevlut Ceylan, need a modicum of understanding of Islamic culture.

Recent emergence of comedy and satire in Muslim societies takes its cue from the resurgence of satirical press in the Arab world and South Asia during the eighteenth and nineteenth century. In the Middle East, the pioneers included Abdullah al-Nadim (1843-1896) with his humorous newspaper *Al-Tanlit wa Al-Tabkit* (Joking and Censure), while in South Asia Akbar Alabadi (1846-1921) regaled the populace with his satirical poetry which poked fun at both religion and modernity. This tradition can now be witnessed in how Arab comedians have wielded their art as a cultural

weapon against the encroachment of politicised religion, chronicled by
Gilbert Ramsey and Moutaz Alkheder in their article 'Let Him Wear it
Himself'. Given the popularity in the Muslim world of crazy preachers
inventing fatwas prohibiting everything from women wearing jeans and
driving cars to credit cards and yoga, satire is the only weapon one can use
against the increasing paranoid piety brigade. Indeed, there is a lot of
unintentional humour to be had in the realm of internet Islamic can-and-
cannot-ery. Here is a sample, randomly picked, of some wise words of
advice from the inimitable islamweb.net:

> Question: *As salam ualaikum*. We have automatic washing machine. The water
> pours down on the clothes but the detergent is put on the clothes first then the
> water pours down on these clothes. Some clothes are above the level of water
> flow … (other) clothes are below the water flow … If the cloth above the
> water flow is impure in 1st round then the detergent may also get impure but
> if the impure clothes is below the water level then all the clothes will be
> considered pure and the detergent also?

> Answer: All perfect praise be to Allah, The Lord of the Worlds. There is no need
> to panic about this issue. If water pours down on the clothes and drains without
> having changed due to impurity, then the water is pure, and so are the clothes.
> The way of pouring the water in washing machines is known. Allah knows best.

As Ziauddin Sardar once said to me: 'For the sake of Allah, Hassan, don't
convert anyone else to Islam, there are more than enough of us in the
world as it is!'

It is fascinating and life-affirming to see humorists emerging from
various Muslim communities, skewering the absurdities in relations
between Muslims and between Muslims and non-Muslims. Interestingly,
they seem to be more numerous in those countries that have been the most
gung-ho in the war on terror, including the USA and the UK. Little did we
realise that Colin Powell's slapstick turn with a vial of pretend anthrax at
the United Nations as a pretext to war with Iraq, and Tony Blair's 'dodgy
dossier' (how we laughed until we cried!) would lead, years later, to
Millennial Muslims on stage and on TV cracking jokes about religion and
politics in front of mainstream audiences. As Eric Walberg perceptively
argues in his essay on 'Comedy and Islam in America', 'there has been an
explosion of Arab and south Asian stand-up comics in the past two decades,

coinciding with 9/11. It's as if Muslims and all 'brown' people, regardless of religion, were pushed so far onto a terrorist limb in public perception, that the only way to deal with it is to laugh, and Muslims in the West rose to the challenge of defending themselves and their heritage with the only weapon they had - the word'. How true.

In Britain, Shazia Mirza was a leading pioneer. I saw her live at a gig in the executive lounge of Charlton Athletic football club in south London (don't ask why). One of the prerequisites of being a stand-up comedian is that you never turn down a gig. In 'Laughing Matters', Mirza writes of the gigs she has done all over the world, including in a toilet in Norway. 'It was a public toilet where I could only fit in eight people; luckily it was a sell-out. I stood on top of the toilet seat holding a microphone telling jokes to local people'.

Apart from Shazia Mirza, one of the first stand-up Muslim comedians (or at least Muslims who is a comedian) I saw perform live was Prince Abdi. This was some years ago, but I'm glad to say he is still around, working the clubs. He has since been joined by a growing number of other UK stand up performers of Muslim heritage. Take Fatiha El-Ghorri, who proclaims herself to be from 'the deep, deep middle east of Hackney'. You have to know the unique crazy nature of the London Borough of Hackney and its denizens to get this one fully. (Ziauddin Sardar also hails from Hackney, which may go some way to explaining its reputation). Fatiha, like many Muslim comics, plays on the perceptions of Muslims, and the mis- and non-understandings:

When I was growing up in school, they used to tease me. They used to say

'Did your mum call you Fatiha 'cos you're fat?'

(Aside to audience) Yeah, laugh it up because you're going to hell anyway.

And I used to be like 'Listen up, yeah, Fatiha's the first chapter in the Quran, it means the beginning or the opening right. What does your name mean, Lisa?...'

(It's noticeable how many Muslim women stand-ups start their show: 'Hi. By the way I'm not Malala'.)

When I see Muslim comedians and humorists at work, I immediately see a direct connection between them and the truly innovative canon of Jewish comedians and writers of the twentieth century, especially in America - Sit-coms. A good example is Ramy Youssef's award-winning series *Ramy*, a semi-autobiographical tale of a New Jersey American-Egyptian young man, trying to navigate between society and religion, which has so many echoes of past Jewish New York family sitcoms. It is the world of the immigrant outsider, nose pressed up against the glass, gazing into the sweetshop of modernity. So, in *Ramy*, you have our young hero straining against religious strictures surrounded by temptation, the middle-aged mother who spoils him rotten, the hard-working strict immigrant father, the resentful caged-in sister, the larger-than-life uncle, the otherworldly religious leader (played by the magnificent Mahershala Ali) and the bunch of mates who give the character Ramy harmless but useless advice. But *Ramy* is none the worse for its Yiddish antecedents. Quite the opposite – it gives him the opportunity to reinvent an already established and rich tradition in American cultural life.

The other distinct observational humour in America is that of the African-American comedic tradition, but that does not come out of the immigrant narrative; it comes out of slavery, Jim Crow, the violence of poor urban life and the Black cultural traditions of resistance and joy. For me, without any doubt, one of the most talented and complex truth-tellers in the English-speaking world is Dave Chapelle, whose work, and the pitfalls he has faced, is eloquently deconstructed by C Scott Jordan in his article on the difference between satire and parody, and the dangers that face humorists in navigating a spiralling insane reality. 'While other comedy shows provided escape', Jordan writes, 'Chappelle essentially said buckle up because we will take reality for the ride it is'. Chapelle is a Muslim, and his faith gives impetus and meaning to his work, rather than providing him with content for his routines. In an interview with US chat-show host David Letterman in October 2020 Chapelle told how he converted to Islam in his teens. 'I wanted to have a meaningful life, a spiritual life, not just what my hands can hold,' he said. 'I felt like I've always had this notion that life should mean something.' Chapelle at his best, teeters between the cracks in US society – class, race, power and lack of power, civilised talk and barbarous acts. I like to call my chosen artform, theatre, the playground of dangerous ideas. It has that spatial dimension, the tangible feel of a citizens' arena and the infinite possibilities of the imagination. Comedy is similar. All forms of art, in their specific way, have the ability to act as spaces for contested ideas and representative thinking, where the outer limits of the truth can be put into play, possibilities pursued, and human consequences revealed. Stories are not virtuous in and of themselves; they are imagined vehicles by which human traits, thoughts, and actions are put to the test by external circumstances.

There is always the chance that attempts at irony and satire, in a world constantly outstripping our deepest fears, can end in situations where we fall through the cracks. As we all know from our early years, playground games can often quickly turn menacing. In his essay 'My Sardonic Tweet,' Hussein Kesvani retells the incident when he sent out a playful tweet that rapidly provoked an international crisis: 'It involved a late-night tweet, a number of far-right organisations and influencers, multiple hospitals across London, and a mischievous paediatrician, who had been allegedly whispering Islamic prayers into the ears of new-born children'. Kesvani uses this incident to map out the ways in which social media particularly is so mired in Islamophobic and hateful cesspools, that it takes a tweet or a joke taken out of context to suck Muslim humorists down into its lower depths, from which they may, or may not emerge. Kesvani talks with up-coming Muslim comics who tell him they employ 'varying degrees of self-censorship' to avoid getting into hot water that might bury their career at its very beginning. This is a common thread to all Muslims working in the arts. This pressure on Muslims to self-censor that which they place in the public arena, is described by Brazilian radical theatre-maker Augusto Boal as 'the cop in the head'.

This pressure to play safe inevitably curtails freedoms of expression that other artists take for granted (and fiercely defend as a universal right). Sometimes it seems like everyone can have their unbridled take on Muslims, except perhaps Muslims themselves. So good on those who rise to that challenge. Kesvani points to the ire stirred up by rising stand-up Nabil Abdul Rashid, who reached the finals of *Britain's Got Talent* in 2020. He managed to rile the TV audience so much with his (fairly mild but heartfelt) stand-up routine against racism, Islamophobia, and for Black Lives Matter, that the TV watchdog Ofcom got more than 3,000 complaints against him, to go with the death threats he received. He got 1,000 complaints for observing that the British police are racist against Black people and another 2,200 the next week when he hit back against the criticism saying: 'They complained because we said Black Lives Matter – thousands of complaints. To be honest I'm shocked that many of them know how to write. They sent in thousands of angry letters. Hopefully if I annoy them today, they can progress onto words.' It was satisfying to see Abdul Rashid double down with this joke about Covid social distancing:

> They constantly make out Muslims to be this force that's trying to take over Great Britain, as if we're trying to take over the culture here. It's so upsetting, they're trying to make out that we are at war with Britain when we're not. While I was out I noticed that people were not shaking hands, they were walking far apart from each other, the pubs were closed and people were covering their faces (pause) and I was like Ooh! We've Won! We Won! Alhamdullilah! (camera switches to judge Amanda Holden laughing uproariously) We won! *La ilaha illallah!*

HUMOURING THE HUMOURLESS

Hussein Abdulsater

'Muslims can't take a joke'—remarked many Western observers. They were commenting on recent occasions when some Muslims reacted violently, oftentimes with tragic consequences, to what others viewed as instances of freedom of expression in comical caricatures: the Danish cartoons (2005), the *Charlie Hebdo* caricatures (2015) and the most recent resurgence resulting in the murder of a French schoolteacher and others (2020). I hear this remark and laugh. It is funny, primarily in a specific sense that the Islamic tradition preserves: 'the worst affliction is that which causes laughter' (*sharr al-baliyya mā yuḍhik*). Have we sunk to comic lows?

Of course, there is much pain in reflecting on this remark as well. Recalling that among the definitions of the human being is that she is a 'laughing animal' (*al-ḥayawān al-ḍāḥik*), it seems that there is an implication—if unintended—that Muslims, in their enmity to humour, are excluded from the universal condition of humanness. But aside from moral outrage, these charges simply make no sense. Before the advent of modernity, Islamic civilisation was the most expansive human experiment to date: geographically, demographically, and culturally. No civilisation could have prospered as much for so long without tolerating humour; much of what we go through as humans, whether in the mundane details of daily life or the grand schemes of history, merits little more than a good joke.

Nevertheless, these observers are probably onto something. Just as humour is a universal human trait, its opposites and contraries, such as being earnest, serious, solemn, sad, angry, and vengeful, are equally human responses. As a result, throughout Islamic history many learned voices were uncomfortable with humour. More often than not, they appealed to religion as the moral justification for their various criticisms of what they saw as the invocation of inappropriate jokes and an invitation to unacceptable laughter. This is not to say that their position was at any point a majority view, but they clearly left a mark on the tradition as a whole.

For Muslims, the Prophet is the best moral example. Whether the best is synonymous with the perfect is a different question; whether it implies absolute sinlessness and total infallibility, are questions we leave to earnest theologians! The Islamic tradition, in its full confessional diversity, imparted sayings from the Prophet in which he praises humour and establishes its benefits. The tradition also preserves anecdotes that clearly show him engaging in gentle humorous exchanges. Muhammad's sense of humour crossed ethnic, social and gender lines: with Suhayb, a poor companion of Greek background who was suffering from ophthalmia; with an elderly lady who was anxious about whether she will enter paradise; with Aisha, Muhammad's competitive wife trying to beat him in a camel race.

His humour was often reciprocal. We read an account where the Prophet is eating dates with Imam 'Alī—his cousin, son-in-law and future caliph. As the two went through their meal, a pile of date pits grew in front of 'Alī, whereas the Prophet's side remained clean; he was liberally amassing the pits of his dates with 'Alī's. Eventually, Muhammad noted the huge pile in front of 'Alī and teased him: 'you are such a voracious eater!' Not to be outdone, 'Alī retorted: 'the truly voracious eater is the one who eats both the flesh and the pits of his dates, O Messenger of God!'

There is, therefore, little doubt about the essential goodness of humour in Islamic teachings. Often the problems appear once we turn our attention to details. Jurists, as befitting of them, tried to carve out a taxonomical classification, a grid of values, that would squeeze acts of humour into the categories of law: obligatory, recommended, licit, reprehensible, or prohibited. We eventually end up with a typical list of legal qualifications. It is okay to engage in humour, as long as you avoid hurting others, disrespecting proper religious values, wasting your time that ought to have been used productively. For Muslim jurists, the *fuqahā'*, this is probably both good and necessary, as it means subjecting one more realm of human experience to the corrective influence of law. For others, it may mean coming close to killing this experience; dancing in shackles might appear as dancing for some, but for others it is nothing but being shackled!

From the broader intellectual perspective, though, it is not difficult to detect a general strain of discomfort with humour. Many authors who decided to include funny material in their work dedicated prime real estate in their introductions to justify their decision to include humour. As if they had violated an unspoken code of morality or a tacit intellectual standard. These authors usually argued that communicating jokes and compiling other humorous materials were licit and beneficial. But often these same authors emphasised the auxiliary value of humour as the handmaid to more serious intellectual endeavours. They intended humour to provide respite from the exhausting demands of theological, legal, linguistic or historical discussions. In so doing, wittingly or unwittingly, our authors implied that unlike these serious discussions, humour had no intrinsic value. I was about to say, the joke is on them!!

In both introductions to his *'Uyūn al-akhbār* (*Choice Narratives*) and *Adab al-kātib* (*The Education of the Bureaucrat*), the traditionalist Ibn Qutayba (d. 889) deals with the problem of the stern puritanical (*mutazammit*) reader. In a mixture of dismay and condescension, Ibn Qutayba instructs his readers not to assume that everyone shares their aversion to humour. Moreover, he invokes the example of the Prophet and early Muslim behaviour to argue for the permissibility of humorous discourse. But Ibn Qutayba is noticeably reserved in his advice. For he always makes sure to qualify the kind of humour he believes is permissible: it must be truthful, timely, and without any trace of foul language. Still, his restraint seems to have not fully removed his doubts, for he concludes by saying humour is neither vile or wrong, neither a grave sin nor a minor one—*inshā'allāh*.

The same Ibn Qutayba, in his *Ta'wīl mukhtalif al-ḥadīth* (*The Interpretation of Conflicting Hadiths*), attacks his older contemporary, the Mu'tazilī theologian al-Jāḥiẓ (d. 868-9), for the latter's sarcastic commentary on material that traditionalists believed to be prophetic *hadith*. For Ibn Qutayba, Jāḥiẓ went too far in his mockery of traditions. For example, traditionalists believe the Black Stone of the Ka'ba was initially white but turned black thanks to the sins of infidels in Mecca. Jāḥiẓ wittily retorts that, well by the same token, it should have turned white after all those Meccan people converted to Islam. Ibn Qutayba did not find this funny—rather, he concluded his commentary on a dark note. Citing a line of poetry to the effect that 'one ought only to commit to paper what she would be glad to face on the Day of Judgement,' Ibn Qutayba thus turned his objections to Jāḥiẓ into an ominous prediction about this wit's otherworldly lot. George Carlin, the American stand-up comedian, known for his dark comedy, would have rejoiced in Ibn Qutayba's sanctimonious attitude on humour. It is almost a textbook example of Carlin's observation: '*have you* ever *noticed* that anybody *driving slower than you* is an idiot, and *anyone* going faster *than you* is a maniac?' '

Upon closer examination, it seems that Jāḥiẓ had given more serious thought to humour. Although he penned a whole treatise titled *Fī al-jidd wa-l-hazl* (*On Earnestness and Jest*), his infamous lack of system and his penchant for sarcasm did not allow these thoughts to develop into a theory. Later scholars felt that even the clumsy title of his treatise ought to be re titled, *In Earnest and Jest*. Jāḥiẓ appealed to the examples of the Prophet and early Muslims to satisfy the traditionalists' need for humour to be traced back to the Prophet, just as Ibn Qutayba would later do. But Jāḥiẓ provides more elaborate justifications for his position on humour. He saw it as a necessary ingredient of proper life, invoking various branches of scholarship to aid his cause. Appealing to the commonplace theory of premodern medicine about bodily admixtures, Jāḥiẓ argues that laughter serves as the first sign of good health in babies. Laughter helps with the absorption of nutrients into their tender bodies. Jāḥiẓ then enlists the support of the linguistic usage of pre-Islamic Arabs. This was almost a necessary normative anthropological practice in the crucible of ethnic tensions during the formative period of the emerging cosmopolitan Islamic empire. The Arabs, he notes, who often chose names like Ḍaḥḥāk (Laughing One), Bassām (Smiling One), Ṭalq and Ṭalīq (Cheerful, Jovial One) for their children is proof of the privileged place of laughter in their worldview. More critically, he invokes the ultimate theological justification. Jāḥiẓ who was aligned to the Muʿtazilī school, believed that God does only what is good in itself. In other words, moral acts do not derive their value from the identity of the agent but can be judged on their own merit. Thus, when the Qur'an declares that 'it is He who makes to laugh, and that makes to weep, and that it is He who makes to die, and that makes to live' (53:43-44), Jāḥiẓ seizes the opportunity to draw two conclusions. First, laughter is the counterpart of life, just like weeping is the counterpart of death. Second, since God cannot ascribe a vile act to Himself, laughter must be good in itself.

Having established the essential goodness of humour, Jāḥiẓ turns to the more controversial details pertaining to its quantity and quality. The easier part concerns the quantitative requirement. Jāḥiẓ perceptively notes that in humour people are prone to err on the side of excess, not of deficiency. Consequently, he acknowledges that humour becomes problematic when it is excessive. A serious and instructive conversation can become silly and ridiculous with excessive levity. This leads to a discussion of the more intricate, qualitative requirement.

It seems that Jāḥiẓ was reluctant to make a clear-cut distinction between humorous and serious discourse. The two are always intertwined, just like fruitful debate (*munāẓara*) and a useless quarrel (*mirāʾ*) are linked. Thus, he repeatedly states that for an author to maintain the attention of readers and listeners—for books were still largely read out loudly to audiences in his day, she needs to strategically include humorous material; otherwise, the benefit of the book, for which it was authored in the first place, would be lost. Therefore, such occurrences of humour should be properly considered as instances of earnestness and sagacity. Conversely, when jokes are told in a pedantic manner, with unnecessary attention to wording and a disproportionate wariness of mistakes, they cease to be entertaining, nor are they instructive.

Nevertheless, when Jāḥiẓ is asked to choose between the value of humour in comparison to earnestness, he rejects the binary choice. Some people argued for the superiority of humour; while others believed it to be equal to seriousness. Instead, he surprisingly counters by saying that a serious discourse is better than a humorous one. However, he introduces a subtle distinction: one must look at the function of each discourse in the general context of human interaction: to be earnest is better in general, but in some cases humour is superior. The reason humour is treated with caution is that unlike injustice and perfidy, which, for a Muʿtazilī, are absolutely evil, humour is morally ambiguous. Humour needs to be exercised in the right amount and at the right time. Otherwise, it can lead to enmity, especially when it becomes a pretext to insult others.

Not much remains in Jāḥiẓ's corpus regarding the requirements that make an account a funny one. In general, he emphasised how authorial choices affect the reception of any text. Therefore, if the author intends to entertain, she should avoid using language that is more suitable for solemn occasions. More concretely, if we are conversing about the pleasures of life and the joys of living, we should avoid citing reclusive individuals and stern jurists as authorities on the subject of joy. The same holds for the composition of amusing discourse. Because the efficacy of any account depends strongly on the characters involved. Thus, we ascribe amusing accounts to individuals renowned for their sense of humour; the characters make these accounts funnier than they really are, just like ascribing good jokes to boring people would render them dull.

In a rare personal admission, Jāḥiẓ states that among the funniest things for him is to watch ignorant people engage in intellectual debate in the manner of theologians. Let us remember that he thought theologians to be among the elite of the Muslim society and Muʿtazilī theologians to be among the elite of the elite. Let us remember, too, that he held traditionalists in exceptional disdain—usually calling them with the pejorative terms, like Nābita (Whippersnappers) and Ḥashwiyya (Ignorami) and firmly associating them with the uneducated. It comes as no surprise, then, that he turns his acerbic tongue against them (among many others). Usually, he presents some of their beliefs as case studies in the extremely funny discourses of ignorant individuals engaging in intellectual discussions. Such case studies include examining their beliefs about moral history and the mythical worlds of various species of animals. How did it transpire that mice, apes, pigs, elephants, rabbits, spiders and catfish were originally humans who went through a metamorphosis as punishment for heinous sins? Why do dogs refrain from barking at anyone who utters the name of the dog that accompanied the Sleepers of the Cave, alluding to 'and their dog stretching its paws on the threshold' (18: 18)? What is the name of the jinn that was heard chanting upon the assassination of the prominent companion Saʿd b. ʿUbāda (637)?

For a detailed example, Jāḥiẓ looks into a relevant Qurʾanic passage 21: 69-70: '*We said, '*O fire, be coolness and safety for Abraham!*'* They desired to outwit him; so We made them the worse losers'. Some traditionalist exegetes, such as Muqātil b. Sulaymān (d. 767), who wrote one of the earliest extant commentaries of the Qurʾan, marked by a strong literalist and anthropomorphist character, used this passage to justify an alleged prophetic injunction to kill geckos by invoking the animal's alleged role in setting Abraham ablaze. In accordance with his disdain for traditionalists, Jāḥiẓ wickedly comments on a belief popular among 'ignorant folks' who used to kill geckos for this presumed crime. Indeed, geckos deserve punishment if proven guilty, he concedes. But Jāḥiẓ is quite unsure whether the geckos of *his* time were involved in that ancient misdeed! Furthermore, it is unclear how those folks verified individual geckos' guilt, or whether the whole species is collectively and thus eternally, responsible.

Which brings us back to Ibn Qutayba. Of course, personal disposition plays a crucial role in defining the threshold of acceptable jokes. People can share the same ideological commitment or religious conviction and yet, still be very far apart in terms of their sense of humour. But regardless of personal disposition, what incensed Ibn Qutayba seems to have been an ideological consideration. The quantitative consideration in Jāḥiẓ's humour—excessive or not—is beside the point. It is the qualitative consideration that irked Ibn Qutayba, particularly Jāḥiẓ's sarcastic attitude towards what Ibn Qutayba and his ideological allies believed to be a sacred component of religion.

Traditionalists in general, and Ḥanbalīs in particular, seem to have allowed for a narrower range of humour in what they considered to be religious matters. This is not surprising in itself. If the sacred is less conducive to humour than the profane, then intellectual trends in which the sacred is more acute, if not less expansive, will naturally have to deal with more challenges in this regard. For theologians like Jāḥiẓ who often appeal to abstract speculation, the sacred tradition is smaller in size than it is for traditionalists. And, to his mind, the pronouncements of this sacred tradition frequently fall short of being endowed with sacred *authority*.

Still, some traditionalist scholars—probably driven by a strong personal disposition—found a way to capitalise on this opportunity to exploit the use of humour. The great Ibn al-Jawzī (d. 1201), who played an instrumental role in propagating the Ḥanbalī school of Sunni jurisprudence in his native Baghdad during the twelfth-century, invoked an impressive group of traditionalist authorities who narrated humorous reports with impeccable chains of transmission (*isnād*). His point was that such highly revered past figures could not have concurred on dissenting from the tradition by endorsing humour. Even more so, Ibn al-Jawzī included a number of accounts that can be religiously irksome—especially for more rigorist schools of thought. For example, he quotes the early traditionalist ʿUthmān b. Abī Shayba (d.849), reading the verse 26: 130 from the Qurʾan. But instead of reading the verse as 'when you assault, you assault like tyrants!', he reads, 'when you assault, you assault like bakers!' —ʿUthmān has misread the Arabic *jabbārīn* as *khabbāzīn*. The reason Ibn al-Jawzī could accommodate such material is that he titled this book *Akhbār al-ḥamqā wa-l-mughaffalīn* (*Accounts of the Dumb and Foolish*). Therefore, classifying these people—or these acts—as dumb or foolish provides an elegant strategy, even in the more conservative intellectual trends, to approach the uncomfortable juxtaposition of the numinous and the humorous.

The Islamic tradition provides vast support for humour. The injunctions of the Prophet, his own example, the behaviour of prominent early Muslims and the legacy of so many celebrated scholars suffice as evidence. Indeed, the material on humour would consume many fat volumes, and is not restricted to any specific group. Irrespective of sectarian, ideological, and disciplinary affiliations, or chronological divisions, there will be ample material for any reader seeking a good joke. These jokes would cover almost any profane theme, and so many—if not most—of the sacred ones.

But this is not to say that the Islamic tradition was a long uninterrupted celebration of the pleasures of laughter. Clearly, jokes about the most sensitive of themes—particularly the person of the Prophet—were not well-received. This thematic consideration notwithstanding, there is a salient common feature in the jokes touching on sacred matters: they all seem to be the work of Muslims and, given the nature of literary material, Muslim scholarly elites. Moreover, the context is mostly one in which Muslims have the upper hand even in humour. Internally, within an Islamic empire, or, externally, when such an empire was a global force to reckon with, Muslims had the last laugh.

What is new is having to deal with humour that touches on the most emotionally charged theme: humour by non-Muslims, at a time when the political and cultural power of Muslims is experiencing a historic low, both internal to majority Muslim societies and externally. It is true, as an eminent Orientalist recently noted, that an Islamic version of a movie like *The Life of Brian* is realistically inconceivable. Scenarios such as the Danish cartoons and the *Charlie Hebdo* episodes move from the realm of humour to the more theologically controversial realm of blasphemy. And, much more poignantly, it also recalls the humiliating memory of colonisation and its lasting tragic effects in the present. Thus, to think of such examples as the yardstick of judging Islamic attitudes to humour muddies the water. These factors, because of their irresistible potency, drastically blur our vision of the subject being analysed.

In the last century, the geopolitics of the world of Islam changed drastically. Among the most powerful changes is the disproportionate dominance, fuelled by lavish funding, of trends that are more puritanical and generally less humorous than most others within the broad Islamic tradition. Then came a mixture of poor theology and social despair, followed by the liberal sprinkling of the salt of arrogant sacrilege on the narcissistic wounds of injured Muslims. But let us cast this aside for a moment. Maybe it is also time that we learn from a tradition that left us so many choices and creative options when it comes to humour. This may well force Muslims out of their comfort zones; but this is the best way for a tradition to grow and mature, instead of being captive to the narrow horizons of its rigorists or the pernicious provocations of its adversaries.

Ostensibly in an act of fulsome praise, a man claimed that God favoured a senior 'Abbāsid bureaucrat over the Prophet himself. Astounded and dismayed, the bureaucrat demanded an explanation for such a bold and borderline offensive speech. The man was ready and promptly offered his justification. God in the Qur'an, he said, addresses the Prophet with regards to his compassionate relations with early Muslims in the following way: 'It was by some mercy of God that thou (Muhammad) were gentle to them; had thou been harsh and hard of heart, they (your followers) would have scattered from about thee'. Well, the man said, the bureaucrat was indeed 'harsh and hard of heart'. Yet, his followers are so committed and loyal to him, they are not discouraged by his harsh speech and conduct. The bureaucrat, Aḥmad b. Khālid, got the joke, was thoroughly amused and then richly rewarded the man for his humorous and kind thoughts.

SUFI SATIRE

Bruce B Lawrence

David Mamet has defined satire as 'a type of wit that is meant to mock human vices or mistakes, often ... to expose political missteps or social inadequacies in everyday life, sometimes with the goal of inspiring change.' It would be astonishing to most readers – Muslim and non-Muslim – to consider that a regional saint from the fourteen century, one whose primary language was Urdu (then known as Hindavi or Hindustani), spoke in Persian to his audience, not only spoke but spoke with such eloquence that his words are still remembered, his counsel revered till today. The words of Shaykh Nizam ad-din Awliya, also known as Mahbub-e-llahi or God's Beloved (d. 1325), are laced with what might be called 'Sufi satire', described in several instances below from his recorded conversations with diverse groups in his open forum or *khanqah* setting.

The impulse to collect saintly discourse is not unique to India nor represented solely by this Chishti master. There exists also a collection of impromptu reflections from Mawlana Jalal ad-din Rumi (d. 1273). A brief comparison highlights differences as much as similarities. The *Fihi ma fihi* (*Signs of the Unseen*) of Rumi was collected after his death by disciples. There is no dating for the selections, arranged in seventy-one sessions, some twelve pages long, others just a paragraph. The tone is apodictic, stressing how saintly behaviour reflects the ability to engage those in power without being subdued to worldly principles or pursuits. The referents are often the urbane, wealthy and powerful of thirteenth century Anatolia, whether jurists and scholars, courtiers or kings, and one imagines they must have been among the primary audience for the published version.

By contrast, the *Fawa'id al-fu'ad* (*Morals for the Heart*) of Nizam ad-din was collected during his lifetime, written down with permission from the saint, and later reviewed – and, one learns, also corrected – by him. There are 188 sessions, sorted out into five fascicles, the shortest seventeen meetings, the longest sixty-seven. They cover fourteen years of the saint at the peak of his public prominence, from early 1308 to late 1322, that is, from his-mid sixties to late seventies. He died in 1325 at about eighty-two years of age.

What is most remarkable is the diversity of those who came to him. His *khanqah* or public audience hall stood near the capital of Delhi by the side of the river Jamuna; it's cool refreshing breeze added to the serenity of the atmosphere. It comprised a big hall in the centre, with small rooms on both sides. An old banyan tree stood in the courtyard, somewhat away from the centre, yet its branches also provided shade to a part of the roof also. A veranda surrounded the courtyard, so a few men could sit there comfortably without obstructing the passage of others. Nearby was the kitchen.

The Shaykh lived in a small room of wooden walls on the roof of the hall. During the day he took rest in one of the small rooms in the main building. A low wall ran around the roof, but on the side of the courtyard the wall was raised higher to provide shade for the Shaykh and his visitors as they sat talking into the morning hours.

From early morning till late into the night, men from all walks of life and all strata of society—princes, nobles, officers, learned men but also illiterates, villagers and town folk—came to pay their respects to the Shaykh. There were persons who came for a short visit just to meet the Shaykh and to seek his blessings. There were others who lived in the *khanqah* permanently or temporarily and were of different categories, from elder followers to local servants. One of his senior disciples, Burhan ad-din Gharib, supervised the preparation and distribution of food in the kitchen and lived nearby.

What concerns us here is the element of satire that runs throughout the discourses of the Shaykh. Always it is aligned with self-criticism, embodied in the concept of *adab*, at once moral exactitude and literary pursuit. As Irfan Ahmad has aptly noted, *adab* in South Asia functions as literature, moral code, and cultivation of self for the collective good, so in *Morals for Heart*, we find a poet-saint, Amir Hasan Sijzi, recording the words of his master but doing so in language that mocks the very fame that make both the saint and his discourse so valued by visitors from near and far, from the upper and lower echelons of fourteenth century Delhi society. As if to discount his own claim to moral purity, Nizam ad-din turns to the topic of saintly fame in his initial discourse:

> Discussion turned to THE MEN OF GOD and how they OUGHT TO REMAIN HIDDEN till God Almighty Himself has decided to reveal their identity. The master then told a short anecdote about Khwaja Abu'l-Hasan Nuri—may God illumine his grave. 'O God,' he once prayed, 'hide me in Your country among Your servants.' From the Beyond he heard a voice: 'For God nothing is hidden, nor is God Himself ever hidden!' In the same connection, the master went on to tell another story. 'In the vicinity of Nagaur there lived a saint known as Hamid ad-din Suwali—may God grant him mercy and forgiveness. He was asked, 'How is it that after their death some of the saints are never remembered by name while in the case of others, their posthumous fame spreads to the end of the earth? What causes this disparity in the states of saints?' Hamid ad-din answered: 'He who strives to become famous during his lifetime—after he dies his name will be forgotten, while he who conceals his identity during his lifetime —after he dies his name will resound throughout the world!'

The irony of this account is that neither of the saints whom Nizam ad-din mentions – Abu'l-Hasan Nuri or Hamid ad-din Suwali – have become famous after their demise. They are remembered but not lauded in the biographies that abound about Muslim Sufi masters. Almost as if to redress the balance between the lesser known and the well-known, the next two episodes discuss very famous saints, first Shaykh 'Abd al-Qadir Jilani, arguably the most renowned and revered of all Sufi epigones, and Junayd Baghdadi, also esteemed among Sufis across time and space.

Yet the most frequent heroes in *Morals for the Heart* remain the lesser or nearly unknown saints, and again the value of these shout-outs to the marginal and oft forgotten is precisely in the *adab* or moral self-cultivation they project, often as a corrective to Nizam ad-dinn himself. In one conversation, after elaborating on the condition of saints as they die or soon after their death, he remembered a person from his hometown, Badaun. We are only told his name, Ahmad, and that he resembled God's most prized servants, the *abdal* or deputies:

> About THE DEATH OF SAINTS, he told this story: 'I had a friend in Badaun. His name was Ahmad. He was very upright and pious and possessed of the qualities of God's deputies (abdal). Though he was illiterate, every day he devoted himself to understanding juridical issues and their implementation.

And he would ask everyone he met about them. When I was on my way to Delhi, he also came to Delhi. One day we met in public. As soon as he saw me, he began to pummel me with legal queries. Then he asked about the health of my mother. He already knew about the affliction from which she had been suffering, but no one had told him about her death. I took it on myself to tell him that my mother had been blessed with God's mercy, that is, she had died. 'May you live a long life' was his rejoinder. But then he became bothered and vexed. He began to cry.' The master—may God remember him with favour—when he came to this point in the story also began to cry. So convulsed was he with tears that I could not make out what he was trying to say. In the midst of his weeping, these verses came upon his blessed tongue. I do not know whether they were connected to the story of that Ahmad or whether he recited them by association. The poem was this:

> Alas, my heart, your careful planning ill served
> To keep even one night for union reserved.
> But united to you or not, O friend, I
> Witness at least this separation preserved!'

After that he remarked, 'Sometime later this Ahmad departed from the abode of this world. On the night after his death I saw him in a dream. Just as he had during his lifetime, he began asking me questions about the law and its application. 'Why are you asking me about this now?' I protested. 'While you were alive that was a commendable vocation, but surely not after death!' In response he asked me: 'Do you really think that the saints of God are dead?''

There are several extraordinary qualities about this anecdote. The saint applauds his friend who is illiterate yet alert to the intricacies of juridical reasoning that depend on deep textual knowledge. His friend Ahmad is also deeply attuned to human suffering, not least the health of the saint's mother, and that conversation becomes so delicate and deeply moving that the saint dissolves in tears: he cannot say anything coherent or memorable apart from a poem, and a poem that evinces pathos. Yet in the immediate aftermath of that meltdown, Nizam ad-din observes that Ahmad dies, and he has a dream of him, a dream in which this illiterate friend is still pummelling him with queries about the law. Nizam ad-din loses patience, and wonders out loud how this deceased holy man can still be concerned about everyday matters requiring legal knowledge and juridical insight.

The query is a self-rebuke, a satire on saintly pretension, here framed as the moral of the entire story: 'Do you really think that the saints of God are dead?'

Monitoring of self, striving for humility along with sanctity – also recurs in other anecdotes, involving both Nizam ad-din and his master, Farid ad-din. He tells this tale of self-rebuke about Farid ad-din. The conversation was about the display of deference necessary in all interaction between the master and disciple, even, and especially, in seeking spiritual perfection, and it prefigures the 'ingratitude' of Nizam ad-din himself revealed in a subsequent conversation:

> Conversation turned to PROPER CONDUCT (of the disciple) TOWARD THE MASTER. 'I have heard from the lips of Shaykh al-Islam Farid ad-din— may God sanctify his lofty secret,' recalled the master, 'that during his lifetime he himself had committed an act of arrogance toward his spiritual master, Shaykh Qutb ad-din—may God sanctify his lofty secret. And it happened in his way: 'Once I asked permission from the Shaykh (i.e., Qutb ad-din) to go into seclusion and perform an inverted fast for forty days (*chilla*). 'There is no need to do this,' replied Shaykh Qutb ad-din—may God sanctify his lofty secret; 'it will give you notoriety. Moreover, no such practice has been transmitted from our masters.' I replied: 'The luminous moment (*waqt*) of God's presence is upon me, and I have no intention of seeking notoriety. I will not do this for the notoriety of it.' Shaykh Qutb ad-din fell silent. After this, for the rest of my life, I was ashamed of what I had said, and I have repeatedly repented of my hasty, disrespectful reply.''

The subtlety of this disclosure of self-censorship is evident in the gap between ascetic desire – performing a fast upside down for forty days – and personal comportment – yielding to the master on every point. It is almost as if that reverse rebuke from Farid ad-din anticipated the much larger rebuke that Nizam ad-din incurred, of special interest because it also involves praise for a saintly woman:

The recorder, Amir Hasan, always begins with his own act of submission, kissing the master's feet:

> I obtained the benefit of kissing the master's feet. Conversation turned to REVEALING MIRACULOUS POWERS. 'Before this time,' he observed, 'there lived in the locale of Indrapat a virtuous, elderly woman named Bibi Fatima Sam. I had seen her. She was a fine woman. She had memorised many

verses pertaining to *every* circumstance of life. I especially remember these two
lines from her:

> For love you search, while still for life you strain.
> For both you search, but both you can't attain.

'Once I was in the presence of this Bibi Fatima,' remarked the master. 'She
turned toward me and said, 'There is a man who has a daughter. If you want
to marry that daughter, it would be a good match.' I replied to her as follows.
'Once I was with Shaykh al-Islam Farid ad-din—may God sanctify his lofty
secret—and a yogin was also present at that time. Discussion focused on the
fact that some children were born without any inclination for the spiritual life
due to the fact that men did not know the proper time for sexual intercourse.
At that point the yogin began to comment that there are twenty-nine or thirty
days in each month. Every day has its special quality. For example, if a man
makes love the first day of the month, such-and-such a child will be born; if on
the second day, the offspring will be such-and-such, and he continued in this
vein until he had given his estimate for every day of the month.

'When the yogin had finished speaking,' said the master—may God remember
him with favour—'I asked him to repeat what he had said about the influence
of each day. As he detailed the qualities of each and every day, I memorised
them, and then I said to that yogin, 'Listen carefully and note how well I have
memorised what you said.' Shaykh Farid ad-din—may God sanctify his lofty
secret—turned to me and said, 'Of these things about which you are inquiring
there will never be an occasion for their use.' The master—may God remember him with favour—concluded: 'When I had finished telling this story to
Bibi Fatima, she remarked, 'Now I know what is your condition (concerning
marriage).' Then she added, 'Indeed, you are right not to seek marriage with
that young woman. I also have spoken with you just to please her father.'

The delight of this story is that the miraculous powers of this saintly
woman are not to produce some dazzling display of transformation but to
register the inner state of her interlocutor's heart. She is an expert on
intuition who also observes adab, correct behaviour, both satisfying the
father of a nubile daughter eager to marry the saint and affirming the
saint's disposition, due to his arrogance with his master, not to marry. The
added element in the story is the intimate, almost matter-of-fact exchange

with a yogin, who also attended the audience with Farid ad-din. There is no sense of unease or dispute about the yogin's reproductive inventory, just on Nizam ad-din's hubris in wanting to use it for his own advantage. There is never even a direct command to Nizam ad-din not to marry, though in fact he never does, becoming the only one of the formative Indian Chishti masha'ikh or saints to remain celibate.

Other instances of satire abound in Morals for the Heart. They include anecdotes that suggest inversion of value: the blind see, the illiterate read. Among those that highlight satire as insight is the following:

> The master continued to speak of THE MIRACLES (*karamat*) OF SAINTS. 'There was once a blind saint. An adversary came and sat down in front of him, wanting to test the saint. To himself he thought, 'Since this person is blind, there must also be some defect in his inner person!' Turning to the blind man, the adversary started to ask, 'What is the sign of a saint?' But as he was asking the question, a fly came and alighted on his nose. The man swatted it away. But it came back. He swatted it away again. A third time this happened, and in the mean while he managed to ask his question. 'The least of the signs of a saint,' replied the blind man, 'is that no fly alights on his nose!''

And then there is another anonymous person – pious and pure of heart – who, like Bibi Fatima, is graced with intuitive judgment:

> The master then began to speak about THE DISCOURSE THAT ONE HEARS FROM SAINTLY AND GRACE-FILLED PERSONS, and how such discourse evokes a pleasure that none other can match. For when you hear the same discourse from someone else it does not evoke the taste for God. Who can match the person who speaks from a station in which he has been touched by the light of divine intuition?

> In this connection he told the following story. 'There was a virtuous man full of grace. He was the prayer leader in a mosque. After prayer he would discourse on some of the dicta and spiritual states of saints. His words would bring comfort to those who heard him speak. Among those who came to hear him was a certain blind man; he, too, found solace in the prayer leader's words. One day the prayer leader was absent and the muezzin, whose job was to call the faithful to prayer, took the prayer leader's place. He also began to narrate stories of the saints and their spiritual states, stories of the same sort that the worshipers used to hear from the prayer leader. When the blind man

heard the discourse of the muezzin, he asked: 'Who is this who is reporting the dicta of the saints and telling stories about them?' 'Today the prayer leader is absent,' they told him. 'The muezzin is substituting for him and telling his stories.' 'Humph!' retorted the blind man, 'I don't want to hear such lofty words from every ne'er do well!' As he was finishing this story, the master— may God remember him with favour—became teary-eyed. 'He who does not have refined conduct cannot evoke the taste for God.' And then some verses from Shaykh Sa`di graced his blessed lips:

> Who else but I can try to talk of loving You?
> Since others have no basis, their words do not ring true.

While the above anecdote is more mockery than satire, it underscores yet again the importance of intent *(niyya)*, whether in conducting prayer, telling stories of saints, or even orienting oneself to the Ka`ba, a ritual necessity for all observant Muslims before performing *salat*. Again, it is the illiterate who often instruct those blessed with natural sight, as in the following anecdote:

Concerning PRAYER AND THE SPIRITUAL AWARENESS (huzur) OF PRAYER LEADERS, the master observed that the indispensable precondition for spiritual awareness is that the prayer leader absorbs the meaning of what he prays in his heart.

After that he told about a certain Muslim who was among the disciples of Shaykh Baha ad-din Zakariya—may God have mercy upon him. 'The disciple was known as Hasan Afghan. The man was a pillar of saintliness, so much so that Shaykh Baha ad-din Zakariya used to say: 'If tomorrow they ask me to bring forward one person from my household (dargah) as a representative to face judgment on behalf of all the others, I would select Hasan Afghan.' Once this same Hasan was passing through a town and arrived at the mosque in time for prayer. The Imam led the prayer and the people followed along. Khwaja Hasan also joined in. When the prayers were completed and the congregation had dispersed, he slowly went up to the Imam and said, 'Respected sir, you began the prayers and I fell in with you. You went from here to Delhi and bought some slaves, came back, then took the slaves to Khurasan, and afterward left there for Multan. I got my neck twisted trying to catch up with you. What has all this to do with prayer?!'

Then, to explain his saintliness further, the master said, 'Once they were building a mosque in such-and-such a place. Khwaja Hasan arrived there. To the people constructing it he said, 'Be sure to make the prayer niche pointing to Mecca (mihrab) here, for orientation to the Ka'ba (qibla) is in this direction.' Having said this, he pointed to a particular spot. A scholar was present there. He disagreed, saying, 'No, orientation to the Ka'ba is in another direction.' Many words were exchanged between them. Finally, Khwaja Hasan said to the scholar, 'Face that direction which I indicated and note it well.' The scholar complied with the saint's demand and verified that the Ka'ba was indeed in the same direction that Khwaja Hasan had indicated.'

After that the master began to explain THE SPIRITUAL STATES OF KHWAJA HASAN. 'He was illiterate. He could not read. People would come to him and, placing a piece of paper and a tablet before him, would begin to write some lines, a sample of poetry, a sample of prose, some in Arabic, some in Persian; of every sort they would write some lines. And in the midst of these lines they would include a single line from a verse of the Word of God. Then they would ask Khwaja Hasan, 'Of all these lines, which is from the Qur'an?' He would point to the Qur'anic verse, saying, 'It is this!' But you don't read the Qur'an,' they would protest. 'How can you tell that this is a Qur'anic verse?' He would reply: 'I see a light in this line that I do not see in the other lines of writing.'

Like others we have observed earlier, Khwaja Hasan is little known, and it is precisely his anonymity and his illiteracy that make him a moral compass for the *imam* or prayer leader, the *qibla* or direction for prayers, and also for the transcendent, translucent quality of the Qur'an. Even not knowing how to read, he could announce: 'I see a light in this line [from the Qur'an] that I do not see in the other lines of writing.'

The ability to see for the blind has as its obverse, the inability to see for the saintly person fixated on his or her saintliness. We have already noted several instances of self-critique, but there is also one about the illustrious master – Hasan al-Basri- recounted in this anecdote laced with satire:

After that the master remarked: 'You should imagine everyone whom you see as better than yourself, even though someone may be obedient and someone else disobedient, since it might be that the obedience of the former is the last of his acts of obedience while the sinfulness of the latter is the last of his sinful acts.' In this vein he told a story about Khwaja Hasan al-Basri—may God illumine his grave. 'He used to say: 'I imagine everyone whom I see to be better than myself. But one day I met my own retribution, and this is how it came to pass. I saw an Ethiopian sitting by the edge of the river. There was a bottle next to him and every moment he was enjoying himself by drinking from that bottle. There was also a woman seated near him. The thought crossed my mind: 'At least I am better than him.' Just as I was thinking this, a boat began to sink in the river. Seven people were in that boat, and all seven began to drown. The Ethiopian immediately plunged into the river. He rescued six people. Then, turning to me, he said: 'O Hasan, you pull out the remaining one.' 'I stood there stupefied,' remarked Khwaja Hasan. 'After that he said to me, 'In this bottle is water, and this woman seated next to me is my mother. It is to test you that I was sitting here. It appears that you see only the outer man.'

Not only does the anonymous Ethiopian oarsman display intuition, which we saw in earlier cases, but he also reverses the implicit racist bias of his saintly observer. It was not just the appearance of this man with a woman and a bottle in the middle of a river, but as an Ethiopian (or *habshi*) he was presumed to be in the lower, servile rungs of society, yet he showed himself to be not only moral and valiant but also a corrective for the saint, reminding him that the outer does not reveal the inner, and that he was sent by the One Beyond to test the saint in the Here and Now. What, of course, redeems Hasan al-Basri, as earlier Farid ad-din and Nizam ad-din had been redeemed, from their acts of arrogance is their ability to recall the moments and the exchanges in which they boasted and then to share with others the lesson learned from these exposures of their own lower, self-preening reflex.

While saintly miracles or *Karamat*, are constantly introduced, they are often couched in subtle exchanges that highlight the need to reserve rather than announce this distinct display of spiritual gymnastics. Consider the following episode where a saint's decision on when to perform his miracle redoubles his status as one of God's deputies or elect.

I obtained the benefit of kissing his feet (recalls Amir Hasan). I was experiencing some anxiety that day, for I suspected that someone had spoken ill of me to the master. When I obtained the benefit of sitting with him, the first words that came to his blessed lips were these: 'If someone speaks ill of someone else, the latter has the intelligence to discern and he knows this much, whether what has been said is true or false, and also what was the motive of the speaker.' When I heard his counsel, I became very happy. I submitted: 'The firm hope of your servants lies in this, that the master's intuition is the arbiter (hakim) in all matters.'

Conversation then turned to THE ABILITY OF SAINTS TO DISCLOSE MIRACLES. He told a story about Shaykh Sa'd ad-din Hamuya—upon whom be God's mercy. 'He was a great saint, yet the ruler of that city had no confidence in the truth of his spiritual state. One day the ruler passed by the threshold of the Shaykh's hospice. He sent one of his retainers to deliver this message: 'Tell this Sufi lad to come out that I might cast an eye on him.' The retainer went in and delivered the ruler's message. The Shaykh took no heed of what he said; he was engrossed in his prayers. The retainer came out and reported what was going on. The ruler's anger subsided. He himself went into the Shaykh's hospice. When the Shaykh saw him enter, he got up and greeted the ruler cordially. The two sat down together in conversation.

'Nearby there was a small orchard. Shaykh Sa'd ad-din signalled his servants to fetch some apples. When they were brought in, the Shaykh cut up a few apples. He and the ruler began eating the pieces. There remained on that tray a big apple. It occurred to the ruler: 'If this Shaykh has spiritual insight and miraculous powers, he will take this apple and offer it to me.' No sooner had this thought crossed his mind than the Shaykh reached for that apple, and picking it up, he turned to the ruler. 'Once when I was travelling,' he recalled, 'I came to a certain city. I saw a huge crowd milling about in that city. A juggler was performing for them. That juggler had an ass, and he had covered the ass's eyes with a blindfold. He then produced a ring in his hand, and gave that ring to one of the onlookers. Turning to the crowd, he announced: 'This ass will find out who has the ring.' Then that blindfolded ass began to move through the crowd. He sniffed everyone till he arrived in front of the man who had the ring. Then he stood still and would not budge. The juggler came and took the ring from that man.' When he had finished telling this story to the ruler, Shaykh Sa'd ad-din Hamuya remarked: 'If a man claims that he has the ability to perform miracles, he is equivalent to that ass, but if he doesn't make that claim and doesn't perform any miracle, someone might suppose that he doesn't possess spiritual insight. ' Having said this, he tossed the apple to that ruler!'

The power of this story is unleashed with the final tale of the juggler and the ass. Had the Shaykh simply tossed the apple to the ruler, he would have performed a *karama* but not undercut the narrow, egotistical intent of the ruler – to have the saint perform a miracle by tossing him the big apple. Through the extended story, the Shaykh is announcing to the ruler that he can perform such physical feats, but despite the glow of the big apple, its role is similar to the ring discovered by the blindfolded ass. It is literally an asinine trick but since there is a common expectation that saints should perform miracles, even the wary Shaykh must satisfy this egotistical urge, casting himself as an ass, the ruler as a mere onlooker, with God Himself a juggler.

The dalliance and delight of *Morals for the Heart* comes through the multiple stories within stories, as well as the clinching verse that marks many of these lessons. Not all are outright jokes but the clever turn of phrase or the emotive response of the master makes them memorable. Above all, it is the constant reversal of roles that provides the leitmotif for much of the satire, and even though political excess is only dimly critiqued, the limits of rulers, such as the ruler wanting a *karama* in the previous anecdote, is often highlighted, even when the reproach is cast as a moral story. The final citation involves an historical person, Tughril Khan, a Turkic slave officer during the Delhi sultanate who ruled Bihar and later part of Bengal. In this anecdote it is the servant who teaches the master, providing fitting closure to this brief reiteration of the subtle art of Sufi satire, originating from Shaykh Nizam ad-din, then recast with edifying simplicity and narrative skill by his disciple-poet, Amir Hasan:

> I obtained the benefit of kissing his feet [notes Hasan]. Conversation turned to THOSE EMPLOYED AS SERVANTS OF OTHERS. On his blessed lips came this statement: 'One should be less preoccupied with servile chores than with attaining peace of mind.' Then he told the following story. 'In former days there was a man named Hamid. In his youth he lived in Delhi as the servant of Tughril, that same Tughril who late in life had himself crowned as king in Lukhnauti. In short, this Farid became the servant of that Tughril, and he remained in his service till one day, as he was waiting on Tughril, a form appeared to him. 'O Hamid,' it asked, 'why are you waiting on this man?' Having spoken, it disappeared. Hamid was puzzled about who this could be. Then a second time, as he was waiting on Tughril, again that form appeared and asked: 'O master Hamid, why are you waiting on this man?' Hamid remained perplexed. Then he saw this form a third time, and again it asked: 'O master Hamid, why are you waiting on this man?' But this time Hamid rejoined: 'Why should I not wait on him, since I am his servant, he my master. I receive wages

from him; why should I not wait on him?' Replied the form: 'You are wise, while he is ignorant. You are free, but he remains enslaved. You are righteous, he is corrupt.' Having spoken, it disappeared. When Hamid understood what the form had said, he went to the king and announced: 'If I owe you some service or have unpaid debts, tell me; for I will no longer be your servant.' 'What nonsense are you speaking?' retorted the king. 'You must be mad.' But Khwaja Hamid stood firm. 'No, I will no longer serve you. I have been blessed with contentment.'

When the master—may God remember him with favour—came to this point in the story, I interjected: 'That form that appeared to Hamid was surely one of the men of the Unseen?' 'No,' replied the master, 'Whenever a man cleans his inner self of defilements, he will see many things of this sort. A myriad of such qualities exist in each of us, but on account of despicable deeds they remain occluded. Only when the inner self becomes completely translucent can a person recognise the many, many wonders within himself.' And then on his blessed lips came this verse:

> That musk-pod you seek will deep inside you remain
> For your fate is such that no scent of it you'll gain.

Making the inner self translucent through constant self-monitoring is the goal of the master's discourse, whether in verse or satire or both: the scent of the musk pod persists, at once alluring and elusive.

'LET HIM WEAR IT HIMSELF'

Gilbert Ramsay and Moutaz Alkheder

In late 2011, a short black-and-white clip from a speech delivered by President Gamal Abdel Nasser, in 1965, went viral on YouTube among Egyptian viewers. The clip shows the Arab nationalist leader on top form, relaxed and charismatic, working a raptured audience with the practised timing of a stand-up comedian. With mock solemnity, the president of the United Arab Republic announces:

> In 1953, we genuinely wanted to cooperate with the Muslim Brotherhood, so long as they went about things in the right way. I met the supreme guide of the Muslim Brotherhood, and asked what his demands were. What did he ask? He said that every woman who walks in the street should wear a headscarf …

The audience erupts in laughter at the absurdity of this proposal. One man heckles: 'Let him wear it himself!'. Nasser goes on:

> So, I said to him, 'Well, if that's what you say, then you want us to return to the days of Al-Hakim bi Amr Allah, who wouldn't allow people to walk by day, but only by night. I am of the opinion that each person in his own house can decide his own rules'. But he said, 'no, you are the ruler, you are responsible'. So, I said, 'well, sir, what about your own daughter in the faculty of medicine? She's not wearing a veil. If you couldn't get one girl to wear a veil, how am I to get ten million of them to do it by myself?'

It isn't hard to see why the video struck a chord with many Egyptians in 2012. As one Egyptian comedian observed, it conjures up nostalgia— among liberals, at any rate—for an apparently more secular past, one in which Islamists were treated not as serious political contenders but as people whose ideas and demands could be regarded as ridiculous.

In 2012, Egyptians with secular inclinations had reason to hanker for this apparent golden age. Following the 2011 revolution, the country's first ever free and fair elections ushered in a parliament overwhelmingly dominated by Muslim Brotherhood and Salafi candidates. Some months later, voters would bring another Muslim Brother, Mohammed Morsi, to power as president.

The year began with an ominous sign of what an Islamist-run Egypt may look like. In January, comedy actor Adel Imam—arguably the country's biggest celebrity—was sentenced to three months in jail, charged with 'insulting religion'. A few months later, another court deliberated over the fate of a group of popular writers and directors facing similar charges: Wahid Hamed, Lenin El-Ramly, Sharif Arafa and Nader Galal. All had, in the past, produced work that outwardly criticised political Islam.

The writers and directors were found not guilty, while Imam was cleared on appeal. It is also worth pointing out that the charges were not brought forth by the government privately, but by the activist Salafi lawyer 'Asran Mansur. Nonetheless, the fact that the cases went to trial at all, and particularly the issuance of a guilty verdict in the most prominent of them, was disturbing not just because freedom of speech was seen to be at stake, or even because of the fact that an actor was being prosecuted for things said by characters he played (or had played alongside) was superficially absurd. On top of all this, the offending films had been released nearly ten years earlier, in a political climate which had apparently welcomed them. For years, Islamists had been marginalised, humiliated and repressed. Now, the cases sent out a clear message: the boot was on the other foot. It was payback time.

But there is a problem with this neat analysis. In its almost ninety-year history, the Muslim Brotherhood and its numerous splinter groups, daughter organisations, and fellow travellers have faced repression in almost every conceivable form. It has been outlawed, manipulated, violently oppressed, and, occasionally, co-opted. Its leaders have been exiled and executed. Its followers, their families and their neighbours have been beaten and bombarded. And yet, for most of its history, this repression occurred, for the most part, offstage. Entertainment media, despite being used for propagandistic purposes throughout the Arab world, was generally slow to turn its attention to Islamists. Far from making them routine subjects of ridicule, for decades, entertainment media largely treated Islamists, militant or otherwise, as if they simply didn't exist. In this regard, Nasser's speech stands less as a product of its time and more as an intriguing false start. The film portrayals of Islamists in the 1990s, for which Mansur was seeking vengeance in 2012, were not the culmination of decades of humiliation. They were almost the first serious attempts by popular Arabic media to turn the weapon of ridicule against Islamism.

Reviewing the history of Egyptian film, we found forty examples that, in some sense, feature themes of problematic religiosity or terrorism. Of these, most do not address anything that could be described as Islamism, but focus on the supposed backwardness and obsolescence of aspects of traditional religiosity or on non-religious forms of terrorism. Of those that do address Islamism, fewer still are comedies; and even among these, most feature Islamists only peripherally. We did not find any film prior to 1994's *The Terrorist* where it can be said to directly address the subject of militant Islamism.

There are two questions to be asked in response to this. The first, and perhaps the most obvious, is 'why'? Why weren't Islamists an apparently suitable subject for mainstream comedy for such a long time, and why did that change? The second question, however, and the one that we address in depth here, is 'how?' When they were finally called upon to do so, how did Arab comedy writers go about negotiating social taboos and adapting the idioms of popular comedy to make Islamists an appropriate object of ridicule?

In a sense, though, there is nothing new about Arab comedians using their art as a cultural weapon against the encroachment of politicised religion. On the contrary, this history of Arabic literature and civilisation offers countless potential precedents.

We need to be cautious at this point. The clash between Islamists and 'secularists' in the Arab world is modern, not ancient. This is because both Islamism and secularism are, to state an obvious truism from an academic point of view, both products of modernity. Before European conceptions of the secular nation-state were introduced into the Middle East, the issue of whether to institutionally and formally distinguish between religion and politics was not even on the table.

Nevertheless, the perceived roots of the cultural conflict between Islamism and secularism do stretch further back, even to the origins of Islam. From the point of view of Islamists, a particular, essentialised reading of Islamic history is all but a definitional necessity. *Muthaqqafun* (Arab intellectuals) on the other hand, while not bound in this way, have drawn on the rebellious heritage of their cultural history, looking to previous golden ages such as the Abbasid era, when the flourishing of art and learning was accompanied by a spirit of libertinism that stood in self-conscious opposition to the stern demands of religious purists, in cultural production characterised by praise of wine-drinking, hashish smoking, bisexuality, philosophical speculation and religious tolerance.

'Wine poet' Al-Hasan ibn Hakami, better known by his nickname Abu Nuwas (the one with the sidelocks), is emblematic of such precedents. Abu Nuwas's poetry, which incurred ire and punishment at the hands of the religious authorities in his time, routinely mocked the sacred rituals and principles of Islam. As one believing attendee quipped during a seminar held at the University of St Andrews on Arabic satire, it contains 'blasphemy in almost every line'. Moreover, in lampooning the tiresomeness of the Ramadan fast, for example, or comparing the prostration of prayer to falling down in a drunken stupor, it has been argued that Abu Nuwas was not just being offensively funny. Rather, he was systematically advancing his own, mystical conception of Islamic piety.

A more explicit example of classical Arabic humour that takes on Islam itself can be found in the work of Abu al-'Ala al-Ma'arri, a celibate and vegetarian, believed to be an atheist, who wrote poetry that outrageously sent up key Islamic tenets. He even produced a spoof of the Qur'an, *Al-Fusul wa Al-Ghayat (Paragraphs and Periods)*, which seems to have been intended to refute the sacred text's key claim to inimitability, whereby Arab poets are challenged to produce even one *sura* (chapter) like it.

While these poets belong to the medieval past, the ideals that they supposedly stood for continue to be of relevance today, as evidenced by contemporary cultural struggles. In 2013, Al Qaeda-affiliated fighters in the Syrian town of Ma'arra beheaded a statue of Ma'arri (though it isn't certain they knew who he was, and may simply have objected to the existence of a statue). In 2015, the hand of Abu Nuwas, clutching a wine glass, was broken off his statue, located on the pleasant stretch of Baghdad corniche named after him. This action seems to have been incited by a local cleric who accused the statue of 'provoking Muslims by manifesting drinking alcohol, which is forbidden in Islam'.

Perhaps the most important precedent for our present purpose is a less well-known writer: Muhammad Ibn Daniyal. Ibn Daniyal is remarkable for two reasons. First, he appears to represent the only obvious example of a medieval Arabic comedy dramatist—one who has specifically served as a model and inspiration for modern-day Arabic comedians writing for theatre and film. Secondly, his writing didn't just serve to express a hedonistically liberal worldview. It seems that it specifically did so as an act of protest and resistance against a political project of religious intolerance.

There are other details of Ibn Daniyal's biography that resonate with contemporary events. Originally from Mosul, which was allegedly renowned as a redoubt of the drinking, carousing culture that Abu Nuwas' poetry previously idealised the city's fate, and that of Ibn Daniyal, was reshaped by the calamitous Mongol sacking of Baghdad in 1258. When, after an uprising, Mosul was also ravaged, Ibn Daniyal took refuge in Mamluk Cairo, where he worked as an eye doctor and acquired a reputation as a comic poet.

Egypt remained a bastion against the barbarian onslaught (as Arabs, Persians and Turks at the time characterised it). Its ruler, Mamluk Sultan Baybars al-Bunduqdari, had, in 1260, defeated the Mongols at the decisive battle of 'Ayn Jalut. And yet, as is often the case, this crisis was accompanied by a reactionary wave of social conservatism. Seeking the political support of Cairo's Islamic scholars, Baybars launched a puritanical public morality campaign in 1267, which included the banning of wine drinking and prostitution. The campaign was apparently violently enforced: 'Taverns were smashed, brothels torn down, and offenders severely punished'.

When, at a high-society dinner, the host was forced to announce that, due to the new restrictions, wine could no longer be served, Ibn Daniyal—a man renowned for his multifarious appetites—seems to have had enough. He responded by authoring a satirical poem sometimes called *Elegy for Satan*, a work which combines stunningly evocative portrayals of debauched carousing with deeply ironic humour, simultaneously spoofing the nostalgic spirit of classical Bedouin verse and offering mock praise to the sultan for his victory over the forces of darkness.

Presumably on the back of this, Ibn Daniyal received an invitation from an unknown promoter of shadow puppet plays, seeking to commission some new writing from him. This was rather remarkable, since Ibn Daniyal was a high-brow writer—a semi-official court poet, even—while the shadow play appears to have been regarded as a vulgar form of popular entertainment. This is akin to John Updike contributing to *Playboy Magazine*. Nonetheless, after considering the offer, he accepted, going on to produce what can confidently be described as some of the most outrageously and hilariously obscene writing created in a trilogy of plays, brimming over with debauchery, prostitution, gay sex and even coprophilia, alongside plentiful lamentations by the sinful characters about the difficulties of Baybars' new regime. In one section, the hero enjoins his lover to anally penetrate him while he is fasting. In another, a poem describes the goings on in a brothel in which a man '... jerks off alone ... aroused by a headscarf'.

Ibn Daniyal has been called 'the Arab Aristophanes', but perhaps it would also be apt to call him the Arab Rabelais. Just as Rabelais—in Bakhtin's assessment—crystallised and preserved the spirit of medieval European folk humour in *Gargantua and Pantagruel*, so too does it seem that Ibn Daniyal's trilogy of plays drew heavily on a bawdy, vigorously alive folk culture in which he was very much a participant observer. This, it is important to stress, was a culture which, for all its profanity, was by no means anti-religious in its core principles, as indeed neither are Ibn Daniyal's plays (at least on the surface), in which the debauched characters ultimately declare their intention to mend their ways and make the pilgrimage to Mecca. Moreover, the institution of the shadow puppet play was part and parcel of the experience of the Ramadan fast, just as it was once traditional in Christian Europe to celebrate Christmas with the sexually explicit genre of song originally denoted by the word 'carol'.

Centuries later, when theatrical comedy returned to Egypt, it came, as before, in the wake of a civilisational crisis precipitated by an invasion. This time, however, the invader came from the West rather than the East, and it was Egypt itself that was occupied by Napoleon's forces. The political response to this shock was not initially religious conservatism, but rather vigorous attempts by the country's new rulers to modernise society along Western lines.

The pioneers of Arabic comic theatre, nonetheless, find themselves in conflict with forces of religious orthodoxy. Marun Naqqash, a Lebanese Christian immigrant to Cairo, cautiously staged an adaptation of Moliere's *The Miser* in his home, but the performance was interrupted when the mufti, who was present in the audience, started to yell out advice to the cuckolded husband he saw onstage. Later, Ya'qub Sanua, an Egyptian Jew, got into more serious trouble by penning a play that made fun of the Islamic practice of polygamy when the ruling khedive (who had two wives) saw this as a personal slight. But this conflict was initially interpreted—as it would continue to be for a long time to come, though increasingly disingenuously—as a straightforward one between forces of traditionalism and progress. In fact, Jamal al-Din al-Afghani and Muhammad Abduh, often regarded as the founding fathers of political Islam, enthusiastically supported Sanua's efforts to establish a popular theatre (including a traditional puppet show alongside his Western-influenced live performances), seeing these as potentially powerful vehicles for politicising the masses.

Indeed, when Egypt did begin to develop a vigorous domestic tradition first of theatre, and then of film, it was not initially Islamic political agitators who represented a major obstacle so much as the institutionalised religious establishment. In her study of film censorship in Egypt, *Censorship: The Expressive Dilemma Between Writer and Producer*, Egyptian scholar Amal Fu'ad notes that laws enshrining the right of the pre-eminent theological institution Al-Azhar to oversee artistic production were established as early as 1911—a power successively renewed in a series of laws and decisions stretching over successive decades. In 1926, Al-Azhar blocked what would have been one of the first Egyptian films ever created: *Muhammad, the Prophet of God*. As the sheikhs of Al-Azhar increasingly mobilised behind a conservative political agenda, the situation reached a point where it seemed as if the official censors, who could, but were often afraid to stand up to the clerics looking over their shoulders, became as much the guardians of artistic expression as its primary obstacle.

This is not to say that the temporal rulers of Egypt adopted a laissez-faire approach either. Indeed, reflecting on the (already heavily censored) films that flourished after the 1930s, Egypt's revolutionary leader Mohammed Naguib complained primly about the 'silliness and indecency' of the country's performing arts. He opined: 'There is no film but that a belly dancer has arbitrarily featured in it. No wonder this happened, because it was just a reflection of the age we have lived in. However, nowadays, we cannot accept from the arts industry and its sponsors anything like what happened in the past.'

Caught between a clerical establishment deeply suspicious of the portrayal of anything pertaining to religion or religiosity, a political leadership demanding nationalist propaganda and a viewing public seeking entertainment, Egyptian entertainment media tended to settle on an escapist formula. The world portrayed on screen became a parallel universe depicting an absurd, carnivalistic fantasy of supposedly ordinary Egyptian life. For film scholar Iman Hamam, Egyptian comedies conform to what she calls the 'sha'abi genre'—deriving from the Arabic word sha'b (people). The key feature of this distinctively Egyptian, popular genre is the way in which it provides 'a distorted view of an already distorted reality' by means of 'temporal dislocation', the 'haphazardness of events' and a 'formulaic and fragmentary storytelling, characterised by 'awkward beginnings, abrupt endings and unconvincing plots'. The films, she insists:

> … highlight common social concerns relating to compromised masculinity amidst corruption and unemployment. The hero's excessive and unruly behaviour mocks social conventions, ruthless authority figures and the disturbed pretensions of class. And yet, for all their apparent subversiveness, these films ultimately end up reaffirming the status quo and maintaining the validity of those same institutions they mock.

It is tempting to suggest that the carnival element at the heart of the sha'abi genre is a more or less direct inheritance from the spirit and style of pre-existing street culture, including that of actual popular carnivals, like the mawlid festivals celebrating various Sufi saints, or occasions such as the Prophet Muhammad's birthday or even, in previous times, the annual flooding of the Nile. If so, then there is a considerable irony.

Film, television and radio are, of course, technically 'modern' media. But more than that, they were used very deliberately and systematically by Egypt's nationalist rulers from the outset as tightly controlled propaganda with the goal of selling to Egyptians the idea of Egypt as a modern, forward looking state. Modernisation, certainly in its nationalist heyday, meant aggressively campaigning against the supposedly backward, embarrassing and un-Islamic institutions of sha'abi folk culture. In short, it seems that Egyptian television and film comedy both killed and preserved the elements of popular festivity similarly to how Hollywood's great silent comedies relied on the skills of entertainers who had cut their teeth in the same popular music hall tradition that cinema was rapidly making obsolete.

Another irony can be identified. In its incorporation of this pre-modern popular ethos, it seems that Egyptian comedy was playing a double game. On the one hand, in presenting a vision of Egypt from which religion and religiosity were largely absent—a merry world of cheeky chaps and curvaceous temptresses with hearts of gold—it may have been reflecting a vision of the progress of a modern, secular nation. And yet at the same time, hiding the sacred symbols and practices of religion behind a discreet veil was, in a curious sense, a characteristically Islamic (or Sunni Islamic) attitude to media representation. Under this approach, storytelling was not a mirror of society, but rather an organ of the social whole with important, if not necessarily praiseworthy, functions. It was a safety valve for jovial impulses that were sinful but also natural, and profanity was not a challenge to religious morality, but its necessary and constant obverse.

At this point, it is useful to make some very general points concerning how the media sector works in the Arab world. For a long time after their introduction, broadcast media tended to be heavily centralised and tightly controlled by the state. In fact, in the case of radio, the states concerned were often not Arab, but the Western powers that were controlling or contesting the region. In a sense, authoritarian Arab media is an inheritance from authoritarian colonial rule. This began to change dramatically with the arrival of the first satellite television station and then the internet. With the emergence of pan-Arab media that paid little heed to national borders, came a large private sector with numerous competing channels. Nevertheless, it would be a mistake to imagine that these are free of political control. The satellites themselves (notably Nilesat and Arabsat) are owned by Arab governments (Egypt and Saudi Arabia, respectively) and the most important commercial channels are owned by tycoons who usually have a close political relationship with a state. Often, it seems commercial considerations are secondary to the advantage accrued from these platforms in terms of media influence. Then, of course, there are the channels, often very popular, which are directly owned and controlled by political actors, whether these be states or movements such as Hezbollah in the case of the popular and largely mainstream Al-Manar TV. For Arabs and other seasoned consumers of Arabic media, it is simply taken for granted that all channels ultimately exist in order to advance some propaganda agenda or other—a level of media literacy which, one could argue, remains comparatively lacking, but increasingly needed in the West.

Against this backdrop, despite changes in Egyptian society, the highly stylised forms of Egyptian popular entertainment came under increasing pressure. Anthropologist Lila Abu Lughod has shown how working-class Upper Egyptian women engaged with Egyptian dramas and the glamorous off-screen lives of their actors (particularly the women) without requiring or expecting that the lives and the values that governed them should in any way resemble their own. And yet, as pious ordinary Egyptians urbanised and began to establish a new, media-savvy middle class, this compact became more problematic. As Walter Armbrust, an anthropologist who specialises in Egyptian popular entertainment, points out, the numerous urban scenes in Egyptian films and television that featured few or any women wearing the hijab began to look less like a merry fantasy all could partake in, and more like a glaring and deliberate writing out of the experience of a vast swathe of people.

There were other reasons that seemed to prompt the push for the representation of Islamists—at least of a particular sort—on screen. For decades, the regime saw that dissident political Islamists, first the Muslim Brotherhood and later its more extreme and violent splinter groups, as representing a threat to national security. Islamists had famously attempted to assassinate Nasser and successfully killed his successor, President Anwar al-Sadat. The religious scruples of Al-Azhar clerics notwithstanding, there were sound political reasons for wanting to make cultural opposition to dissident Islamists visible.

Ahmed Salim, an Egyptian Islamist who has written about the cinematic representation of his ideological brethren, concurs, pointing out that Islamist characters in film and TV 'were very marginal and very weak until the beginning of the 1990s. Before that, neither Nasser, Sadat, nor even Mubarak in his first decade employed these two tools in their struggle with Islamists'.

Film scholar Hani Darwish offers an alternative perspective. In his view, the artistic motivation for making films about jihadis may not be as transparent as it seems. 'Terrorism', he points out, is an exciting, action packed subject that 'represents an excellent space for political thought' and is less likely to be confronted with 'the traditional censorship experienced by works which treat of political expression or dictatorship'. In short, it is important to be mindful of the possibility that films ostensibly about terrorists may be intended to, and be understood to, indirectly criticise the targeting of those in positions of power.

However, at the beginning of the Mubarak era, when Egyptian artists were first attempting to introduce Islamist themes to their work, these were initially rebuffed by the censors. Salim draws attention to *The Elephant*, a novel by Fathi Ghanem that Yahia al-Alami turned into a TV series of the same name. 'In this case, the censors intervened to remove everything related to this character just a few hours before the series aired. Occurrences like this were repeated on more than one occasion.'

This seems to imply that the religious establishment constituted the biggest obstacle, rather than a fundamental unwillingness on the part of Egyptian writers to broach the subject. Such things had happened before. Fu'ad quotes a former Egyptian film censor describing the struggle faced by 'the first film about extremism in the Egyptian cinema', *The Man from the Sixth District* (1984). Even after having 156 passages recommended for deletion, the film's backers struggled to get the film cleared, perhaps doing so by means of further concessions.

Salim suggests some reasons for this. There is, he suggests, a 'dominant tendency in modern Arabic culture towards covering up and concealment, believing that disclosing and displaying wrongdoing risks tempting people towards the very wrongdoing it seeks to fight.' This is a propagandist's dilemma that stretches well beyond Arabic culture.

Salim's second suggestion, one with which Darwish's account correlates, is, if not the most intellectually satisfying, certainly the most plausible. Despite everything that happened in the 1970s and 1980s, the assassination of Sadat notwithstanding, it was only in the 1990s that Islamism achieved enough momentum at every level of society that it became impossible for state media and the Egyptian media elite not to address it.

As we just noted, some Islamists had posed an immediate threat to the heads of Egyptian state since the 1950s. By the last two decades of the twentieth century, however, Islamism represented a more deeply entrenched and omnipresent threat to the established order. The most extreme manifestations of this were the campaigns of terrorist attacks launched by Al-Jama'a al-Islamiyya and Al-Jihad, both essentially offshoots of the Muslim Brotherhood. Often targeting the foreign visitors on whom Egypt's tourism industry depended, and sometimes killing Egyptian lives in the process, these attacks were a direct and palpable threat to sections of Egyptian society as well as political leaders. Though, attacks against individuals also escalated dramatically in the 1990s. In 1990, Rif'at Mahgub, the speaker of the Egyptian parliament, was assassinated by Al-Jihad. That same year, jihadis gunned down outspoken public intellectual Farag Foda. An attempted assassination of the Nobel Prize-winning novelist Naguib Mahfouz followed in 1994, and, one year later, President Hosni Mubarak completed the clean sweep of Egyptian presidents to face attempted assassination at the hands of militant Islamists.

By this time, Islamist movements were also able to present a direct cultural challenge to Egypt's media creators, which was just as threatening in its own way. As ostentatious public piety became increasingly mainstream—for example, a number of formerly prominent female actors decided to put on the veil and abandon their careers in what was now presented as an inherently sinful industry.

As producers, actors, writers, and directors began to fear for their careers and sometimes their lives, many began to see making a stand as essential. As a 1992 article in the *Christian Science Monitor* put it:

> Artists critical of Islamic extremism are not necessarily motivated by patriotism. It is also in their best interest to fight its spread. Muslim groups, critical of sex and immorality in the media, have an assassination hit list, which includes many artists. Adel Imam, the main character of 'Terrorism and Kebab' and the most popular actor in Egypt today, is on this list. Reportedly, he is under 24-hour police protection.

In short, by the 1990s, the perceived interests of Egypt's creative industries and government cultural policy had aligned, presumably outweighing any scruples felt by the religious censors. Where, according to Salim, writers had been impeded by government censors in their attempts to present Islamist characters, now the government was eagerly pushing for anti-Islamist films, and Egyptian film-makers were obliging, out of a genuine desire to do so but also in the hope of placing themselves in the government's favour.

There are several notable examples of this new enthusiasm. The television drama *The Family* and the abovementioned film comedy *Terrorism and Kebab*, both written by veteran screenwriter Wahid Hamid, were two. The former addressed Islamist extremism, but not humorously. The latter was a notably successful comedy, but one that touched on Islamism obliquely, via the character of a Salafi government employee who used incessant prayers as a pretext to avoid work. Particularly important is the 1994 film *The Terrorist*, written by Lenin el-Ramly, directed by Nader Galal, and starring Adel Imam, which is significant because it marks the first sustained portrayal of Islamist extremism in an Egyptian comedy—at least in the formal sense.

The considerable cultural significance of this film was recognised at the time and continues to be today. Despite being generally regarded as a work of indifferent artistic quality, it is among the most written about Egyptian films in in the scholarly literature in English and, to a lesser extent, in Arabic. It features in numerous articles and books on Egyptian popular culture, notably by Armbrust, Shafik, Khatib, Hammond, Baker, Allagui, and Najjar Leaman, and Ahmed Salim also devotes considerable attention to the film, offering the only extensive critique of the film from an Islamist perspective of which we are aware.

Despite the attention the film has received, however, it has not, so far as we are aware, been specifically analysed in the sense with which we are primarily interested in it—that is, as a work of *comedy*. This assumes that *The Terrorist* actually is a comedy—a point that could be contested. It is only sometimes referred to as such, and, as we will consider in due course, a good deal of the content is clearly not intended to be funny. The film, as with other Egyptian comedies, contains elements that resemble generic serious action and melodrama more than humour. Even the more convincingly comic parts are typically played rather straight, especially compared with the over-the-top clowning one would normally expect.

At the same time, cinema audiences going to watch *The Terrorist* probably expected a comedy and likely interpreted, at least some of the film, through this frame. Imam was, particularly at this time, primarily known as a comic actor, and Ramly, the film's screenwriter, was known as a comedy writer. Moreover, the film's essential plot depends on what is clearly a comic premise. When interviewed in Cairo, the late Hazem Azmi, a close personal friend and perhaps the most well-informed expert on Ramly's work, insisted 'the film is unquestionably a comedy—whether it is funny or not is, of course, another matter'.

The Terrorist, then, marks a pioneering moment in the development of anti-Islamist satire. As a popular film with artistic ambitions, it upholds elements of the *sha'abi* comedy formula and violates others. Much of what Hamam sees as integral to the genre is present, including the 'body swap' topos, the 'unruly behaviour' of the male protagonist, pretensions of class and the problem of compromised masculinity arising from socio-economic challenges. However, the film's central reversal is, for the most part, used to re-assert the dominance of state sanctioned ideology rather than challenge authority figures. It is also clear that the film is trying hard to be meaningful and shed the label of 'meaninglessness' that is typically applied to Egyptian *sha'abi* comedies, often intended as escapist films.

The plot of the film, in brief, is this. Ali (played by Imam) is a violent Islamist extremist. We know that he is an Islamist extremist because he and his fellow extremists dress in uniform white robes with full beards and completely shaven moustaches. We know that he is violent because at the outset of the film we see him leading a group who smash up and torch a Coptic jewellery store and then a video shop.

Soon after, Ali is revealed to be a simple, uneducated man in the thrall of a sinister and hypocritical sheikh, who speaks in stilted classical Arabic and demands unquestioning adherence to his every word. Ali, as with the protagonists of countless other Egyptian comedies, turns out to be sex-starved and desperate to get married, a fact which the sheikh uses to manipulate and control him, parading a potential fiancée in front of him. However, his hopes of marriage are dashed when, after shooting up a busload of tourists, killing a nearby Egyptian child but none of the foreigners, Ali is forced to go into hiding, where he is tormented by sexual thoughts and aroused when he catches sight of a buxom woman hanging out laundry on her balcony—another commonplace burlesque motif in such films.

Subsequently, Ali is dispatched on another operation, this time to assassinate public intellectual Fu'ad Mas'ud (closely modelled on the real life Farag Foda). In order to carry out this operation, Ali is obliged to shed his Islamist clothing in favour of jeans and a shirt, to shave his beard and to steal a car, which contains a briefcase belonging to the vehicle's owner.

When the operation goes awry, Ali finds himself on the run from the police, but is run over by Sawsan, a wealthy and naïve young woman from a liberal, upper-class family. Panicked, the family bring the unconscious Ali into their home, with the help of their neighbour Hani, a Coptic Christian doctor.

Based on the documents they find in the briefcase; the family believe the convalescent Ali to be a poetry-writing philosophy professor from Cairo University. Ali is initially shocked and morally outraged by the family's liberal lifestyle but gradually finds his prejudices challenged. He also becomes acquainted with Hani who, in an ironic subplot, turns out to be henpecked by his obsessively religious wife.

Just as he is beginning to build a relationship with Sawsan, who has fallen in love with him after reading what she believes to be his poetry, Ali sexually harasses Sawsan's younger sister Faten due to her revealing clothing and gregarious manner, which he considers signs of sexual availability. Faten then becomes suspicious and investigates Ali's identity, discovering the truth by contacting the real professor whose identity he has stolen. Meanwhile, Ali attends Sawsan's birthday party, at which he drunkenly travesties a religious sermon before collapsing. Shortly after recovering consciousness, Faten returns and exposes him, forcing him to flee, holding the family at gunpoint.

Returning to his jihadi comrades, though he no longer believes in their cause, Ali discovers a fresh plot against Mas'ud. He phones him up to warn him of the plot, but the intellectual, refusing to be intimidated into changing his plans to appear in public, dies a martyr. An aborted escape attempt brings Ali to the house of his adopted family, where he is slain in a hail of bullets, calling out their names as he collapses before their door.

As we already pointed out, and as the plot summary will have reinforced, the film is not a comedy throughout. It is unlikely that this generic heterogeneity—the distribution of identifiably comical and serious moments throughout the film—is accidental. There is balance in the film between laughter and what, following Billig, we might call 'unlaughter', which, more than just the absence of laughter, is the clear expression that certain things are not to be laughed at. This merits careful examination.

If we consider where humour is and is not made possible within the internal logic of the film, it seems that the key factor is the progress of Ali's character through four different incarnations. In the first, we are presented with Ali in his supposedly 'true' identity: an Islamist extremist and terrorist. These sections are fairly consistently melodramatic. Occasional flashes of comedy are permitted to peek through only when the rigid, fundamentalist personae slip a little, revealing the urges and frailties beneath. In a moment that could be interpreted as mockery, the sheikh character feasts on grilled meats, eating in a manner reminiscent of the culture of the Persian Gulf, one that is intended to appear savage and uncivilised to Egyptians. The moment is sinister and reveals an animalistic hunger beneath the veneer of religious propriety, but it can also be seen as comic. A more plausibly humorous scene comes later, when Ali finds himself sexually tempted. Though he is far from home and already operating incognito, Ali still has an Islamist appearance. But the Islamist persona is already beginning to slip.

In his second incarnation, the protagonist is forced to disguise himself in order to carry out the assassination plot. An irony here is that, although Ali is supposedly in disguise, it is tempting to see this version of him as the 'true' one: resourceful, attractive, invested with agency—a model of capable Egyptian manhood in line with Imam's other leading roles in previous films. These sections are devoid of even slightly comic moments. Instead, they follow the generic conventions of action movies.

The third iteration of Ali, which makes up the bulk of the film's plot, is the one in which the most comedy can be found. Here, Ali is forced to adopt not only a new appearance but an entirely false identity. This is a classic comic set up. So much so, that, according to Wickberg, it is quite literally the origin of the word 'humour' in its present sense in English.

Finally, at the film's dénouement, Ali re-adopts an identity similar to his second incarnation. In this situation, he is no longer in the thrall of the Islamists, but must pretend to be in order to try to escape. Once again, he is presented as tough and capable, and this section of the film is a mixture of action with a touch of melodrama and even tragedy.

This tonal division of the film is revealing. Ali, understood as a sort of distorted representation of the *sha'abi* everyman, spends the bulk of the film occupying one of two essentially false guises. One of these gives him a horrific, hateful yet pitiable facet—another comic aspect. When, however, he assumes his true identity, he is neither horrific nor laughable. Stripping Ali of fundamentalist trappings and his action-hero skills is essential not just to setting up an incongruously comical situation, but also to making him a viable subject for comedy.

Then, *The Terrorist* derives humour from Ali's situation in two ways. The first of these is familiar territory for Egyptian comedies: a working-class protagonist trying to fake it in an upper-class world. Unlike the pattern identified by Hamam, in which a cheeky, folksy anti-hero would exuberantly rise to this challenge, milking the situation for all it is worth and lampooning the stuck-up pretensions of those around him in so doing, in this case the joke is usually squarely on Ali, whose backwardness becomes an object of derision as he is baffled by seemingly ubiquitous products of the modern world like Nescafe.

There is, however, an arguably more sophisticated comic discourse also at play. Here, the humour revolves around a series of misunderstandings between Ali's inflexible, literal understanding of religion, and the more complex modalities of faith he gradually uncovers. In a lengthy discussion with Hani, Ali is pleased to find another person who takes religion seriously, unaware that their religions are not the same. On another occasion, Ali asks one of his hosts about a picture of Che Guevara hanging on the wall of his bedroom who, he is told, is:

> 'One of the most important *mujahidin*'.
> 'In Afghanistan?'
> 'In Cuba'.

In the linguistic theory of humour developed by Raskin and Attardo, it might be said that the humour in these lines derives from a 'script opposition'. For Ali, the word '*mujahid*' carries a very particular set of associations, all of them deriving from a narrow, exclusionary attitude to Islam. For his interlocutor, on the other hand, the word carries a more general meaning of anyone fighting for a just cause. The two scripts are linked by a visual gag in this case—Guevara's unkempt beard, which fits with the narrow reading assumed by Ali.

Another theoretical resource from the discourse analysis tradition which can be usefully applied in this case is AS Berger's typology of the comic and the tragic:

The comic	The tragic
Chance	Inevitability
Freedom	Determinism
Optimism	Pessimism
Survival	Destruction
The social	The personal
Integration	Separation
Low status	High status
Trivial	Serious
Lowly characters	Elevated characters
Pleasure	Pain
Cathexis	Catharsis

The section of the film spanning from the car accident up until Ali's unmasking contains numerous comic elements. The accident itself involves the comic element of chance, bathetically undercutting and thus ending the first 'action' sequence of the film. Even though Ali is trapped by his injury and because he is on the run, he enjoys greater freedom than before, as he is no longer hemmed in by religious restrictions and the demands of his leader—something which, intentionally or not, seems like a metaphor for the often-promised trade-off between personal and political freedoms presented by Arab dictators. This section is characterised by Ali's sometimes inept attempts to survive and adapt in this situation and, ultimately to integrate into a new society—one which can be read as a stand in for the Egyptian nation itself—a process involving numerous mishaps stemming from Ali's ignorance and low social status.

In sum, *The Terrorist* was a tentative step towards treating Islamist extremists as subjects for comedy. The film avoids being comical altogether wherever it directly encounters militancy or fundamentalist Islam, instead presenting their otherness as a melodramatically emphasised threat to the state. Similarly, in depicting the state's response, the film is never anything other than reverential. Comedy is confined to the domestic sphere and often the comparatively safe realm of class politics. But even here, a key ingredient is missing: neither Ali nor his upper-class hosts are capable of representing the rebellious, carnivalistic *sha'abi* spirit normally central to

Egyptian comedy. This reinforcement of social order based on class hierarchy without any legitimised conduit for rebellion seems to lend the film a rather stifling feel.

One could counter that the awkwardness of the way *The Terrorist* juxtaposes traditionally comic and tragic-action elements means that it works as a sort of meta-comedy, inviting the viewer to choose whether to live in the broadly comic realm offered by existing societal structures, or in the tragic one that will inevitably result from rebellion of the sort initially chosen by Ali. The risk here may be that some could see the dignity the tragic arc grants Ali's character, even as a villain, as preferable to the sometimes humiliating comic role he is thrust into.

As Armbrust observes, *The Terrorist* was a watershed moment in the sense that, after its release, Islamists became relatively commonplace in popular Egyptian film and television—the taboo was, apparently, lifted. However, most portrayals of Islamists on the screen before 2011 also tend to be even narrower and more stereotyped.

In comedies like *Hello America* (also written by Ramly, as the final instalment of his popular Adeela and Bakheet trilogy) and Youssef Maaty's *The Embassy in the Building*, Islamists represent a more or less undifferentiated mob of fringe loonies, who serve as a punch line in their own right. (Of these, the former is perhaps slightly more sophisticated in so far as it presents Islamism in the context of American hyper-individualism and consumerism.) Even in serious films with artistic ambitions, it is common to see portrayals without much more depth. Wahid Hamid's *Blood of a Gazelle*, for example, despite featuring a radicalisation narrative, nonetheless presents Islamists as de-individuated and mindlessly violent. A possible partial exception is *The Yacoubian Building*, which critic Ahmed Salim compares favourably with *The Terrorist* for its acknowledgement of brutality on the part of the security forces towards Islamists as a key factor in their radicalisation. But even here, Islamism is presented as a reaction to poverty, exclusion and humiliation; very little is said about its actual attributes.

One interesting exception to this, which came at the end of the period with which we are concerned, is the comedy *Three Men Deceive Her*. The plot of this film revolves around the misadventures of Nagiba, a young woman from a poor family who excels in academic studies, but is socially awkward and naïve. Entering university to study archaeology while holding down an elementary school teaching position, she is attracted, in turn, to three men: a Westernised playboy, a Marxist revolutionary and an Islamist television personality. Unlike most previous representations of Islamists in Egyptian films, the character of Sheikh Amir Hassan—probably a caricature of real-life Islamist Amr Khaled—is presented as suave and handsome, wearing a smart suit and with his own television programme. When Nagiba gets to know him better, however, this appearance turns out to be a façade. Amir's use of modern media is hypocritical—he scolds his adoring female followers for wasting time on Facebook, while simultaneously asking Nagiba to follow him. Even his eating habits display a similar double standard: he takes Nagiba out to a sophisticated restaurant, but proceeds to disgust her by eating simple Gulf style dishes of rice and meat, including bones and animal testicles (another trope present in *The Terrorist*). His teachings too are revealed as two-faced: on the one hand, he incites Nagiba to an act of rebellion, smashing pharaonic statues on the grounds that they are heathen idols (in shocking anticipation of the Islamic State's real life actions in this regard). But when asked to publicly comment on this, he condemns the act, using the smooth language of moderate Islam.

In its treatment of Islamism, *Three Men Deceive Her* represents a curious and, in some ways, jarring blend of the highly artificial world of Egyptian comedy and elements of realism, and not only in its central plotline. For example, various establishing shots throughout the film present groups of Egyptian students a significant number of whom, naturalistically, are wearing the hijab in a realistic modern style. The segment of the film dealing with Nagiba's dalliance with Sheikh Amir opens with her being consoled by two *muhajjibat* (women wearing the hijab) who are presented as pious, but not dangerous or unsympathetic. On the other hand, Nagiba (a working-class girl who, in real life, we would probably expect to wear the hijab herself, as well over 90 per cent of Egyptian women do) corresponds to the logic of film convention. For most of the film, she acts as if religion simply does not exist. When she does become religious, however, she immediately puts on an *abaya*, and transforms her school class likewise into a traditional-style religious *madrasa* (school). Nonetheless, the film is clearly innovative not only in the way in which it represents Islam and Islamism, but also in the way it extracts humour from the subject matter. While *Three Men Deceive Her* does invoke the old crude stereotypes of backwardness, savagery and ignorance, it relies more on incongruity than on simple mockery in order to obtain laughs. Islamists are funny now not so much because of their backwardness, so much as because of their duplicitous attempts to conceal their backwardness.

If Egyptian media took a long time to get round to representing Islamists on screen, it was still well ahead of most of the rest of the Arab world. Indeed, *The Terrorist* was seen as controversial enough for a number of other Arab states to ban it. This was not for a lack of appropriate vehicles for such an output. While Egypt was, and to a lesser extent it still is, the leading producer of Arabic entertainment media in general, most Arab states produced topical domestic comedy of their own. Operating within the limits of what Lisa Wedeen has influentially called 'licensed parody' or even 'licensed acts of subversion', a number of such television shows gave voice to the frustrations of citizens, while stopping short of directly blaming governments or proposing systemic change. Notable examples included *Buqa'at Daw'* (*Spotlight*) in Syria, *Bas Mat Watan* (*The Nation Just Died / Smiled*) in Lebanon, *Watan 'Ala Watar* (*The Nation on a String*) in Palestine, *Dababis* (*Needles*) in Jordan, *Caricature* in Iraq, and *Tash Ma Tash* (*You Either Get it or You Don't*) in Saudi Arabia. Some of these shows, or their successors, would go on to produce episodes tackling Islamist extremism—but only after the rise of IS had dramatically changed the cultural and political climate.

Where satirists did engage with Islamism, the examples conform to the same general pattern—it seems that Arab popular cultural production only addressed the topic when it became all but unavoidable not to do so. In Lebanon, *Bas Mat Watan* attempted a skit in 2006 involving a spoof interview with Hezbollah Secretary General Hassan Nasrallah, though this example is perhaps a tenuous one in so far as, for many Arabs, the Shia Islamism of Hezbollah, together with its focus on Israel, makes it categorically different to the extremism of groups like Al Qaeda. More directly relevant, by this rubric, are the sketches making fun of Sunni militants that were incorporated into the Iraqi comedy show *Caricature*, reflecting the violence that followed the US-led coalition invasion of the country. In both cases, these comic interventions prompted violent responses: *Bas Mat Watan* were forced to apologise after an outbreak of pro-Hezbollah rioting in Beirut. In Iraq, Walid Hassan Ja'az, one of *Caricature*'s stars, was gunned down by unidentified militants.

Probably the most important show to broach the subject of Islamist extremism was *Tash Ma Tash*. This is due to the fact that the series addressed the subject both earlier and more frequently than similar series elsewhere and also because it did so in the context of Saudi Arabia. This meant on the one hand that its creators were immediately face to face with the forces of Islamic fundamentalism at their most institutionally powerful, representing an important element within the Saudi state itself, and also that it was in a position to play a role within the wider context of the increasingly well-resourced and determined media campaign waged by the Saudi and Emirati states against Islamic 'extremism'.

On the face of it, Saudi Arabia was a radically different context to that of Egypt. While Egypt is a fiercely nationalist republic, Saudi Arabia is a monarchy run, at least theoretically, as an Islamic theocracy in which the Qur'an is the constitution and the Islamic *sharia* is the law of the land. Egypt had for decades been the most culturally exuberant Arab state, with a thriving film, music and television industry. Saudi Arabia's main cultural export, by contrast, was fundamentalist religion, while its traditional culture remained largely insular and unknown outside the country.

Even so, there were some notable parallels with the Egyptian situation. Saudi Arabia had its own history of anti-state religious insurgency, notably the shocking capture of the Grand Mosque in 1979 by millenarian radicals and, like Egypt, it had initially dealt with this by trying to sweep it under the carpet to some extent. As in Egypt, cultured Saudi elites had to battle with the power and influence of fundamentalist religion from both above and below. According to Saudi critic Abd al-Rahman al-Nasir, *Tash Ma Tash* did not feature any women characters for its first three seasons as a direct result of clerical censorship, a situation which changed only after a direct intervention from the Ministry of Information. Again, like their Egyptian counterparts, these restrictions from above were matched by increasingly vigorous cultural challenges arising from below in the form of an Islamist movement—in Saudi Arabia's case the *Sahwa* or Islamic Awakening movement—which commanded a loyal following from among a broad swathe of the emerging middle class.

Finally, in 2002, Saudi Arabia found itself dealing with a wave of jihadi violence bearing significant similarities to that experienced by Egypt in the 1990s. Like Al-Jihad and *Al-Jama'a al-Islamiyya* in Egypt, Al Qaeda in the Arabian Peninsula was the offspring of a longer history of domestic radicalisation. Like the Egyptian groups, it carried out domestic violence with a clearly internationalist agenda. In both cases, militants set out primarily to target non-Muslim foreigners within the country, but ended up killing locals in the process. Finally, and most significantly, both groups triggered concerted, if belated, efforts by the state to combat Islamist radicalisation by soft means as well as hard.

From 2003 onwards, Saudi-controlled media aired a number of documentaries and dramas on the subject of Islamist extremism, most of which treated the subject with great earnestness. These included *Al-Hur al-'Ayn*, a drama which was co-scripted by former Al Qaeda member Abdullah al-Otaybi and, apparently, actively facilitated by the Saudi government, which gave its writers access to state archives.

In treating this subject with grave seriousness, the comedy show *Tash Ma Tash*, interestingly, was initially not exceptional—at least, not completely. From 2003 on, the show began to focus much more squarely on issues of religious extremism, but it did so initially in two ways. On the one hand, there were episodes that dealt with absurd situations arising from Saudi Arabia's highly conservative laws and norms relating to issues such as the compulsory segregation of men and women or the prohibition on women driving. These episodes, among the most celebrated in the series, are bitingly satirical and extremely funny. On the other hand, however, the series also produced episodes which dealt with Islamist radicalisation and political violence head on. To begin with, episodes of this latter sort struck a very different tone, with comedy appearing to be all but absent, except occasionally, when very subtle black humour could be inferred.

These episodes (most of which were initially banned) include 'Nothing Makes Things Right Except the Truth', 'Oh Education!' and 'Blind Faith', among others. In each of them, Nasser al-Qassabi, a gifted comic actor and the leading star of the series, plays a moderate Muslim character pitted against the encroaching menace of Islamism. The Islamists are consistently portrayed as disciplined and cynical entryists, corrupting and co-opting Saudi institutions in order to brainwash young people into a militant and xenophobic mentality. In each case, these social processes are set against the backdrop of a changing and modernising society. Characters become vulnerable by, for example, travelling to live in an unfamiliar city, or by attending a mosque far from the family home. In 'Blind Faith', parents worry that it is no longer appropriate for their children to play out on the street, and so enrol them in a Qur'an recitation class which turns out to be presided over by a jihadi sheikh.

While, of course, they don't seek to be even handed, these episodes are significantly more subtle in their representation of the nature of Islamism and Islamists than most Egyptian portrayals. While some of the same tropes are used, with Islamists presented as sinister, cynical, hypocritical, blindly obedient and violent, they are seldom presented as obviously coarse or backward. The model of radicalisation they seem to invoke is closer to models actually favoured by political scientists. In the Egyptian film narrative, becoming an Islamist is explicable only as a result of extreme ignorance or nihilism, where in *Tash Ma Tash*, it is more about belonging. Finally, in these episodes of *Tash Ma Tash*, there are often significant attempts to engage with actual theological arguments put forward by extremists.

It was not until 2006 that *Tash Ma Tash* presented an episode that dealt with Islamist extremism from an overtly comic angle, in the form of 'Terrorism Academy'. Despite striking a very different tone, the episode is in some ways a continuation of the earlier episodes dealing with similar subject matter. This time, Qassabi plays an idiotic young man from the city of Jeddah who is staying with his uncle in Riyadh. Looking for an activity to keep him occupied, his uncle enrols him in what he thinks is a youth club, which of course turns out to be dominated by extremists who promptly brainwash him and send him on a suicide mission to blow up the American embassy. Unable to find the embassy, Qassabi's character returns, to the exasperation of his handlers, who decide to set up a reality-TV style talent contest in the hope of finding better recruits.

It should be obvious from this description that 'Terrorism Academy' is not a total departure from previous attempts by *Tash Ma Tash* to address the issue of Islamist extremism. It plays, for example, on the same theme of social dislocation. Where, exactly, does the humour in the episode derive from, and what is its discursive significance? There are two basic jokes in

'Terrorism Academy'. The first one is the ancient device of idiocy and incompetence. Qassabi's character is a straightforward clown. He is brainwashed with comical ease, because he doesn't fully understand what is going on. When he is tasked with carrying out an act of terrorism, we don't need to take it seriously because he is incapable of carrying it out. But Qassabi's character is also a sort of wise fool. When he is radicalised, he takes to imitating his fellow extremists' habit of addressing each other as 'my brother in Islam'. When he gets lost on the way to the American embassy, he stops and asks a passer-by, whom he also addresses as 'my brother in Islam', for directions. This is, of course, correct, since he is a Muslim, but the fact that it violates the convention of the Islamists reveals them, at least implicitly, as *takfiris* who believe that only they are the true Muslims.

The larger joke of the episode, of course, is the incongruity of juxtaposing Islamic fundamentalism with the triviality (and for such fundamentalists, immorality) of talent contests like *Star Academy*. At a superficial level, the joke here is simply this: the incongruity between strict religious propriety and the sexualised glamour that is normal on television. More deeply, however, the contrast seems to make the claim that despite being superficially grounded in Islamic piety, Islamist extremism, too, is really just a kind of show business. Terrorism, like pop-stardom, is about the self-regarding pursuit of fifteen minutes of fame. Unlike *The Terrorist*, this comic device makes it possible to represent actual Islamist terrorists as objects of fun. And yet there is still an important underlying similarity. The comedy in both cases requires transplanting the terrorists from their own realm to the glamorous, make-believe carnival that is the world behind the screen.

We end, chronologically, at the threshold of the Arab revolutions and the seismic upheavals that followed. Up to this point, attempts by comedy writing in Arabic to tackle the subject of Islamist extremism and jihadism were still rare and tentative, especially outside of Egypt. Nonetheless, an important precedent had been set, a foundation to be built on. What, exactly, did this foundation look like? What lessons can be drawn from these attempts?

The first lesson is straightforward: whatever development there may have been in society and media, it isn't easy in the Arab world to laugh at Islamists and get away with it. Doing so has been and remains dangerous on a personal level. Islamists make vindictive and frightening enemies, and state protection—if and where it is offered—can seldom be relied on. We have noted the prosecution of Imam and the key Egyptian writers who took on Islamists in the 1990s. In Saudi Arabia, the actors and writers of *Tash Ma Tash* faced numerous death threats and state censorship.

Even once the matter of personal danger is set aside, there is the issue of public scorn or indifference. The public popularity of *The Terrorist* was never as great as the importance accorded to it by critics. Today, the leaked version available on YouTube has a million views—respectable, compared with other popular Egyptian comedies—but of the four thousand people who have rated it, a quarter dislike it. 'Terrorism Academy', unlike other episodes of *Tash Ma Tash*, even previously banned ones dealing with extremism, is almost impossible to find online.

For those writers who have braved the subject, what are the key areas of commonality and difference? One important commonality is the way in which comedy has attempted to bring the fight with Islamism to the sphere of everyday life and the family. This is logical. Popular comedy is almost always concerned with everyman themes, and presenting itself as standing for the idealised everyman, triumphing against a mad and confusing system. But Islamism also seeks to base its power in this same realm, presenting family values and personal morality as under siege and their correction as the purifying step necessary to create a just society.

By pitting *sha'abi* characters against Islamists, or by placing Islamists in *sha'abi* contexts, popular Arabic comedy strives to reframe this, portraying Islamists as belonging to a perilous, strange world that sits outside the warm hearth of the comic realm, whether because they are literally foreign, as in the Egyptian association of Islamists with the customs of Saudi Arabia, or, as in Saudi Arabia, because they represent a source of social relationships with unknown strangers beyond the bounds of the local neighbourhood or the extended family circle. Despite claiming at one level to speak for progress against regression, what lies beneath is a clash of rival conservatisms.

Extracted from *Joking About Jihad: Comedy and Terror in the Arab World* by Gilbert Ramsay and Moutaz Alkheder, published by Hurst, London, 2020

WAR OF THE WORDS

Boyd Tonkin

'You believe that venerability and sublimity are to be found only in frowning. However, the books of jurisprudence don't say that laughter is a sin or is reprehensible and you – God protect you from envy! – are quick and intelligent.' (*Leg Over Leg*: 5.1.2)

'The rights of women are too many to list.' 'I have taken that in,' I said, 'lock, stock and barrel. But tell me, what sort of men do women love most?' 'If I tell you,' she replied, 'you'll kick up a row.' 'Speak,' I said, 'and don't worry! Conversation's carpet has been unrolled and will not be rolled back up until we reach its end.' 'At the End of Days, then!' she replied.' (*Leg Over Leg*: 4.9.13)

I.

Ahmad Faris al-Shidyaq (1805/06-1887) ended a long life full of jokes and paradoxes with a final farewell jest. Although buried in a Christian cemetery near his birthplace in Lebanon, he had asked for his grave to be marked with a crescent, not a cross. 'Intellectually and personally,' Rebecca Johnson writes, this piously sceptical Muslim Christian scholarly comedian was 'a series of irresolvable paradoxes'. One could, however, disagree – and the value of disagreement drives almost every verse or paragraph he wrote. The precious quality that will eventually resolve every paradox, inside the literary work if not in the warring world at large, is humour.

In al-Shidyaq's unruly, pioneering masterpiece *Leg Over Leg*, the hero's wife and soulmate has one complaint above all else about the 'Franks' – that is, the English and French – among whom the couple have passed several years. Forget the grey skies, the starchy manners and the quite deplorable cooking of greens. For all their wealth, the Franks, in contrast to the merriness of daily life in Cairo, Tunis or Damascus, just don't have enough *fun*. 'Life is not to be valued according to the length of its nights or the number of its days, by views of green land, or by observing instruments and machines. Rather, its value lies in seizing the convivial moment with those who are dear'. Banter lends shine and sparkle to our days, and 'The world's worth lies in exchanging *bon mots*.' (4.12.11) Good laughs and good sex, the narrator maintains, go hand in hand. They even rhyme. So let's hear it for a marriage spent in 'carousal' and 'arousal', 'in witty contestations' — 'and conjugal relations'... 'in joking' — 'and poking'.' (4.12.12) For al-Shidyaq, laughter really does make the world go round.

It counts as a pretty poor joke that it took 160 years for the all-embracing, all-conquering humour of *Leg Over Leg* to find its way into English — especially since its author devoted large chunks of his career to translations between that language and Arabic. Only a partial, flawed French version of this sprawling, unclassifiable, encyclopaedic book, first published in Arabic in 1855, had appeared before Humphrey Davies got to work on al-Shidyaq's maverick epic. Yet when New York University Press began to release the volumes of *Leg Over Leg* in a dual-language edition in 2013, it came as a thunderbolt of revelation to specialists as well as curious lay readers. Here was a genre-defying sort of total book from the Arabic *Nahdah*, or nineteenth-century Renaissance: a literary counterpart to the kind of *Gesamtkunstwerk*, the unified art-work, that Richard Wagner sought on the European musical stage at this time. But much funnier. Al-Shidyaq's not-quite-a-novel, but not-really-a-memoir-either, seemingly broke every rule, crossed every boundary, shattered every convention, in its tumultuous onrush of punning, ingenious, erudite, and acrobatic prose and verse. Learned opinions differ as to how much al-Shidyaq borrowed from the traditional forms of classical Arabic literature, and how much he imported from the 'Frankish' writing he read abundantly. As a headline designation of *Leg Over Leg*, it's not entirely misleading to call it the Arabic equivalent of Laurence Sterne's *Tristram Shandy* (which he knew well).

However you parse the Eastern and Western strands in its literary DNA, the book struck, and still strikes, its readers in English as a comet-like prodigy. It streaks across the sky of nineteenth-century culture, illuminating the entire firmament and redrawing our map of its literary stars. Humphrey Davies's heroic English version ranks as a marvel in itself. It matches the torrential original pun for pun, gag for gag, right up to the borderlines of orthodox translation – and then, when al-Shidyaq's unstoppable eloquence crashes through them, pulls some dazzling stunts of its own. Davies raids the furthest reaches of the English thesaurus as he pursues the author's compulsive logorrhoea. Miraculously, he finds equivalents for every hue of a stylistic spectrum that runs from the deepest purple lyricism to lurid shades of blue. After a (typical) twelve-page list of words for 'feminine charms', all the way from 'a thin, cute, jolly girl' to 'a female who slumbers deeply in the forenoon', al-Shidyaq for once wilts, and writes that 'I have no strength or energy left and imagine my reader doesn't either'. (2.14.30) Astonishingly, over the four volumes and 1100 pages (in the NYU Press paperback edition) of *Leg Over Leg*, Davies never seems to falter in his wit, invention and resourcefulness – like a scarily tireless djinn of words from the *Thousand and One Nights*.

Leg Over Leg may escape all definition, but newcomers do deserve a brief sketch of the principal contours on its outlandish map. To begin with, it tells the story of a life: that of 'the Fariyaq', its author's alter ego. The title page announces that '*Leg Over Leg or The Turtle in the Tree*' will concern 'The Fariyaq, What Manner of Creature Might He Be' and will recount his 'Days, Months and Years spent in Critical Examination of the Arabs and their Non-Arab Peers'. A separate voice narrates the Fariyaq's various adventures, although the storyteller and the autobiographical persona often overlap. Born near the start of the nineteenth century into a Maronite Christian family in a village in Mount Lebanon, the Fariyaq converts to the Protestantism brought into the area by missionary activity. As a youth, he clashes with the religious and political hierarchies of his community. He begins scholarly work first as an Arabic copyist for local emirs, then as a translator for missionary societies. His travels first take him to Egypt, both Alexandria and Cairo. He moves to Malta, where his professional status as a Biblical translator into Arabic grows, then back to Egypt. In Cairo he woos and eventually weds the woman who becomes his sparring partner, sidekick, conscience and bantering antagonist for much of *Leg Over Leg*: 'the Fariyaqiyyah'. Further journeys take him back to Malta, to Tunis and home to Lebanon, before translating commissions for the missionaries send him to London, Cambridge, rural Hertfordshire, and finally Paris, for long spells.

These elements of memoir and travelogue, however, just supply the bare skeleton around which the book's muscle, sinew and vital organs grow. It is also a euphoric celebration of the Arabic language itself, filled to bursting with lexicons, inventories and catalogues of all kinds that scour every corner of the historic word-hoard, and delight in the ribald, scurrilous and obscene byways of high and low vocabulary. It is a marathon stand-up performance, stuffed with puns and wordplay of every conceivable sort (from the title onwards, as *Leg Over Leg* alludes both to the traditional storyteller's pose and copulating limbs). It is a sort of epic rapper's act: not as loose an analogy as it sounds, since al-Shidyaq adores the virtuoso techniques of rhymed prose in Arabic, or *saj'*. They turn up on almost every page and sometimes settle into the formal rhyming narrative known as *maqamah*. It is, beyond all this, an eclectic sheaf of anthologies of poetry, from odes and quatrains to epigrams, love lyrics and rhetorical exercises of sundry types. In its grammarian's delirium, *Leg Over Leg* both mocks the lunatic excess of Arabic scholars and outdoes them in comical performative pedantry.

Its prose delivers sharp and witty satires too, on religious and social institutions and customs in Lebanon, Egypt, Malta, England, and France. Al-Shidyaq explores the nature of belief, the principles of the good society and – supremely – the role and rights of women, and the proper nature of sexual love and marriage. Many readers, I suspect, will come to cherish it above all as an extraordinary portrait of one marriage in particular. The Fariyaq and the Fariyaqiyyah debate, bicker, flirt, wrangle, snipe, canoodle, break up and make up, across the years, the countries and the continents they share. Perhaps only one other literary work of the 1850s can vie with *Leg Over Leg* in its compendious, miscellaneous, world-devouring genius: Herman Melville's *Moby-Dick; or, The Whale*. You might say that the great cetacean al-Shidyaq hunts is the Arabic language itself. Compared to his Lebanese contemporary, however, the New Yorker falls short in both jokes – and love.

II

The author, and the Fariyaq, warn the reader against treating this yarn as a reliable memoir. Do so and you'll fall into the category of slow-witted literalist asses for which *Leg Over Leg* always has an insult or twenty. All the same, the outlines of the Fariyaq's progress do (save for a couple of cases of scrambled chronology) follow Faris al-Shidyaq's adventures. In his youth around Mount Lebanon, he did scandalise the upland Maronite community by abandoning the denomination of his forebears for missionary Protestantism. The local church authorities persecuted, jailed and even tortured his brother Asad, who had chosen the same course. Asad's suffering and premature death casts one of the few tragic shadows to fall over the Fariyaq's odyssey. Its scorn for the Maronite hierarchy does not fade. Al-Shidyaq did sustain a long career as a theological translator for missionary bodies, primarily the (Anglican) Church Missionary Society and the Society for Promoting Christian Knowledge (SPCK). At the same time, while his official duties took him to Egypt, Malta, and then London, Cambridge, and Paris, he worked to become a noted Arabic linguist, poet, lexicographer, and editor. In Cairo, where he served Egypt's official gazette as well as translating the Bible and teaching Arabic to foreigners, he did court and eventually marry Wardah al-Suli, the daughter of a Roman Catholic merchant from Syria. He would immortalise her in *Leg Over Leg* as the quick-witted, sharp-tongued, back-chatting but generous-hearted Fariyaqiyyah.

Leg Over Leg closes in Paris in the mid-1850s. Al-Shidyaq's years of widest influence, however, were still to come. He quit the missionary translation business and moved to Istanbul. There he founded and edited *Al-Jawa'ib (The Answers)*: a pioneering Arabic periodical that helped root modern journalism in the Sultan's domains. He flourished in the Ottoman capital as a philologist and lexicographer, managed printing presses, and played a key part in entrenching print culture across the Levant as a luminary of intellectual reawakening in the *Nahdah*. He died, after a final trip to Egypt to consult on his new edition of a thirteenth-century Arabic dictionary, at Kadiköy on the Bosphorus in 1887.

Al-Shidyaq's formal conversion to Islam (hence the adopted name 'Ahmad') may have come around 1857, but everyday Muslim phraseology punctuates *Leg Over Leg*. Besides, the story of his double-coded resting-place suggests that he liked to keep his options open. *Leg Over Leg*, which mercilessly mocks the pomp, idiocy, and cruelty of puffed-up clerics but never simple faith of whatever stripe, hardly ever gets preachy across all its immoderate length. But when the narrator tells us that 'The wise and well-guided man sees in others only their common humanity, and any who pays attention to incidental matters such as colours, food, and costume distance himself greatly from what is central to humanity,' we don't need to doubt that the author speaks for once with no ironic veil. (2.1.19) On his return to Lebanon, the Fariyaq upbraids the Mountain emirs for their factional bigotry and tells them: 'Know, God guide you, that difference of views over religion does not preclude familiarity and friendship.' (3.12.25) Or, to put it even plainer, 'All people are God's children, and the person God loves best is he who is of greatest benefit to His children.' (2.1.19)

Like many satirists, even the most outrageous, al-Shidyaq comes across as something of a moral conservative. Yes, he can be richly obscene, bawdy, scatological, and vitriolic towards folly, ignorance, and arrogance in high places. And he does insist on the literary originality of his genre-busting work, proclaiming that 'I am no chain-man and will not form the rump of the line' in relation to earlier authors. Rather, 'I follow what I see to be good, seize what I find appealing by the forelock, reject the impositions of tradition.' (1.17.10) When it comes to religious and social customs, though, hypocrisy, deceit and pretence goad him into righteous mockery, not the faith of any humble believer. The Fariyaq is keen as well to honour the satirist ancestors who twin-tracked learning and piety in public office with scurrilous antics in print: 'the celebrated Dean Swift, though only one rank below a bishop, wrote a long essay on the anus.' (4.11.4) Al-Shidyaq goes on to enlist another of his most prominent European forerunners, one more wise-cracking cleric, in the uproarious combination of low jesting and high thinking: 'the first to follow the path of bawdiness was, I believe, the celebrated Frenchman François Rabelais, who was also a man of the church.' (4.11.4)

To paraphrase Oscar Wilde, his mouth may be in the gutter (as the Fariyaqiyyah regularly scolds) but his eyes are on the stars. On his travels, the Fariyaq always seems to be searching for a wise, just authority to compensate for the primal disenchantment of his flight from the corrupt emirs and patriarchs of his youth around Mount Lebanon. He never quite finds one – not in Cairo, Malta, Cambridge, or Paris – and his thwarted quest for an honest polity fuels much of his book's fulminating comedy. If the Maronite clergy disappoint, even disgust, him, then the Protestant missionary bureaucrats who give him his position and livelihood hardly escape the Fariyaq's whiplash tongue.

Throughout *Leg Over Leg*, al-Shidyaq shrinks the confessional rivalries between Christian sects in the Levant into a single, vastly extended, running gag. The region's Maronites and Catholics became 'Market Men', stationary stallholders and warehouse-keepers, while the itinerant Protestants go by the name of 'Bag-Men', wandering pedlars touting their wares from the back of some weary ass. Although a paid-up Bag-Man himself, the Fariyaq never forgoes a chance to ridicule the sectarian narcissism of small differences – much as Swift did in *Gulliver's Travels* with his Big-Endians and Little-Endians, going to war over how to eat a boiled egg. As for al-Shidyaq, in his rapper's *saj'* mode he upbraids the nit-picking clerics: 'were you placed in this world only to *quarrel?* Were you commanded to fight and *squabble?* How come the doctors of mathematics, geometry, and astronomy don't differ over their *proofs,* or if they do, don't set the world to the torch to assert their *truths*, while you set fire to it at every chance you *find*, with every fancy that comes to *mind?*' (3.1.36) In Egypt, Malta, and England, his Protestant employers fare little better under the Fariyaq's withering gaze. Just as the scrapping churches of the Levant become rival hagglers, so his Biblical translator's post in Malta is transformed into a job as 'Interpreter of Dreams' for the master of the 'Oneiromancer's Chamber'. In one episode, the master goes mad and starts preaching the virtue of nudity: not another piece of farcical hyperbole on al-Shadyaq's part, but an affliction that periodically seized Christoph Schlienz, leader of the Church Missionary Society in Malta in the 1830s, after he was struck on the head by a bargepole in Egypt. No, you couldn't make it up…

III

The couple's sojourns in England and France during the 1840s and 1850s allow al-Shadyaq to add the picaresque travelogue to his portfolio of comic genres. The Fariyaqs, Mr and Mrs alike, put the Orientalist gaze smartly into reverse as they swap verdicts on the weird ways of the Franks. If they don't think much of the food, the clothes or the poetry (especially the poetry), they concur on the splendour of Western hygiene and the need to lavish fulsome praise on it to your hosts: 'How sweet-smelling are your latrines! How aromatic your drains!… How elegant your sewers! How clean your lintels and doorsteps!' (4.11.8) Behind the travel-writer's knockabout, and the genial to-and-fro of stereotypes, al-Shidyaq has some shrewd and surprisingly balanced (though never dull) points to make about early-Victorian English life in particular.

He does appreciate the widespread literacy, the scientific prowess, the respect for rights and individual liberties, even if imperfectly applied: 'one who comes to their country is not asked whether he has a passport or a permit... Moreover, the rabble aside, they love strangers, are compassionate to the poor, and go in aid of those in need.' (4.11.13) Along with these civic values go lashings of sexual hypocrisy, pomposity and – above all – a stifling joylessness that drains life of its zest and flavour. Unusually for a non-European foreigner, al-Shidyaq lived not only in London and Cambridge but also a Hertfordshire village, Barley, where a co-translator occupied the rectory. His strictures on the monochrome monotony of peasant and urban working-class life remind us that these observations date from the mid-1840s, as the 'Condition of England' novel reached its peak: 'how can it be that this sort of person creates the adornments of the world, makes it a delight to live in, and creates its prosperity, while they themselves are excluded from it and have but little share in it?' (4.12.2) We can speculate that al-Shidyaq, the comic unmasker of greed, falsity and cruelty among the prosperous, might have walked past Charles Dickens on the streets of London. But the Arabic wizard of inspired nonsense, of logical and verbal gymnastics, could also (just) have bumped into the student Charles Dodgson, aka Lewis Carroll, on his research visits to Oxford.

As he weighs up the virtues and the vices of the English, the Fariyaq concludes that among their worst faults ranks sheer incuriosity about ways of life beyond their island. Hence 'in their ignorance they believe everyone else in the world to be less then they'. Along with that wilful ignorance, he deplores the strait-laced, sobersided gloom that left him in 'loneliness and hardship' there, despite the welcome and recognition he received as an Arab Christian engaged in God's work. Back home, he vows to return to 'belly laughing, splitting one's sides, laughing like a horse... peeing oneself with laughter, chuckling, chortling, checkling' and so on, all of which 'bring the heart greater relief from worry than unbreakable vessels or unshakable buildings'. (4.12.10)

Al-Shidyaq finds plenty to ridicule not only in England but France as well. In Paris, the Fariyaq succumbs for a while to a conventional male taste for the alleged oh-la-la seductiveness of the local womenfolk. Like any salivating Victorian sex tourist, he assures us that 'the French make no distinction between the respectable woman and the harlot' and that 'no people are more lascivious than they in their desire for intercourse'. (4.17.11) With her husband clearly thinking not with his head but a lower part of his anatomy, it's up to the Fariyaqiyyah to catalogue the manifold drawbacks of Paris – not least the open sewers of the streets 'and the blood, filth and waters of varied colours that flow along them, part green like pond scum, part yellow like turmeric, and part black like coal'. (4.18.2) For her, 'the modest decency of the young Englishmen', not to mention London's exemplary drainage and street-lighting, suddenly come into their own. As for that vaunted Parisian café culture, 'are a few people sitting on chairs enough to make one judge in its favour?' (4.18.10) The London-Paris rift becomes, like everything the couple encounters, more grist to the mill of the matrimonial dialectic. Its wheels of backchat and badinage keep spinning without pause.

For the globe-trotting duo, bad governors mean good copy. When the Fariyaq does at last benefit from the patronage of a leader he admires, Ahmad Pasha, the Bey of Tunis, he slips, both in prose and verse, into a stilted laudatory mode that utterly cramps his usual style. The same goes for an interminable ode of praise to the Ottoman Sultan Abdulmejid as the Crimean War breaks out: 'Our Most Exalted Sultan, through whom our days/ have been rendered happy and bright… Has spread justice throughout the land…' (4.20.12) And so, numbingly, on. At these few unctuous moments, we wish we were back in some agonisingly well-mannered dinner party among Cambridge scholars, where the Fariyaq – accustomed, after all, to the refined cuisine of Lebanon and Egypt – reminds his wife that you have to wait meekly to be served some gristly lump or other by the host, 'and should he offer you a fragment of meat from a rabbit that was strangled a month ago and has been hanging in the air till it has gone rotten, praise the soil on which such a precious animal and its species was raised, as well as the one who strangled it and the one who cooked it.' (4.11.10)

Whether on a donkey, a sailing-ship, a steamer or a railway train, the Fariyaq hunts far and wide around the Levant and the Frankish lands for virtue, justice – and, not least, the finest literary style. Al-Shidyaq both parodies and indulges the runaway verbosity of Arabic literary tradition. The whole of *Leg Over Leg* amounts, whatever its other aims, to a lexicographer's carnival in which impossibly extended lists of synonyms and set phrases tumble over page after page. The book begins as it means to go on, with a catalogue of words for female and male genitalia, and for sexual activity of various kinds. Humphrey Davies has counted them: 255. In such gigantic rosters of ribaldry, whether it be 'the spontaneous leaping of she-camels by he-camels', 'emaciation resulting from incessant intercourse', or even just 'the clitoris said with a funny accent' (1.1.6), al-Shidyaq disputes the assumption that all the words he cites signify more or less the same thing. Words themselves make meanings multiply and proliferate, 'synonymous only in the sense that certain of them may take the place of certain others'. (1.1.7) Likewise, one man may take the place of another in a woman's bed – and, of course, vice versa. The comic motor of endless substitution, and inexhaustible fecundity, applies to language and sexuality alike.

Desire, conversation and wordplay can and should never run dry or come to a full stop. Verbal abundance breeds an inherent ambiguity, which breeds misunderstanding, which breeds discord, which breeds comedy, which breeds another bounteous harvest of words. As the Fariyaq says to the Faryaqiyyah when they're quarrelling, as usual, about sex, lies, and lexicons, 'most of these misunderstandings are generated by our language, which is so wide that it allows every expression to bear numerous possible meanings.' She replied, "I would rather it were tight!" "That," I responded, "goes with the other!" To which she responded "and the other goes into this!" "And on top of it," I said. "And underneath it," I retorted. "Better not to say anything then." "Not while going to it", I said. "You men," she said, "all snort, groan, and talk dirty like women when you're having sex" "How come you know that?" I asked. "Back to delusion and suspicion!" she said.' (3.20.2)

IV

If there exists another portrait of a marriage from mid-nineteenth-century literature to match that of the Fariyaq and Fariyaqiyyah, I have yet to find it. While, in the backwaters of Normandy, Flaubert's *Madame Bovary* self-destructively seeks an escape from solitude in ashen adulteries, Mr and Mrs F keep on talking till the Nile – or the Fenland – cows come home. Given its crowing delight in obscenity, its lexical spurts and gushes over female anatomy, its recourse to a traditional yarn-spinning voice in which women feature as wily houris and insatiable cheats, it may seem strange to invoke 'feminism' in relation to *Leg Over Leg*. (The socialist thinker Charles Fourier first used the term in 1837; the *Oxford English Dictionary*'s earliest English-language reference dates from 1852.) Everything here, however, turns on the bedroom dialectic between husband and wife in which she gives not only as good as she gets but, often, much better. The Fariyaqiyyah delivers most of the wittiest sallies, the punchiest punch lines, the killer retorts. Al-Shidyaq declares at the outset that he wants women – still largely excluded from his work by illiteracy – to understand that he has written 'a book about women that gives them precedence over all other creatures, declaring them to be the adornment of the universe, the comfort and pride of this world, the joy and hope of life,' and so on, right down to 'the embellishment of the age and the glory of every place and dwelling'. (1.1.8)

Leg Over Leg is no tract, however progressive or enlightened. Its debate on the rights and powers of women flies up in showers of rhetorical sparks struck from the scintillating repartee of its central couple. In place of theoretical argument, al-Shidyaq's happy battle of the sexes takes the form of a cross-border screwball comedy driven by flirty, waspish badinage. True, before the Fariyaq's marriage he goes in for more old-fashioned, and sometimes dull, enumeration of the supposed virtues and weaknesses of women derived from the ancient authorities: 'a certain scholar has said that if God wishes to do something good on earth, he chooses a woman as the means to its accomplishment, and if the devil wishes to do something evil, he also uses a woman for his ends.' (2.14.89) During such passages, you sense that al-Shidyaq would really rather be launching into yet another frenzied string of arcane synonyms for buttocks and bosoms, as per usual.

The Fariyaqiyyah's arrival changes everything. The pair's long bouts of sparring – affectionate, seductive or plain exasperated – tilt the tone of the third and fourth volumes away from rhetorical virtuosity towards realistic dialogue, even if al-Shidyaq can still break off into a mini-anthology of flowery verse at the drop of a tarboosh. The stark contrast, when he first gets to know her, between the Fariyaqiyyah's quick and keen wits and her lack of basic instruction leads her husband to place women's education at the heart of his exhortations to reform. For 'if women discover for themselves that they are men's equals in understanding and knowledge, they will use this knowledge as a shield against them and deploy it to make

themselves unassailable when men treat them without due respect.' (3.5.5)
When his wife comes to take an equal, or more than equal, part in their
matrimonial cut-and-thrust, she pinpoints not just education but language
itself as a root cause of patriarchal inequality: 'it is men's habit to claim that
women were created only to please, entertain, and flatter their husbands,
and they have created the language in such a way as to serve their exercise
of tyrannical power over and violence against women.' (4.9.9) When her
husband, on a losing pitch, lamely proposes that 'all books bear witness to
the trustworthiness of men and the treachery of women,' she's ready with
the riposte: 'weren't the ones who wrote those books men?... They're the
ones who made up those stories.' (4.2.5) *Leg Over Leg* both exalts an ideal
of marital equality and gives the wife the lion's share of winning arguments
in its favour. Nothing, from Maltese balls to Cambridge chit-chat to Parisian
couture, escapes her piercing scrutiny and swift judgment as the pair shuttle
between Egypt, Lebanon, Malta, England and France. As the Fariyaq
admiringly acknowledges, 'your quickness of understanding, acuteness of
mind, and genius make everything difficult easy to you'. (4.11.2)

Leg Over Leg tells a second story, within its hero's verbose peregrinations
around the eastern Mediterranean and into the lands of the Franks. It
shows how a man obsessed with language and learning marries a woman
who not only acquires those tools herself but comes to master them in a
way that stimulates, infuriates, and – in the end – satisfies both partners.
The heart of al-Shidyaq's comic vision lies not in his hypomanic riffs on
obscure words for the penis or vagina, nor in his recondite parodies of
Arabic rhetorical devices, nor even – though these matter much to him –
in the boisterous satire on flawed sects and societies, both his own and
those he observes abroad. Humour alone can bridge the gap between two
minds that love and language both draw together, and keep apart. At one
point, the fed-up Faryaqiyyah complains again about her husband's
lubricious fixation on the lexicon of sex: all that daily 'muttering about
women with quivering flesh, women with firm and swelling flesh, women
with fleshy flesh, women with masses of plump flesh...' His dirty talk, she
avows, would 'make the Baptist salivate and excite a hermit'. To which he
feebly replies, 'they're just words.' Her answer is truly unassailable: 'every
war begins with words.' (4.2.8)

Because words, as *Leg Over Leg* shows us, divide and subdivide, replicate, shatter and fragment. They explode in a fractal multiplicity of meanings that no single voice or reductive doctrine will ever manage to control. Humour, however, especially the humour of a free and loving exchange, can mimic the divine power not just of making many things out of one thing, but one thing out of many. It was a bizarre accident of Middle Eastern religious history that made a writer of al-Shidyaq's carnivalesque gifts pass so much of his time in the employ of solemn Evangelical prigs. But it gave him an unequalled treasure-trove of comic raw material. It sharpened, too, the insight that the Fariyaqiyyah voices, and which might almost serve as motto for the book: 'that in seriousness is humour and in humour seriousness'. (4.2.2)

OLD ARAB JOKES

Robert Irwin

The twelfth-century Syrian warrior, poet and memoirist, Usama ibn Munqidh, found the liberty that the Franks of the Crusader principalities allowed their women quite extraordinary. He also did not think that the Franks were very bright and he told this story about a Frankish wine-seller in Nablus, at that time part of the Kingdom of Jerusalem:

'So one day he came back home and discovered a man in bed with his wife. The Frank said to the man, 'What business brings you here to my wife?'

'I got tired,' the man replied, 'So I came in to rest.'

'But how did you get into my bed?' asked the Frank.

'I found a bed that was all made up, so I went to sleep in it,' he replied.

'While my wife was sleeping there with you?' the Frank pursued.

'Well, it's her bed,' the man offered. 'Who am I to keep her out of it?'

'By the truth of my religion,' the Frank said, 'if you do this again, we'll have an argument, you and I!'

As Aristotle noted in the *Poetics*, 'Comedy represents the worst types of men; worse however, not in the sense that it embraces any and every kind of badness, but in the sense that the ridiculous is a species of ugliness or badness.' A great deal of medieval Arab humour aimed at ridicule or disparagement. Common butts included Franks, Kurds, Bedouin, schoolteachers, drug addicts, misers, gluttons, cuckolds and stupid people more generally.

One particularly stupid and tubby man was unlucky enough to attract the hostile attention of the stylish polygraph, al-Jahiz (c.776-869). Al-Jahiz, irritated by the claim of Ahmad ibn 'Abd al-Wahhab that round things were better and more natural than square things, went on to compose *The Square and the Round* (*Kitab al-Tarbi' wa al-Tadwir*). In this treatise al-Jahiz, having noted that Ahmad was prejudiced in favour of round things because he was so very fat, went on to ask the would-be omniscient scholar a long string of unanswerable questions regarding the parentage of the phoenix, the origins of toothpicks, the builder of Palmyra, the colour of peacocks' tails and much, much else. Al-Jahiz, who lived in Basra and Baghdad was certainly the best and most interesting writer of Arabic prose in pre-modern times. *Munazara* is the Arabic term for the literature of rivalry or comparison. Al-Jahiz excelled at this and, among many other examples, he composed treatises on *The Superiority of the Blacks to the Whites*, *Women's Superiority to Men* and *The Superiority of the Belly to the Back* (The last was actually an attack on homosexuality). It is difficult to determine whether he was always being serious in his comparisons. Al-Jahiz also excelled in sarcasm, as in an epistle which purported to be in praise of singing slave girls, but was actually no such thing.

Examples of *munazara* can be found in *The Thousand and One Nights*, including 'The Dispute about the Merits of Men and Women' and 'The Story of al-Ma'mun the Yemeni and the Six Slave Girls'. The arguments are often playful and *munazara* was a genre which could lend itself to spoofs. Abu al-'Anbas al-Saymari, (828-88) was an Iraqi who doubled as a qadi and a buffoon and who found high favour with the Caliph al-Mutawakkil. He deployed both erudition and comedy in his work, *The Superiority of the Ladder over the Staircase*. Al-Saymari once ascended a mosque's pulpit during the Friday prayer and asked his congregation 'Do you know what I have to tell you?' They chorused back 'No'. To which he replied 'Since you do not know, it is not worth the trouble that I should tell you,' and he descended from the pulpit. The following Friday he ascended the pulpit and asked the same question. This time the congregation shouted back 'Yes.' Then he said, 'Since you know, there is no need to tell you.' And once again he descended from the pulpit. The third Friday he asked the same question from the pulpit and this time some in the mosque said 'Yes', while others said 'No'. As he left the pulpit again, he suggested that those who knew should inform those who did not.

To get back to al-Jahiz, members of the Arab literary elite were terrified of being thought boring. It seems possible that it was al-Jahiz who invented the literary technique of *al-jidd wa al-hazl*, instruction mingled with jokes, or earnestness with triviality. Certainly, he made a great deal of use of this way of carrying his audience along, and 'Lest I tire the reader...' is a recurring phrase in his writings. Other later writers followed al-Jahiz in defending *al-jidd wa al-hazl*. The twelfth-century religious scholar, Ibn al-Jawzi wrote 'The mind tends to get annoyed when staying earnest for too long, and it delights in a pleasurable pastime'. He wrote the first books entirely devoted to jokes, most notably, the *Akhbar al-Hamqa wa'l-Mughaffilin* (Information about Fools and Simpletons). The fourteenth-century scholar al-Nuwayri in his encyclopaedia, *al-Nihayat al-'Arab*, introducing his chapter on 'Entertaining, Witty and Bawdy Anecdotes, wrote that 'this chapter is on a subject to which all souls incline, and that all minds are in agreement about, a source of comfort for the weary and excitement for the fatigued. The soul, after all, cannot bear continuous labour and finds a change in affairs to be pleasing. So, if you engage with entertaining stories from time to time, and oblige it with witty anecdotes every now and then, it will return to earnest work refreshed and renewed, pursuing knowledge with great ease.' So, humour was widely approved of as a didactic tool. Here now is one of the jokes included in al-Nuwayri's encyclopaedia: 'A man claimed to be a prophet. They asked him 'What are the proofs of your being a prophet?' He said, 'I shall tell you what is in your mind.' They asked him, 'What is in our minds?' He said 'You are thinking that I am a liar and not a prophet'.

Despite the endorsement of many of the learned, it was more or less inevitable that some of the more puritanical *'ulama'* should denounce comedy, satire, and even laughter itself. Some thought that Jahiz's levity was a threat to the social order, and they were able to produce passages from the Qur'an which, taken out of context, seemed to condemn laughter. But various orally transmitted traditions concerning the Prophet and his companions suggested that Muhammad enjoyed a good joke as much as anyone and that sometimes he would laugh so heartily that he would show his molars (In the centuries that followed, falling over backwards helpless with laughter, was the other way of responding to a really good joke).

Nevertheless, a great deal of Arab humour does not belong in the laugh-out-loud category. The hyper-sophisticated wit displayed by such erudite stylists as al-Jahiz and al-Hariri are cases in point. The Iraqi man of letters, Abu Muhammad al-Qasim al-Hariri (1054–1122) produced one of the greatest classics of medieval Arabic literature, the *Maqamat* (literally 'standings' but more comprehensibly 'sessions'), a sequence of narratives in rhymed prose and poetry, in which Abu Zayd, an eloquent and erudite fraud who deploys his eloquence for his own profit, is encountered in various disguises. Abu Zayd's hyper-sophisticated wordplay more often provokes astonishment than laughter. As the Moroccan literary critic, Abdelfattah Kilito noted, 'The palindrome in particular is a device much favoured by al-Hariri. For example, one poem by Abu Zayd reads the same from beginning to end as it does from end to beginning: even when read backward the content remains consistent. One letter, a remarkable accomplishment, when read produces one text, and when read backward reveals an entirely different one: a disturbance has taken place, an astral and cosmic one, so to speak whereby the sun rises at one and the same time in both East and West,' (By the way, fans of the English palindrome may be interested to learn that a falindrome is a string of letters which looks like a palindrome but is not).

The variety of linguistic tricks and (somewhat obscure) jokes has encouraged a recent translator, Michael Cooperson to translate each *maqama* in the manner of a different Western model. Thus, the ninth *maqama* is presented like a Gilbert and Sullivan operetta, the twelfth is modelled on the manner of Jerome K. Jerome and the nineteenth has borrowed the style and vocabulary of P.G. Wodehouse. Here then are medieval foreshadowings of Gilbert's 'over-the-top wordplay', Jerome's jauntiness and the cheerful deployment of slang by Wodehouse.

Though jokes, puns, and other kinds of wordplay were the common currency of the soirées of clever people, a great deal of what was also transmitted on such occasions celebrated the alleged sayings and deeds of both wise fools and foolish fools and much of the humour was pornographic or scatological. In the early centuries, Ash'ab al-Tamma' (Ash'ab the Greedy) was the top fool. Allegedly this poet and comedian flourished in eighth-century Medina. Various literary anthologies celebrated his greed and meanness. On one occasion when he was being pestered by a gang of children, he got rid of them by telling them that free gifts were being distributed at a certain place elsewhere, but then he ran after them in case what he had said was true. Ash'ab's girlfriend once said to him 'Give me your ring, so I may remember you by it'. Ash'ab replied 'Rather remember that I refused it to you. I like that better.' 'A man asked

Ash'ab why he was not grateful to him for the kindness he had shown him. Ash'ab replied: 'Your kindness came from someone who did not seek a reward, and thus came to one who was not grateful'.

Someone said to Ash'ab; 'If you were to relate traditions [*hadiths*] and stop telling jokes, you would be doing a nobler thing.' 'By God' answered Ash'ab, 'I have heard traditions and related them.' 'Then tell us,' said the man. 'I heard from Nafi,' said Ash'ab, 'on the authority of Ibn 'Umar, that the Prophet of God, may God bless and save him, said 'There are two qualities, such that whoever has them is among God's elect. 'That is a fine tradition,' said the man. 'What are these two qualities?' 'Nafi forgot one and I have forgotten the other,' said Ash'ab.'

Gurning, the pulling of grotesque faces, together with contortionism, used to be a popular form of entertainment. Ash'ab was a master of gurning, able to press his face together, widen it and then contracted it. Ash'ab challenged a member of the Quraysh tribe to match what he could do: 'If you are a man of my calibre, do now what I am doing!' With these words, he pressed his face together and widened it and contracted it until its width was greater than its length and it assumed a shape in which nobody would have recognised him. He then let his face go and said to him: 'Now this!' And he lengthened his face until his chin almost went beyond his breast and his face came to be like that of a person who mirrors himself in his sword. Then he took off his clothes and gave himself the appearance of a hunchback. There actually appeared upon his back a hump like that of a camel. Its length was a span or more. Then, he took off his trousers and started to extend the skin of his testicles until he scratched the ground with them. Then, he let them go and walked. He started to move backwards while his testicles were drawing lines upon the ground. Then he got up and extended and stretched himself until he became as tall as any man could be. Those present really laughed until they lost consciousness.' The Qurayshite rival was confounded and had nothing more to say.

In the long run Ash'ab's reputation for comic stupidity was to be eclipsed by the legendary figure of Juha who allegedly lived in the eighth century. He seems to have made his first appearance in al-Jahiz's *Kitab al-Bighal* (Book of the Mules). Thereafter his comic sayings and exploits (many of which were obscene) featured in numerous literary anthologies. So, for example, we learn from Ibn al-Jawzi's, *Akhbar al-hamqa* that one day Juha's father wondered what to do with the soil that had accumulated next to his house, as the neighbours had started complaining and the soil in question was not good for making bricks with. Obviously expecting a reward for his advice, young Juha proudly suggested digging a hole in which to deposit the soil. This was a joke which travelled and essentially the same story can be found in Baldassare Castiglione's sixteenth-century *Il Cortegiano* (The Courtier). Though Juha was a famous fool, as fools go, he was pretty cunning, as the following examples suggest:

Juha bought three pounds of meat and asked his wife to cook it. This she did, but she ate the meat with some of her relatives. Then, when Juha came and asked for the cooked meat, she told him that the cat had eaten it while she was busy preparing other things. Juha took hold of the cat and weighed it; it was, he found, exactly three pounds. 'You cunning woman!' he said to his wife. 'If this is the cat, then where's the meat? And if this is the meat, then where's the cat?'

Juha had two wives. One evening, when he was sitting with them and enjoying their company, they decided to trap him by asking him which one of them he loved the best. 'I love you both the same,' he told them. 'Oh no,' they said, 'You can't just slither out of it like that. You're in trouble this time! Now, there's a pool over there. Just choose which of us you'd rather drown in it. Which one of us are you going to toss in the water?' Juha hesitated, pondering his dilemma. Finally, he turned to his first wife. 'I've just remembered, my dear,' he said. 'You learned to swim some years back, didn't you?'

Juha married a woman who was very fat, and he was afraid that she'd be too strong for him and do him harm. One day, when she was chasing after him with a cane in her hand and, he hid under the bed, where she was too fat to follow him. 'Come here after me,' he yelled, feeling safe at last. 'If you're man enough!'

'Which is more useful,' someone asked Juha, 'the sun or the moon?' He didn't hesitate for a moment. 'The moon,' he answered firmly. 'No question about it.' 'Why is that?' they asked. 'Because,' he answered, 'the sun rises during the day, when you don't need it. But the moon comes out in the dark. And that's when you need it.'

It was reported of Juha, that 'his mother once went to a wedding party and left him at home, telling him, 'Watch the door!' He sat there until noon. When she was late in returning, he took the door from its hinges and carried it on his shoulders.'

All sorts of strange professions flourished in the medieval Arab world, including professional farters, gurners and gate-crashers. Farting featured prominently in literary anthologies. Abu Sa'd al-Abi's seven-volume *Scattering of Pearls* was a compendium of thousands of anecdotes and jokes, especially regarding prostitutes, transvestites, homosexuals and farters. A professional farter was known as a *darat*. Of course, he faced plenty of competition from amateurs.

The story of 'How Abu Hasan Broke Wind' is found in Burton's version of *The Thousand and One Nights*. A wealthy Yemeni Bedouin wanted to get married, but during the wedding ceremony he let out an enormous noisy fart. Humiliated, he fled town and went to live in India for ten years. After the passage of some years, he thought it safe to return to his home town. As he once more walked its streets, he heard a girl ask her mother when she was born. The mother replied 'You were born on the day that Abu Hasan farted'. So, Abu Hasan returned to India where he died. Again, this was a joke which travelled. Effectively the same joke is found in John Aubrey's *Brief Lives*. Edward de Vere, Earl of Oxford, was making low obeisance to Queen Elizabeth when he let out an enormous fart. Humiliated, he went travelling for seven years. On his return, the Queen greeted him, 'My Lord, I had forgot the fart'.

According to Emily Selove's translation of al-Khatib al-Baghdadi's *Al-Tatfil wa hikayat al-tufayliyin*, his treatise on the *tufayli* (gate-crasher), 'The *tufayli* enters a party uninvited. The word is derived from the root *tafala* which refers to the encroaching darkness of night time upon the day. It is implied that the *tufayli* brings darkness upon the party, for the rest do not know who invited him, or how he got in.' Although there were always plenty of freelance gate-crashers, gate-crashing was for a while a regulated profession in medieval Baghdad and the Shaykh of the *Tufayli*s would allocate members of his guild their daily and nightly assignments. Stories about these freeloaders abounded. Al-Khatib al-Baghdadi (1002-1071) was a religious scholar who was chiefly famous for his biographical dictionary of religious scholars who transmitted traditions concerning the Prophet and his Companions, but here are some of the stories he collected about gate-crashers:

'I once said to a party-crasher, 'Woe unto you! You eat what is forbidden!'

'I've never eaten a bit that wasn't allowed,' he replied.

'How's that?' I asked.

'Because when I go into a party I head for the door to the woman's quarters, and everyone says, 'No, not there!' Here!' Their saying 'Here!' *is* the invitation, so therefore I don't eat anything that isn't allowed.'

'Once a man crashed another man's party. 'Who are you?' the host asked him. 'I'm the one who saved you the trouble of sending an invitation!' he replied.

Although there was scarcely anything that can be classified as live theatre in the medieval Arab world, three remarkable shadow play scripts survive from the late thirteenth century. They were the work of an Iraqi ophthalmologist called Shams al-Din Muhammad Ibn Daniyal (d.1310). He had fled to Mamluk Egypt in advance of the Mongol occupation of Mosul and his plays were performed in Cairo in the 1290s.

All three plays feature disreputable low-life characters and the scripts are thick with pornographic and scatological double and sometimes triple *entendres*. The late English journalist and satirist, Malcolm Muggeridge once observed that 'good taste and humour... are a contradiction in terms, like a chaste whore.' In Ibn Daniyal's plays cripples, women, beggars, and homosexuals are ruthlessly mocked and it is hard to imagine his plays being staged in Britain today. *Tayf al-Khayal* (The Shadow Spirit) has a hunchback protagonist in search of a bride (His name Wisal means copulation). The play satirises an earlier Mamluk anti-vice campaign. Ibn Daniyal makes use of religious language for obscene purposes. The play ends with the protagonist being trapped into marriage with a hideous old woman who farts a lot. *'Ajib wa Gharib* (The Amazing Preacher and the Stranger) presents a parade of street entertainers, charlatans and other representatives of the dregs of Cairene society. One can admire the inventive parade of low-life grotesques, as well as the elaborate word play, yet it is hard to imagine a citizen of the twenty-first century actually laughing at these dramas Ibn Daniyal's humour is dark and the concluding line of this play is 'My grief, my poverty and my art are strange, very strange and amazing, and very amazing.' *Al-Mutayyam* (The Love-Stricken One) is a bawdy homosexual love story in which al-Mutayyam and his beloved, a beautiful boy, witness a cockfight, a ram fight and a bullfight and then all sorts of sexual perversions are celebrated. But, in keeping with Ibn Daniyal's dark moralism, the play ends with the appearance of the Angel of Death.

Though the concentration on disreputable low-life characters and vulgarity of the language may tempt one to think that these shadow plays were targeted at a plebeian audience, this was probably not the case. Ibn Daniyal was held in high favour by the Mamluk elite and was a close friend of the Sultan Qalawun's two sons Salih and Ashraf. There was not a clear distinction between high culture and low culture in the medieval Arab world. There is plenty of evidence from Mamluk times and earlier for the delight that many members of the military and civil elites took in lower-class humour and in mastering popular slang. Some Muslims today have an idealised view of the mores that prevailed in the days of the medieval caliphate. The following is recorded in the polygraph al-Tha'alibi's *Yatimat al-dahr* (The Unique Pearl) as a regular event during the reign of the 'Abbasid Caliph al-Mustakfi (944-6): 'At the residence of the Vizier al-Muhallabi, the qadis. . . met twice a week, all with long grey beards like that of the Vizier. At the summit of their merry-making each holding a golden cup in hand, filled with Qatrabul and Ukbara wine, would dip his beard into it and they would sprinkle each other with it and dance in variegated dresses and adorned with garlands'.

'Ali al-Bashbughawi Ibn Sudun (c.1407-64) was the son of a mamluk slave soldier. There were periodic attempts in Egypt to ban shadow plays as indecorous, but although Ibn Sudun wrote no shadow plays, his coarse sense of humour was similar to that of Ibn Daniyal. He started out in life as a poor Sufi scholar, but then he gave up being poor and respectable to become poor and unrespectable. According to the historian and biographer al-Sakhawi 'he followed a path that was excess in buffoonery, jest, wantonness and dissoluteness; he became well-known and his fame became widespread because of it, and the fashionable people fought over his Diwan [his collection of writings].' The first part of Ibn Sudun's *The Delight of the Eye and the Garden of the Mind* was devoted to *jidd*, that is, serious themes, but the second half must be classified as *hazl*, for it is full of jokes, silly pun-laden poems, riddles, obscenities, parodies, and other frivolities. He was particularly fond of sweet delicacies from the pastry shop, wine, hashish, and love. Sweet foods in particular loomed large and the second part was prefaced with the following doxology:

Praise be to God the Almighty, Who bestowed upon His servants various nice-ties. He taught man what he did not know and inspired him when He taught him to make, as he was taught, from sugar stuffed pastry. He made sellers subservient to swallowers, those who sit in their shops and those who are ambulant. He made the kernels of pistachio nuts, having been cracked, whole. He made streams of sugar syrup descend from the firmly anchored mountains of sugar, down the bellies of wadis of syrups...

Among other things, he offered this dubiously useful piece of dietary advice regarding a dish of rice mixed with ghee, honey, or other comestibles:

He who eats two platefuls after lunch and two platefuls after dinner for forty years on end will never fall sick, except from some disease, and he will not die, except when his allotted time is up; and if he should die a Muslim he will enter paradise.

The oldest substantially surviving manuscript of *The Thousand and One Nights* also dates from the fifteenth century and has already been cited for a fine farting joke. Many of the collection's jokes look as though they are targeted at the stupid, as in an episode in which a dim-witted Bedouin allows himself to be crucified in exchange for the promise of fritters. But looking at the story in another way, it can be seen to be a celebration of cunning, as the offer of fritters is just one of the cunning exploits attributed to the string of *Nights* stories about the Baghdadi criminal Crafty Dalila. Similarly, the cycle of *Nights* stories known as 'The Craft and Malice of Women' are double-edged, as they simultaneously celebrate the cunning of women and mock the stupidity of cuckolded or otherwise cheated men.

To stay with Mamluk Egypt, a little later in the early sixteenth century the Sultan Qansawh al-Ghawri (1501–16) used to preside over twice-weekly soirées in which religious, political, literary, scientific and historical issues were discussed. Though stern on some religious issues, Qansawh enjoyed a good laugh and jokes also featured frequently in these soirées. For example, on one evening a story was told about Nasr al-Din

Khoja, a sly fool who features as the protagonist in hundreds of medieval Middle Eastern jokes. An Ottoman sultan had commanded Nasr al-Din to bring him a goose, but Nasr al-Din had already eaten one of the legs. So, when he presented what was left of the goose to the ruler he claimed that it had been a one-legged goose. Then, as they travelled along, they saw a flock of geese indeed standing on one leg and the Ottoman ruler was reassured that Nasr al-Din had not been deceiving him.

It is not a great joke, but then not a lot of medieval jokes have travelled well. I have done my best to pick out ones that struck me as funny or clever (as well as not going on too long), but this involved me in ploughing through much would be that was humour that was either limp, or starkly incomprehensible. For an example of the latter, 'Ash'ab was asked about the number of men around Muhammad at the Battle of Badr. He replied: '313 dirhams'. I have not the faintest idea what the joke is here.

Sigmund Freud's *Jokes and Their Relation to the Unconscious* was first published in German in 1905. In it he argued that jokes are transgressive of cultural norms, either bitingly sarcastic and hostile, or comfortingly mild, depending on the strength of the superego and what it would allow the ego to express. The jokes he uses as test cases date from turn-of-the-century Vienna and, like so many old Arab jokes, they have not travelled well. They do not strike me as very funny. I will cite the late English comedian Ken Dodd in my support: 'The trouble with Freud is that he never played the Glasgow Empire on a Saturday night after Rangers and Celtic had both lost.' And perhaps the ninth-century physician Ishaq ibn 'Imran had it more right when he wrote 'Laughter is defined as the astonishment of the soul at observing something that it is not in a position to understand clearly.'

The superego does not seem to have a role in many of the best jokes.

Finally, my current favourite medieval Arab joke: The 'Abbasid Caliph al-Mutawakkil asked a slave girl whom he was inspecting, 'Are you a virgin or what?' 'I am or what, O Commander of the Faithful,' she replied. And my current favourite British joke: 'My great-great-grandfather died at Waterloo.' 'Oh really? Which platform?' 'Don't be ridiculous. What does it matter which platform?'

COMEDY AND ISLAM IN AMERICA

Eric Walberg

Comedy is a protest art form. It's an honest art form. You reveal your inner secrets. It's positive. You get things off your chest, make them hilarious, positive.

Mohammad 'Mo' Amer, American stand-up comedian

We've seen an explosion of Arab and south Asian stand-up comics in North America in the past two decades, coinciding with 9/11. It's as if Muslims and those of south Asian origin, regardless of religion, were pushed so far on a terrorist limb in public perception, that the only way to deal with it is to laugh, and Muslims in North America rose to the challenge of defending themselves and Muslim heritage with the only weapon they had – the word. My focus here is on comedians who are challenging Islamophobia armed only with this – 'the word', touring the world and therefore playing an important role in breaking down anti-Muslim prejudice in their own unique ways.

But before we can look at specifically Muslim humour today, we must begin with the lower common denominator of the 'brown immigrant' stereotype, whether Muslim or not, which has entered American culture via *The Simpsons*. Most Americans were brought up on the stereotypical south Asian immigrant (whether Hindu or Muslim, not important) as portrayed in *The Simpsons'* Apu Nahasapeemapetilon, a naturalised PhD in computer science, who runs a Kwikie-Mart, notorious for its high prices and the poor quality of its merchandise. The character was created in 1989 at the very start of the series as a servile, devious, goofy, but endearing merchant with the thick, musical Indian accent, spoken by Hank Azaria.

There is little doubt that *The Simpsons* is smart, funny and political all at the same time, making it the longest running show in TV history. And Apu gets in many anti-racist digs. To a racist customer: 'And soon you will be telling me I should be going back to a place I'm not actually from. Thank you please come again'. But the stereotype leaves Americans with brown skin chaffing, immigrant or native, Muslim or non-Muslim, slotting them into a demeaning TV image for life. The subject of bullying in school, mocking of all ages.

Apu was, at the time, the only figure of south Asian heritage to appear regularly on mainstream US television. Apu is very Indian, but less prominently Hindu, and became the default south Asian stereotype. Indians have indeed become a regular feature of small-town commerce, taking the place of Koreans (and a century ago, European Jewish immigrants). Hindu immigrants have also become the main owners of small motels across the US, as Paul Theroux describes in *Deep South* (apparently many are invariably all run by Mr Patels), so the stereotype sticks, as does the other cliché of the Indian immigrant doctor or scientist (often, yes, a Dr Patel running a rundown motel in the boondocks).

However, new so-called 'woke' Western culture decries all stereotypes, and the widespread bullying of brown-skinned children as 'sons/ daughters of Apu' is a reality. The racism of the character was exposed in the 2017 documentary *The Problem with Apu* by American stand-up comic and film maker, Hari Karthikeya Kondabolu. Kondabolu interviews a string of South Asian comedians about the impact of Apu on their own lives, and the racism and slurs they have experienced as a result. Aziz Ansari, Karl Penn, Aasif Mandvi, Hasan Minhaj and others recount being called Apu in their childhood, and having the characters' catchphrases thrown at them by perfect strangers. They also recall being asked to deliver lines in Apu's accent. Kondabolu concludes that Apu is actually an equivalent to blackface, the practice of white actors to use black theatrical makeup to portray a caricature of a black person. He talks to Whoopi Goldberg, who collects and specialises in collecting racist material; Goldberg agrees that Apu is a form of blackface. *The Problem with Apu* contextualises Apu within minstrelsy and other tropes in American pop culture history that have historically stereotyped minorities.

The Simpsons responded to Kondabolu's film in a 2018 episode, 'No Good Read Goes Unpunished'. In it, Marge finds that a book she loved as a child contains elements that would now be considered offensive, and edits the book herself to remove these elements. In doing this, she finds the book loses its 'emotional journey'. She and Lisa then look to a picture of Apu, and Lisa comments that 'something that started decades ago and was applauded and inoffensive, is now politically incorrect. What can you do?' Kondabolu came back on Twitter to say that he was disappointed that the message of his film had been reduced to the concept of political correctness. In an interview with *USA Today*, *Simpsons* creator Matt Groening dismissed the criticism of the Apu character: 'I think it's a time in our culture where people love to pretend they're offended'. *The Problem with Apu* became a popular, even cult, documentary on the internet. So, on *The Late Show* with Stephen Colbert, Hank Azaria said that he would be 'perfectly willing to step aside' from the role of voicing Apu, saying that he was increasingly worried about the character causing harm by reinforcing stereotypes and that 'the most important thing is to listen to Indian people and their experience with it … I really want to see Indian, South Asian writers in the writers' room, genuinely informing whichever direction this character takes'. Indeed, in January 2020, Azaria announced that he 'won't be doing the voice anymore, unless there's some way to transition it or something.' In June 2020, in the wake of the murder of George Floyd, the show's producers announced in a statement that *The Simpsons* will no longer have non-white characters voiced by white actors.

Through all this, I couldn't help thinking that, as the American psychiatrist E Fuller Torrey wrote in 1992, it is:

> scientifically incorrect to refer to races as still existing. Attempts to characterise a genetic trait which may exist among a group of people as a racial trait simply indicates ignorance, because 85% of human genetic variation exists *within any group*. Genetic differences between individuals overwhelm all other attempts to differentiate mankind, while *genetic differences between groups have no predictive value* for any single individual.

It is perceptions that are the problem, words, which humour attacks. Fighting fire with fire. Hence, the 'second American Revolution' (abolition of slavery in 1865) and the ongoing struggle to overcome these perceptions today. Humour has an ambitious role cut out for society. It's no laughing matter.

The events of 9/11 put Muslims front and centre in the world, feared and respected, often hated. The anti-Muslim bigotry and the need to face it down can be seen most sharply via comedy and satire. The most celebrated of TV shows is still *Little Mosque on the Prairie*, created by Zarqa Nawaz, originally broadcast from 2007 to 2012 on CBC, filmed in Toronto, Ontario and Indian Head, Saskatchewan. The centre of the small Muslim community is the mosque, presided over by Imam Amaar Rashid, and located in the rented parish hall of the town's Anglican church, and Fatima's Café, a downtown diner run by Fatima Dinssa. The community patriarchs are Yasir Hamoudi, a construction contractor who originally fronted the money to establish the mosque under the pretence that he was renting office space for his business, and Baber Siddiqui, a college economics professor who served as the mosque's temporary imam until Amaar was hired. The town of Mercy is governed by Mayor Ann Popowicz. Sarah Hamoudi, Yasir's wife, works as a public relations officer in Popowicz's office. The title is a play on the name of the classic American book and TV drama series, *Little House on the Prairie*, though the stories are not related. There actually is a (now legendary) 'little mosque on the Prairies', Al-Rashid Mosque founded in 1938 in Edmonton, which was moved to Fort Edmonton Park in 1988 as a 'heritage site'. The sitcom developed an enduring cult following in the US and Europe, exploring through humour the thorny issues of media bigotry, conversion to Islam and Muslim-Christian relations. There have been other TV sitcoms with Muslims, but none so tasteful.

As well as an explosion (pun intended) since 9/11, in the number of Muslim comedians, humour festivals and forums have also proliferated. These have given a platform to many talents. Most noted amongst the post-9/11 generation of comedians that have emerged are Aziz Ansari, Ramy Youssef, Mohammad 'Mo' Amer, Azhar Usman and Ahmad Ahmad. Aziz Ansari is a stand-up comic and actor who first gained attention with his TV sitcom *Parks and Recreation* (2009–2015), playing Tom Haverford, a lazy, feckless landscaper. Later he starred in the Netflix series *Master of None*, which ran from 2015 to 2017, for which he won two Emmys and a Golden Globe, the first award received by an Asian American actor for acting on television. Ansari also authored *Modern Romance* in 2015, in which he concluded that humans pretty well figured out all things romantic, long before computers. He was most impressed interviewing octogenarians, happily married for sixty years, who met through family or in their neighbourhood, and practised a strict 'no sex before marriage' rule. (Does this sound familiar?)

Ansari was raised Muslim, his parents are Tamil, but insists he is 'not religious', though for all his flirting with 'haram', there is a strong moral sentiment underlying his humour. In his Netflix *Buried Alive* special which aired in 2013, Ansari poo-poos having a child. He tells his friends: 'You'll have to look after it for the rest of your life! All my options are still options.' He spoofs social media full of not just baby pictures, but baby videos, and feels sorry for the kids who have had the misfortune of being born to his wild, ignorant friends, and declares that at thirty, he still feels unready to be a father. His skirting with racism is clever: 'And white babies? Disgusting, gross! Like unripe fruit.' He was troubled by the reality show *16 and Pregnant* which ran on MTV from 2009 to 2014 (spawning multiple spin-offs), for using the abandoned teen as a 'reality show', not actually helping the poor mother-to-be. His own careful Muslim upbringing tells him how important experience and extended family support is in raising children, and how tragic it is to give birth without the maturity and commitment. He also tackles child molestation: 'Why did no camp councillor try to molest me? I guess because I was super cute, so maybe they were all intimidated. And I can see you're feeling sorry for the scared molester. But if my football coach had tried it, I would have told my mother: you want me to go back so he could stick his dick in my mouth again?'

Ramy Youssef, an Egyptian New Yorker is more subtle, and sophisticated in his style of humour. The Hulu series *Ramy*, written by and starring Ramy Youssef, is, according to *The New Yorker*, a 'charming, melancholy meditation on the verboten.' Youssef's standup material is drawn from the comedy of errors that is his life. He is a practicing Muslim, a diaspora kid who has spoken of being profoundly changed by the rise of anti-Muslim sentiment after 9/11. As a storyteller, he alternately resists and embraces the role of representative for all Muslim-Americans. 'Just make your story narrow!' Youssef said in an interview with *GQ* in May 2020. In *Ramy*, Youssef's persona is a contradictory mess—by turns holy, horny, and prone to playful chauvinism. In the first season, when Ramy's parents set him up with a Muslim woman, her sexual agency freaks him out and he cowers, unable to bring himself to please her. 'I'm in this little

Muslim box in your head,' she laments. 'I'm the wife or the mother of your kids, right? I'm not supposed to come.' Youssef won a Golden Globe Award for Best Actor – Television Series Musical or Comedy in 2020. He jokes that whereas he feels sorry that his gay friends have to come out, they feel sorry for him in LA being a religious person who struggles to come out to the gay community. In 2017, Youssef appeared on *The Late Show* with Stephen Colbert with his tongue-in-cheek homily:

> Hi. I'm a Muslim. You know, from the news? Have you guys seen our show? You listen to Fox, any news show? They're all about us. Sometimes I feel like I'm just going to turn thirty and get a 'Hogarth's letter' from ISIS.

> I believe in god. Yah, God god, not yoga. In the hope that there's more to life than what's in front of us … I'm not trying to be preachy. Just submit to Islam. It's the truth. That's the only way. You'll be saved. Seriously, trust me.

Quoting Youssef doesn't do his delivery justice. His reference to Hogarth was thrown in for the knowledgeable. Hogarth is the 1918 messenger for Sykes Picot to Hussein bin Ali, Sharif of Mecca, following Hussein's request for an explanation of the Balfour Declaration.

Mohammad 'Mo' Amer, of Palestinian descent, became, overnight, a media celebrity, when he was upgraded to first class on a flight from New York to Britain in 2017. Mo, who is best-known for his work with comedy troupe 'Allah Made Me Funny', was headed to Scotland to launch his Human Appeal Comedy Charity Tour. He found himself sitting next to political activist and former reality show personality, Eric Trump, who also happens to be the son of the former president, Donald Trump, from his first wife, Ivana Trump. Eric was also flying to Scotland, to check in on the Trump International Golf Links. 'I'm sure the lady that upgraded me to that seat was a Clinton supporter', he said. 'I looked at Eric immediately and said "Look man, FYI I'm not doing that shit". He's like "what?" I said, "I'm not going to get a Muslim ID number bullshit. I'm not doing it". "That's not gonna happen", Trump assured him, adding, "Come on man, you can't believe everything that you read".' Mo complimented Eric on his sweater, which featured an embroidered Trump crest.

Trump: 'Wouldn't you, if you had a crest of your family?'

Mo: 'I don't want to scrutinise that too much, but if I had a dope-ass logo, I'd pimp that too'.

Mo was on a roll. 'Build all the walls you want, Eric. I flew in. I can't help myself. My name is Mohammad, I'm a comedian, I came here as a refugee. Ha, ha'.

Eric tells Mo to take it easy on the Trumps; and claims to have Muslim friends and, though a bit embarrassed, seemed to enjoy his flight. Three weeks before the presidential election in 2020, Eric was the star at a gun owners' rally in Michigan, not far from the organisers of a failed attempt to kidnap the Michigan governor, of which President Trump showed epic complacency, ridiculing the governor for 'whining'.

Mo milked this 'material from God' (and his name Mohammad) thoroughly, making it the centrepiece of his 2018 Netflix comedy special *Mo Amer: the Vagabond*, in Austen Texas, which is mostly about his this-is-not-a-passport passport, trying to obtain US citizenship, and anti-Muslim prejudice rampant in America. He is asked for his given name in a telephone interview inquiring about his US citizenship application (which he and his mother had waited twenty years for):

Mo: 'My name's Mohammad'.

Receptionist: 'No. Stop joking. ... You ain't gonna get your citizenship baby'.

When he is particularly furious over this ad nauseam reply, Mo thinks: '... and if this continues, I'll blow up the whole airport! (Just kidding!) Or when stopped by a policeman for dangerous driving, but who himself had been speeding and almost hit Mo, the policeman asks: How come you're still alive? Mo replies: Because of our lord and saviour Jesus Christ. 'Amen', retorts the policeman. And no ticket. The closeness of Islam and Christianity shines through at such moments.

The youngest of six children, Amer's father worked as an engineer for the Kuwait Oil Company. In October 1990, at the age of nine, Amer, his sister, Haifa, his brother, and mother fled his birth country of Kuwait during the Gulf War, his mother sewing their dollars in the lining of her and Haifa's clothes, as they gambled the likelihood of a mother and daughter being strip-searched was slim. His escape from Kuwait as the 'first Gulf war' got underway is riveting, culminating in 'my mother the gangstah'. Then Mo looks at his mother in the front row, the camera pans to her beaming face. His mercurial style, perfect English (his early schooling was in Kuwait at the international school, with British teachers), has served him well. He can play Jose, white Mr Amer, or black Mohammad as necessary. When in school, he would feign Hispanic with the Mexican gang and with the black gang, Mohammad was a plus. 'I use my super white voice on the phone to get shit done, late checkouts.' His sending up of the wall: I just flew in. Or, I'll just jump over the unfinished fence'. It is a feat for a Palestinian refugee to rap for an hour without any overt political statement. The closest Mo gets is in Germany. The airport official queried his this-is-not-a-passport stateless citizen passport. 'Palestine's not a state', he replies. 'So get a state, the German says. 'It's all your fault we don't have one', Mo retorts. Mo has adoring followers, mostly non-Muslim. He is proud that he has performed to troops on over 100 US bases, including Iraq and Kuwait, even before he was granted US citizenship, the only Arab-American refugee comic to perform for US and coalition troops overseas, and has performed tours in over twenty-seven countries on five continents, including Germany, Italy, Japan, South Korea, and Bahrain. He has also performed in Tel Aviv. Amer joined American-Israeli rabbi Bob Alper and Ahmed Ahmed for four nights of comedy in Ramallah, West Bank.; and made his US network television debut in March 2017 on *The Late Show* with Stephen Colbert. Amer's work promotes art and understanding between the diverse cultures of the world, and his ethnic and family background enables him to speak about the problems of religion, terror, and current politics through the lens of personal stories about his family and himself. He talks about his Palestinian background, family histories and growing up American. In 2009, Amer became a US citizen which enabled him to travel to Amman, Jordan and visit family he had not seen for almost twenty years. He also returned to Kuwait and Baghdad for the first time since his family fled. In 2003, Mo joined Preacher Moss and Azhar Usman in the 'Allah Made Me Funny' comedy tour. By 2006 they were performing to sold-out shows worldwide, including the Royal Albert Hall.

Azhar Muhammad Usman is an American Sufi Muslim, comedian, actor, writer, and film producer of Indian descent. He is a former lecturer, community activist and lawyer and has been referred to as the Ayatollah of Comedy and Bin Laughin. He jokes about being mistaken for a terrorist, Muslim customs, religious holidays, families and himself. Usman is also co-founder and director of The Nawawi Foundation, an Illinois non-profit Muslim think tank dedicated to contemporary Islamic research; and serves as an Arts and Culture advisor to the Inner-City Muslim Action Network (IMAN) in Chicago. In 2005, ABC Nightline ran an entire episode about Usman.

Ahmed Ahmed is an Egyptian American, winner of the first annual Richard Pryor Award for ethnic comedy at the Edinburgh Festival in Scotland in 2004. Ahmed was a member of the Axis of Evil Comedy Tour (2005–2011). He was also a notable guest for Axis of Justice which is a rock and heavy metal band which fights for social justice. Following 9/11, and through 2004, Ahmed Ahmed and the comedian Rabbi Bob Alper toured the United States with their ground-breaking show 'One Arab, One Jew, One Stage' about interfaith harmony and essential human dignity. His name matches the alias used by an Osama bin Laden acolyte, noting that he is frequently stopped by airport immigration officials on suspicion of terrorism, including a twelve-hour stint in a jail in Las Vegas. Alper and Ahmed Ahmed celebrated their bar mitzvah together in Jerusalem in a show in 2015 in Tel Aviv and Haifa. The duo has been performing together since 2002, making people laugh in synagogues, churches, mosques, theatres, and most often, colleges, where Arab and Jewish student groups jointly co-sponsor their appearances. Ahmed starred in the cult Adam Sandler 2008 movie *Don't Mess with the Zohan* in which Sandler starred as an over-the-top stereotypical Israeli and Ahmed played a clothing store owner named Walid.

Also worth mentioning is *The Muslims Are Coming!*, an overly earnest 2013 American comedy documentary film co-directed and co-starring Negin Farsad and Dean Obeidallah. It follows a team of Muslim-American comedians as they tour the American South and Southwest performing free stand-up comedy shows, and engaging in community activities, with an aim to 'reach out to Middle America' and counter Islamophobia. Though not a smash hit, its premise is thoughtful and its script innovative. Some samples:

In Lawrenceville, Georgia, they set up an 'Ask a Muslim Booth' in the town centre.

At the Islamic Center of Columbus (in fact, Masjid Al-Jannah), performing during Ramadan, they stop to have iftar.

At AMF Peach Lanes in Columbus, they invite community members to 'Bowl with a Muslim'.

After performing in Birmingham, Alabama, they invite passers-by to play 'Name That Religion' where they try to guess if a quote read to them came from the Old Testament, New Testament, or the Quran.

In Salt Lake City, Utah, they perform at The Complex, and in front of the Salt Lake Temple they hold a sign inviting passers-by to 'Hug a Muslim'.

Obeidallah is co-creator of *Stand Up for Peace* which he performs across the country with Jewish-American comedian Scott Blakeman, bringing Arab-Americans, Muslims and Jews together through comedy in the hopes of fostering understanding and supporting a peaceful solution to the Palestinian-Israeli conflict. In June 2019, a federal judge ordered Andrew Anglin, editor of the neo-Nazi website *The Daily Stormer* to pay $4.1 million to Obeidallah, whom Anglin had accused of orchestrating the Manchester Arena bombing.

On a very sour note, there is Bassem Youssef, the Egyptian doctor who showed with a vengeance what a fickle taskmaster humour on the internet can be. Youssef used YouTube to launch *El-Bernameg*, a satirical show which spoofed mostly Muslim Brotherhood politicians in a way unprecedented in Egyptian history. *El-Bernameg* ran from 2011 to 2013, uncensored despite its increasingly ad hominem attacks on Egypt's first democratically elected president, Mohammad Morsi, promoting the opposition's distorted exaggerations of actual events, claiming that Morsi was becoming a dictator. Anyone watching Youssef skewer Egypt's Islamists, learned nothing, but was titillated in the cynical style of Western political satire. The most famous media byte was Morsi looking silly in a ceremonial hat. As the campaign of subversion intensified on all fronts, Youssef (dubbed the Jon Stewart of the Arab world) let his programme, fresh from witnessing the overthrow of a real dictator (Mubarak), set the stage for el-Sisi's coup in 2013. In June 2012, American satirist Jon Stewart invited Youssef to *The Daily Show* in New York. Youssef recorded one of the highest viewership ratings in the world on both TV and internet, with 40 million viewers on TV and more than 184 million combined views for his show on YouTube alone. He was a political power created by social media, the biggest Egyptian star in the West since Omar Sharif.

Youssef's humour looks maudlin and shameful in retrospect. This American-style humour is poisonous in a troubled context, a doctor using his cold-blooded skills to inject Egypt with US cultural poison. He handed Morsi's head to Sisi, though Sisi hesitated, leaving Morsi languishing, sick and dying. How convenient that he just gave up the ghost during his trial. Human Rights Watch official Sarah Leah Whitson said Morsi's treatment in prison was 'horrific, and those responsible should be investigated and appropriately prosecuted.' The United Nations High Commissioner for Human Rights, called June 18 for a 'prompt, impartial, thorough and transparent investigation' into Morsi's death. *The Toronto Star* highlighted the goulish last minutes, Morsi in a glass cage blinded by bright, garrish light, disoriented, collapsing. Such a vision makes for powerful theatre, but has little effect on the official level. Morsi – and Youssef – already footnotes in a Muslim tragedy with no comedy.

So many stories. America outdoes the world in anti-Muslim bigotry, but at the same time in positive Muslim response – Ansari's embrace of multiculturalism, Ramy Youssef's moral dilemmas and struggle to practice Islam in today's decadent, violent world, Mo Amer's subtle witness as Palestinian, the *Axis of Evil* cheering up US troops occupying Muslim lands, Ahmed Ahmed's engagement with the political nitty-gritty of America. Only Bassem Youssef's humour leaves a bad taste behind. Identifying Ramy Youssef's attraction in the 'verboten' really goes for all these contemporary humorists. In a secular age, religion is the ultimate verboten. It is heartening to see the Other breaking down prejudice through laughter.

THE OTHER HUMOURS

Leyla Jagiella

Humour is a strange word, in so far as we mostly use it in a very limited way today, a way that does not reflect the original wide range of its meanings. But such could be said of a host of other words in our current common parlance, which we use to describe certain instruments of human perception and expression. 'Intellect' being another one, a word that originally was never meant to be limited solely to a dry rational faculty. The constant confusion between words such as 'spirit', 'self' and 'soul' in modern language is another example (at least the learned people in medieval Europe and in the classic Islamic Era knew quite well that these three are completely different parts of our being). The word humour has also changed its meaning in a way that has made it more precise in some ways but also caused it to lose much of its original subtlety.

The word *humour* is originally a Latin transliteration of the ancient Greek χυμός (*chymos*), a word that literally means juice or sap but that, similar to the Sanskrit *râsa*, can also metaphorically mean 'flavour'. According to the medical theory of the ancient Greeks, a tradition that we identify with ancient scholars such as Hippocrates and Galen, four 'juices' are flowing within every human being's body: blood, yellow bile, phlegm and black bile. And it is the precise mixture and balance of these juices that determines both the character of an individual and their state of health.

The contemporary reader will recognise three of these juices easily as actually existing fluids of the human body. But the fourth will probably be a mystery to many. What is this enigmatic 'black bile'? Blood and phlegm are easy to recognise. We also know the 'yellow bile' that we usually just call 'bile', even though we also know that it is somehow related to bilirubin, the source of the characteristic skin colour that sufferers of diseases such as 'yellow fever', hepatitis and liver cirrhosis often acquire. Strangely, as a remnant of the old Greek idea of a connection between these humours and character traits, we also associate 'bile' and 'bilous' with unpleasant behaviour. But this 'black bile' is a stranger to most of us. At least it seems to be. In truth, it isn't that much of a stranger to us. We only use words derived from it in their ancient Greek form. In ancient Greek, 'black bile' was called μέλαινα χολή (melaina chole). From which derives our word 'melancholy'. A person who is melancholic is literally a person who suffers from an imbalance (usually an excess) of 'black bile'.

Black bile is, in fact, nowhere to be found in the human body. There has been speculation that the idea may be based on a Greek misunderstanding regarding the formation of gall stones or the function of the spleen. The Greeks did not simply make up their theory of humours, however. It was based on their scientific understanding of the time and on observations and examinations. Naturally, during that era people were unable to observe the work of bacteria and viruses the way we can today so they developed a different theory of health and disease. The idea of the four humours formed the most significant element of their theory, but there were other important factors as well – such as the influence of 'cold' and 'warm' elements around us. Interestingly, even though we know that a tangible substance called 'black bile' does not exist in our bodies, we still use various concepts that eventually hark back to the ancient Greek theory. The idea of 'melancholy' being one of them. But we likewise employ an expression based on this theory when we say that we have caught 'a cold'. We call certain people 'phlegmatic', a word that refers to an excess of phlegm. And others we name 'choleric' referring to a preponderance of yellow bile (chole). The word 'sanguine', indicating an excess of blood, isn't used as often anymore, it seems, but it is still part of literary language.

Greco-Roman medicine, as mediated by Assyrian Christian and later Muslim scientists such as the great tenth century philosopher and physician Ibn Sina, was for centuries the default theory of medicine in a geographical region stretching from the British Isles to the Tianshan mountains. For much of the European Medieval and Renaissance period the most progressive developments and advanced state of knowledge was to be found in the Muslim World. At that time, Europeans often looked to translations from Arabic texts to broaden their medical knowledge. Some even ventured towards the East to gather first-hand information on the most recent breakthrough in the field of science. One such journey has been fictionalised in Noah Gordon's 1986 novel *The Physician*, which relates the tale of a Christian English boy of the eleventh century studying medicine in Isfahan, Persia. Indeed, up until the eighteenth century Ibn Sina`s *Canon of Medicine* (*Qanun fi'l-Tibb*) was a major standard reference work taught at European medical colleges and consulted by all learned medical practitioners. But a shift of paradigms had already begun in Europe in the sixteenth century, with a new medical theory emerging thanks to the efforts of the Swiss alchemist Paracelsus. Paracelsus's theory was still quite different from our current ideas on disease and health but it set medicine on a new journey of discoveries. Inspired by his knowledge of alchemy, itself also an import from the Muslim World with Greco-Roman ancestry, he shifted attention away from the 'humours of the body' and to the study of substances such as toxins, thereby eventually enabling the rise of what we today understand as modern allopathic medicine. Granted that in the sixteenth century the glorious times of a Greco-Roman Islamic medicine based on humoral pathology were not yet over. The Muslim World still made important medical discoveries even at that time and this would later contribute to the current modern allopathic understanding of medicine as well.

In 1616, for example, Mughal emperor Jahangir, a man with a strong personal interest in medicine and other sciences, mentioned in his *Jahangirnama* that there seemed an apparent connection between rats and other rodents and outbreaks of the Plague amongst human beings. He credited this observation to his own niece. Much later, in the eighteenth century, as Iftikhar Malik writes in the *Virus* issue of *Critical Muslim*, Lady Mary Montagu learned the technique of smallpox inoculation from the women of Ottoman Istanbul and subsequently introduced it to England. Nevertheless, the Paracelsus paradigm had started to turn the tides as far as progress in medical science was concerned. From then on, European medicine seemed to have advanced steadily while the Muslim World appeared to have lost its leading role. While humoral pathology once used to be the default theory of medical science, it is now only used in some forms of alternative medicine, such as the traditions based on the medicine of the medieval German saint Hildegard of Bingen that remains popular amongst some people. Expressions such as 'catching a cold' and the romantic concept of melancholy belong to some of the very few persistent survivals of humoral pathology in our world.

It is fascinating that of all the humoral types, melancholy remains one of the most popular. Even though we still use words such as phlegmatic and choleric in certain contexts, but these terms never seem to carry the same weight that the idea of melancholy seems to convey. Melancholy is at the same time dreaded and loved. It is a type of depression but unlike the idea of clinical depression it also seems to carry inherent notions of beauty and creativity. The melancholic is often imagined as a genius or an artist, unlike the depressed, who more than often seems to be perceived as some sort of social failure. Melancholy is a mood related to yearning and nostalgia. But it may, just as clinical depression, also lead to suicide. In the *Canon* of Ibn Sina, already melancholy is something that may in some cases have to be treated. The presence of too much 'black bile' must be curbed to guarantee the health of a human being. But on the other hand, people also carry their own particular mix of humoral juices within themselves and thus it is quite natural that some people have more 'black bile' than others and may be more inclined to melancholy than their counterparts. As such, unlike clinical depression, melancholy does not always have to be pathologised or treated.

Just as in the West the word 'melancholy' has a strange afterlife that is disconnected from any knowledge of humoral pathology, the Islamicate terminology surrounding 'black bile' has acquired a certain autonomy from medical theory as well. More often than not, the idea of 'melancholy' is connected to specific types of music and poetry. The Arabic word for black bile is *sawda*. In the Islamic East this word became the *takhallus* or pen name of a famed Urdu poet, Mirza Muhammad Rafi 'Sauda', who died in 1781, something that led to an abundance of clever allusions to both him and the concept of melancholic madness both in his own poetry and the poetry of opponents and admirers alike. In modern Turkish, *sawda* is transcribed as *sevda*. An interesting assimilation of the word has happened here, for the Turkish verb *sevmek* means 'to love'. Many modern Turks nowadays think of *sevda* as a word that is etymologically derived from sevmek. It is therefore understood as a kind of love. But according to its original meaning it can only be seen as an unhappy and unfulfilled love, a melancholic love. In the post-Ottoman Balkan nations, a whole genre of

music is seen as the perfect expression of this kind of love, the *sevdalinka*.
Bosnian Muslims see the *sevdalinka* and the melancholic spirit that comes
with it as their very own, but it has its fans and its equivalents in all the
other Balkan nations as well. Its orchestration draws on old Balkan folk
music as much as from Sephardic Jewish and Turkish elements with lyrics
full of broken hearts and shattered hopes. But even someone unable to
understand its lyrics will immediately grasp the melancholic nature of this
particular style of songs.

Another type of music often associated with intense feelings of
melancholic desire is the Portuguese *fado* and it is therefore only slightly
surprising that this type of singing is also associated with a word that seems
somewhat reminiscent of the Arabic *sawda*: *Saudade*, a mood often described
as a 'profound longing for something or someone lost', a type of bitter sweet
romantic yearning. In the case of *saudade*, the etymology is not as clear as in
the case of the *sevdalinka*. The ultimate origins of the word have actually been
a mystery to linguists. Many have tried to derive it from the Latin *solitudo*
but that etymology has not convinced everybody. There is a certain tendency
in the linguistic study of Iberian languages to explain away Arabic influences
and to stress an uninterrupted Romance heritage but the fact cannot be
ignored completely that Portugal has been a part of Islamicate Al-Andalus
from 726 until 1249 and the last Portuguese Arab speaking Muslims were
expelled only at the end of the fifteenth century. Cultural influences from
that historical period persisted for a long time and even though what we
know today as *fado* only emerged centuries later, in the 1820s, it has often
been noticed that the musical style does have audible similarities to North
African Berber and Arab and Sephardic Jewish styles of music. We see a
strong Arab influence in Portuguese cuisine even today – with the popular
Portuguese comfort food *açorda* for example derived from the Arabic
al-thurda, allegedly the favourite dish of the Prophet Muhammad – and as
British food historian Rachel Laudan notes in *Cuisine & Empire*, the
transmission of Arab recipes and techniques of cooking to the cuisines of
later Catholic Iberia was often accompanied by a transmission of medical
knowledge based on humoral pathology. In fact, it was most probably the
Iberian peninsula where the work of Ibn Sina entered the awareness of
Catholic Christian Europeans for the first time and gave birth to a renewal
of medical sciences in Europe. *Sawda* was certainly a concept known to the

Portuguese in the medieval and early modern period and the idea most likely had an influence on the emergence of *saudade*. It is also quite possible that, as in the case of the Turkish *sevda*, two etymologies merged into each other and *saudade* may be a love child of *sawda* and *solitudo*.

Thus, an Islamicate conception of the influence of 'black bile' has taken a musical form both in the most south-western and the most south-eastern parts of the European continent while it also still lingers on in the languages and folk medical ideas of Central and Northern Europe. The humoral tradition of medicine is still very much alive in other parts of the world, of course. In South Asia in particular there still exists a very vibrant tradition of alternative medicine that still carries the name *Yunani*, literally 'Greek', etymologically *Ionian*. In countries like Afghanistan, Pakistan, India and Bangladesh it functions as a Muslim equivalent to the more Hindu-influenced Ayurvedic medicine and as a competitor to the likewise very popular homeopathic system. Yunani medicine directly carries on the legacy of Hyppocrates, Galen and Avicenna and up to this day many of its professionals often still consult the Canon of Ibn Sina in their practical work. For centuries Yunani medicine has coexisted with Ayurveda, however, and throughout the ages the two systems have become more and more similar to each other. Sometimes this similarity becomes a contentious object of nationalist sentiments. Hindu nationalists may often feel that Yunani medicine has borrowed far too extensively from Ayurveda, which they understood as the true origin of all medical knowledge. In fact, we can detect a lot of Ayurvedic borrowings in the writings and practices of Yunani practitioners, but there has also been a great deal of visible influence of Yunani medicine on Ayurveda. The connection between the two medical systems may run even deeper than the Islamic period, for the *dosha* theory on which Ayurveda is based has so many strong parallels with the Greco-Roman humoral pathology that some scholars have speculated that it may have its origins in the Indo-Greek kingdoms that ruled over parts of today's Afghanistan, Pakistan and North India in the period between the exploits of Alexander the Great and the beginning of the Common Era. Strong similarities also exist between both systems and other medical systems of Asia, such as Tibetan, Mongol and even Traditional Chinese Medicine. One may speculate that all of these systems owe something to mutual influences and exchange of knowledge along the Silk

Roads, from the Hellenistic Age up to the times of Ibn Sina. We also have to acknowledge in this context that the ancient Greeks probably did not entirely invent their humoral medicine on their own but that they were strongly influenced by the vast medical knowledge of the ancient Egyptians and Mesopotamians, who in turn had interactions with the people of the Indus Valley Civilisation.

The idea that very different medical theories can nevertheless all benefit human beings often bothers the human mind. There has for long been a consensus amongst Western allopathic physicians that alternative theories of medicine are just quackery. But in recent decades Traditional Chinese Medicine in particular has made some strong inroads in the West and the results of its methods of treatment have been baffling to many people schooled in modern allopathic medicine. The theory behind practices such as acupuncture, for example, appears as complete nonsense according to the standards of modern allopathic medicine but nevertheless it has become a more and more accepted fact that acupuncture can seriously help people suffering from certain ailments, such as migraines, and that relief is based on more than just a placebo effect. These realisations have also engendered a more thorough scientific investigation of medical systems such as Yunani and Ayurveda. In India, in particular, it is nowadays not uncommon to find medical institutions where Yunani and Ayurveda are both studied and used along with allopathic medicine.

We should indeed not forget that, eventually, both Yunani medicine and modern allopathic medicine go back to the work of Ibn Sina. Even if the sceptical scientistic allopath cannot accept Yunani medicine as a valid alternative to his own theories and practices, he must at least regard it as an old relative, maybe one that is a little out of tune with the developments of the world. In reverse, to the Yunani practitioner, allopathic medicine would often look like a young man filled with vigour and energy but not yet able to entirely grasp what life is about and how to keep its quality in balance. Due to this old relationship, it is therefore not surprising that many of the practices and treatments of Yunani medicine actually do make sense from an allopathic perspective, even though the theories behind the two have diverged so significantly from each other. Hippocrates, for example, prescribed tea made from the leaves of willow trees to reduce high fever. Modern allopathy has identified acetylsalicylic acid as an active ingredient of willow that brings down fever and fights pain and we still use it today in the form of aspirin. Humoral pathology has no knowledge of this chemical substance, instead it assigned certain humoral characteristics to willow leaves. The patient may or may not be aware of both the properties of acetylsalicylic acid or of his humoral constitution but whether treated by an allopathic physician or a specialist in Yunani medicine, he will notice that the treatment is successful and will give him relief.

In the case of melancholy, Ibn Sina prescribes for mild cases a treatment with lavender. His *Canon* notices that it purges out an excess of black bile. And, indeed, modern placebo-controlled studies have found that lavender has sedative, anxiolytic and neuroprotective properties and can give some relief in mild cases of clinical depression and anxiety attacks. Modern medicine has quite a different understanding of why some active substances in lavender may have these properties, according to Ibn Sina's findings, but in practice the results are the same. Some other treatments suggested by Ibn Sina seem almost shockingly modern: Basing his claims on the works of Galen he writes in his *Canon*, 'When a live electric-ray-fish is brought near the head of a patient, it serves as a sedative'. A surprising precursor to electrotherapy.

Sometimes we may today notice that allopathic medicine is in some ways turning back to the principles of Ibn Sina and the ideas of Yunani medicine. Modern medicine now accepts, for example, that the mental constitution of a person may be influenced by his nutrition, and may also have an influence on his immune system and his physical constitution. It was the observance of interactions such as these that originally gave rise to humoral pathology and produced ideas such as the concept of melancholy. Generations of modern medical professionals have treated phenomena such as clinical depression as either a purely psychological problem that could be changed through psychotherapy or as an imbalance in the brain that could be treated easily with antidepressants. Further study of the matter has then led many specialists to favour a combination of both. But a more recent understanding of clinical depression suggests that this disease can be rooted in a number of intersecting problems, some of them psychological and related to brain chemistry but some others also related to social factors, life circumstances, organic inflammation, lifestyle and nutrition. Ibn Sina and the masters of Yunani medicine did in fact keep an eye on most of these factors when treating a supposed excess in 'black bile'. Ibn Sina would not just have given a person suffering from melancholy some concoction of lavender and other substances. He would have asked the patient about his daily routine, his food habits and his socio-economic situation. Where possible he would have suggested changes in diet and lifestyle. In fact, according to the principles of humoral pathology, unhealthy nutrition is one of the most common sources of humoral imbalances. At the same time, some of Ibn Sina's treatments remind us of certain modern types of therapy employing nutritional and pharmacological knowledge as much as talking therapy.

A widely cited anecdote often told about the great man, first related by the Persian poet Nizami, is about how Ibn Sina cured a prince from a madness caused by an excess of 'black bile'. The prince suffered from melancholy and gave up eating properly. His excess of 'black bile' only increased and his madness intensified to the extent that he imagined himself to be a cow. And not only had he started to think of himself as a cow, but again and again he asked the people around him to slaughter him, cook him and eat him. Eventually Ibn Sina was called to help the young man. When he examined the prince for the first time he said, 'this cow is too lean. If we want to slaughter it and eat it we should first fatten it properly'. Ibn Sina designed a diet for the young man, both providing him with proper nutrition and with medical substances to balance his humours. Under the pretence of being fattened for slaughter, the prince agreed to eat the diet prescribed by Ibn Sina. He examined him every day, talked to him, and showed his care while never trying to convince him that he was not a cow. Eventually the prince recovered from his madness.

Melancholy is not a humour that is meant to make us laugh. But Ibn Sina's wit in healing the melancholic prince is something that should make us smile at least and it is certainly something that many modern medical professionals can still learn from.

NO LAUGHS TO GIVE

C Scott Jordan

Let's start with a distinction. It is not essential but it would clarify a common mistake. The distinction is between *parody* and *satire*. Often these words are used interchangeably, and incorrectly. Skimming through various dictionaries, satire comes off as an exposé. It exposes a flaw or lacking of intelligence. Using humour, particularly irony or exaggeration to ridicule another through the use of artistic expression. It is mostly seen in literature, performance, and song but is widely applicable and is often tied to anything concerning politics or hot topics of the period the work is produced in. Satire is often made synonymous with any sort of political tongue and cheek. Parody at first glance would seem a broader tent under which satire can fit. Parody is just an inspired representation, an imitation. Yet, while some imitations seek to emulate the original subject or take them beyond projection, parody only does so to the ends of setting up a comical jab. Traditionally, these two phrases are rather simple forms. Tools in the comedian's toolkit. Yet, with repeated use, like copies of copies, the lines become blurred and complexities are birthed in this opportunity.

The first major complexity between satire and parody arises in that they are both terms which contain each other within them. Satire can be attained through parody. This is what occurs with caricatures and political cartoons. Likewise, parody can be used for satirical ends. This, I would argue, is what happens with fake news shows, which to avoid confusion, I will refer to as satirical news shows in accordance with popular parlance. I make a distinction between these two concepts, which may seem arbitrary at the moment, because I believe there has been a historical evolution – or devolution, depending on your perspective – from satire to parody, and we are on the brink of another evolutionary step that we ought to consider the ramifications of.

Fake news for the sake of comical entertainment, what will develop into satirical news, begins in the US with a young journalist, Samuel Clemens, the man who would become immortally known as Mark Twain. While comedy and satire had a special place in various published works, Clemens would be the first to use serious mainstream media to satire the society of his day. His radical new style caused great outrage throughout the western United States between Missouri, Nevada, and California during his journalistic odyssey. News was news. What he wrote was taken as truth. Audiences did not know how to take fake news or even satire within the serious papers. The result was Clemens having to run from town to town to flee duel challenges and the wrath of local police. The danger of such a job description alone shows why the style did not catch on immediately. While the locals of mid-nineteenth century America did not appreciate Clemens's satire in their serious papers, he would find better appreciation when he used the form in his novels.

For almost a hundred years, satire news would lie dormant. On April Fool's Day some papers would print a completely fake story to only print a correction the next day in celebration of the holiday. MGM tried a short-lived reel show by having deadpan narrators read fake news over actual news footage in the 1930s. Aside from this there would be no major establishment for fake satire news until the 1960s. I should also note here that although yellow journalism and muck raking became popular a couple decades after Samuel Clemens's run, there is a major difference between what Clemens did and what followed. Clemens used the seriousness of mainstream news to provoke a humorous irony in the audience to emphasise a deeper social ill. In contrast, Joseph Pulitzer, then editor of the *New York World*, and William Randolph Hearst, then editor of the *New York Journal,* were competing with each other to sell papers in one of the worst adherences to 'if it bleeds, it leads!' in the history of print journalism. The exaggerations of yellow journalism, at least to Pulitzer and Hearst, did not break the laws of journalism. The main point would not be a lie or an attempt to expose a deeper meaning. The stories just added a bit of flourish to reality. And there's no harm in dramatising the news a bit, even if it provokes American military aggression and war on foreign soil for the financial gain of the one percenters, right? The important distinction is that to Clemens, his news was, to use the words of Harry G. Frankfurt, bullshit, to Pulitzer and Hearst, while their news was undoubtedly propaganda and produced a plethora of satirically critical art pieces, it was still journalism in the traditional sense, given minor cosmetic surgery to increase profits.

But the fake, satire news I talk about here would not be seen as worthy to propagandists until much later. Satire news as we know it today really takes it origins in the 1960s. And like most things that have become super popular in the US, it started in the UK first. Everything was changing in the 1960s, so why not entertainment and news. Perhaps there is some credence to the zeitgeist's addiction to postmodernism and the question of 'is any news actually unbias or even true', or perhaps it was simply the rebellious spirit of the age and a restlessness around the 'thirteen wasted years' of Conservative patrician pomp, but however it transpired, the satire boom kicked off a renaissance in the early 1960s.

The first major products of this Boom, both in the UK and US, arose out of disgruntled and talented university graduates. In the UK, the period was kicked off with the performance of the stage revue *Beyond the Fringe* by Peter Cook, Allan Bennett, Jonathan Miller, and Dudley Moore in 1960. Following this success, writer and producer Ned Sherrin would team up with David Frost, the journalist who would gain international notoriety for his interviews of British and American leaders (most infamously his interview with former President Richard Nixon), as the presenter of the first satire news show *That Was the Week That Was*, popularly known as *TW3*, which was shown on the BBC for eighteen months between 1962 and 1963. The writer's room of this show saw many satire greats, including Peter Cook, John Cleese, and Roald Dahl. *TW3* made famous the defining deadpan reading of ridiculous news headlines, broke ground in lampooning political figures and the Royal Family, and not only satirised the elitism of British politicians, but the irony of their becoming involved in rather saucy sex scandals. Both of these seminal formats would attempt to make the leap across the pond, but ultimately fizzle out as the high-brow blend of comedy was not exactly America's cup of tea.

But what goes up in the UK eventually gets a demented American version fit to the humour more palatable in the US. A decade after, but similar to the satire boom in the UK, disgruntled university graduates in the US took to the stage and television, print media, and eventually film through *National Lampoon* and *Saturday Night Live*. The American version of the satire boom would officially hit televisions around the US from 1967 until 1973 with Dan Rowan and Dick Martin's stint on NBC's *Rowan and Martin's Laugh-In*. This was largely a sketch comedy show that featured some satire news, also commenting on topical political issues, as the Laugh-In was a play on the popular protest style of Sit-Ins. It was more a vaudevillian variety show focused on criticism of hippie culture and sexual innuendo. The first American satire news show would come from one of the sketches known as 'Laugh-In Looks at the News' where Dick Martin would anchor. This would directly inspire *Saturday Night Live's* 'Weekend Update' a popular satire news programme that began with the show's inception in 1975 and continues today. *Rowan and Martin's Laugh-In*, with its more pop culture focused angle would give rise to the, often forgotten, first iteration of Comedy Central's *The Daily Show* hosted by Craig Kilborn, running from 1996-1998, which embodied the apathy and cynicism of 1990s Americana. Think of the postmodern film *Reality Bites* (1994) meets MTV in baggy clothes with frosted tips. In 1999, Jon Stewart would be given the helm of *The Daily Show* and a whole new generation of comedy would follow.

The 1990s were an age of tumult for the arts. New technologies and decreased production prices coupled with a lack of confidence in the established studios, opened the door for an age of independent art. Indy was all the rage. Genre-less, garage-band produced popular music led by Grunge, films made on shoe string budgets, and a proliferation of new television channels met with an American public eager for something fresh with lightened censorship standards. The definition of the next age of American popular culture was waiting for whoever would claim it. Meanwhile in comedy, a blending was occurring. The barriers between literary humour, performance comedy, television, and film comedy were being torn down and the conventions mixed. Stand-up comedy was more common, as it also had a greater potential to be lucrative, with the invention of cassettes and CDs and even being seen on television. With format and standards changed and production barriers torn down, writers jumped around more freely and had greater agency and mobility in their careers. And while there were a lot of opportunities and new avenues opening up, many things had to adapt or die, so American satire took a new evolutionary step.

For fake news shows up to this point, satire, as I distinguished above, was the mode. The content was not the focus. The crux was put on taking the piss on the subject, to get the audience to think and then laugh at the expense of the subject. The news itself was inconsequential. Often the report would be on news that was not 'newsworthy' to expose and ridicule how news works in the UK and US or the ludicrousness of public figures and politicians. The flip comes in the backdrop of the 1990s, at least in the US, where we move from satire to parody. Parody then turns the focus to the content in order to mirror the absurdity of both the subject and concept. Sitcoms are the major utilisers of parody as a primary form of political humour and the longest running sitcom in US television history gives us some insight to the power of parody.

It is no accident that Fox's *The Simpsons* has remained on air for over thirty years, beginning in 1989, but it is curious how an animated series has become the champion of the sitcom. Sitcoms are fundamental parodies. And in the 1980s and 1990s these shows parodied various facets of American life: the prototypical American family, the American workplace, American social circles, dating and sexuality, and even dived into a variety of issues related to identity and ideas of masculinity, beauty, or heroism. The reflection of reality in the television provided a fruitful common place for some tension dissolving humour. *The Simpsons*, in a sense, was lightning in a bottle. Good writing goes a long way and simple, yet established characters allow for future plug-ins for arcs and plot. And the sky was the limit on the number of characters that one could introduce to the town of Springfield, and the writers showed little restraint in this regard. Also using the form of animation, the characters never have to age, aiding in the series' rewatchability. While *The Simpsons*, and parody in general, relies heavily on referential humour, this is not the only trick in the long playbook for this series. Shows like *Family Guy* rely, almost entirely, on not only referential humour, but pop culture referential humour. This produces a show that is hilarious when watched live in the moment, but is almost unwatchable today as the references are out of date and much of the humour that the show banked its jokes on would today be perceived as insensitive to contemporary standards of political correctness. Indeed, recently *The Simpsons* too has had to deal with the 'pc problem', but adapted by removing certain ethnic characters that embody insensitive stereotypes. It is in this adaptability that *The Simpsons* separates itself from other sitcoms and did not share in their fate.

This adaptability is the reason I focus on *The Simpsons*. In earlier seasons it did dabble a lot in satire, but pretty consistently embodies parody right up to today. The Simpson family is a parody of the traditional American family, a distorted reflection of reality. The American dream itself is parodied in the adventures the Simpson family find themselves within. Meanwhile numerous elements of American society and community are parodied, from fanatical evangelical Christians, to evil one percenter misers, to celebrities who differ greatly from the characters they portray on television, incompetent police, fast-talking hustler businessmen, and corrupt politicians to name a few. Parody as a mirror of reality is seen so strongly that *The Simpsons* even gives off the appearance that it can predict the future. Yet, the occasions where the show has spoken of future happenings have been largely coincidental and more an effect of America's (and even the world's) trajectory being so horribly predictable. And as more and more things appear to be the correct prediction of *The Simpsons*, we watch as parody falls victim to the comedy killer. The parody and the reality have merged and real life events are beyond what comedians could have imagined.

When Jon Stewart took over as host of *The Daily Show* in January 1999, he completely revolutionised the show, turning it into what many hailed as a proper fake news satire show. But instead of taking the form of prior satire news shows, his aim was to make the subject of the satire reality and by way of a cunning use of parody, he saw this out. In the early days, some of the satire persisted as his correspondents would give the classic deadpan deliveries of news poking fun at both the situation and what broadcast journalism had become by that point. And while his correspondents and writing staff would also be a farm for future comedy talent, as was the case with *TW3*, Stewart's content was not dramatised or exaggerated. The humour came in his delivery which exposed elements of irony, contradiction, and absurdity in what was happening in the real world. The content had to be honest news, that was what made his comedy so powerful. Not only that, but while he was witty and clever, he also knew how to ask questions and conduct an interview. He read the books of the authors he would have on the show and drilled them on their arguments. The jokes did not feed the content, he took the content for the news it was, and by using clips where a subject might contradict themselves or have gotten away with saying something in a different context, he wrote them into a trap. Jon Stewart's *The Daily Show* was so popular because at its heart it did not have a grand stand political agenda to push, it ridiculed left-wing and right-wing all the same. It pointed out the hypocrisies that existed in our world of twenty-four-hour news and hyper-speed instant gratification. While he was a showman, Jon Stewart was also a good journalist who knew how to conduct an interview and was able to flip between the laughs and the reality of certain situations. On 10 November 1963, the day after the assassination of US President John F. Kennedy, *TW3* held a tribute show that featured no satirical content out of respect. Likewise, Jon Stewart took at least two shows off from telling jokes. On their first show after the 11 September 2001 attacks, Jon delivered a shaken, tear-filled monologue about mourning and refusing despair, referencing his own experience as a child when Martin Luther King, Jr. was assassinated. Similarly, on 17 June 2015, following a mass shooting event at a traditionally African American church in Charleston, South Carolina, that left nine people dead, Stewart changed the show to have a real talk about racism, devoid of jokes, and filled the rest of his show with an extended interview with Nobel Prize winner and Taliban survivor, Malala Yousafzai, focusing on activism and opposing hate.

Only five years into what would be a seventeen-year tenure, Jon Stewart would rocket into celebrity and fame for his style of telling it like it was. And this would garner a false rumour, one that the Pew Research Center would discredit in 2010 and again in 2015, when Jon Stewart left the show. There was a belief that people, particularly young and liberal people would tune into *The Daily Show with Jon Stewart* as their only or primary headline news source. And this was before social media actually became a primary place Americans would get their daily news from. It turns out that only ten percent, and no more than twelve percent when the show was most popular, of the show's audience tuned into *The Daily Show* as their primary news source. A vast majority of the audience would tune in for the entertainment value. Interesting enough, this is much in line with the audiences of British satire shows, as the way they were written, if you do not also watch mainstream news or read the papers you would not understand half of the jokes being made. This false rumour was intoxicating and many mainstream news outlets picked it up and ran with it making Jon

Stewart and his subsequent successors from Stephen Colbert to John Oliver, Samantha Bee, Hasan Minaj, and Trevor Noah persona non grata in the eyes of most 'real' journalists. In fact, this disdain might be one of the few things that brings together pundits of the extreme right and left.

When it stopped being funny

The peak of the style of parody comedy was found in a spin-off from *The Daily Show* featuring one of Stewart's original correspondents, Stephen Colbert's *The Colbert Report*. Colbert, a proud son of South Carolina, would become the ultimate parody of American exceptionalism, Fox News and Partisan style punditry, and the 'compassionate conservativism' of George W. Bush's America. Such a dedicated character, and therefore a strong mirror of all the insanity in America at the time, there was even cause to question whether he was serious or a comedian. This pinnacle of parody resulted in the coining of the terms 'truthiness' (truth based on a gut-feeling, regardless of logic or reason), 'wikiality' (reality as decided by majority vote), and 'freem' (freedom without having to 'do' anything), 'the creation of an actual Super Pac (political action committee legally permitted to raise funds), being immortalised as a Ben and Jerry's ice cream flavour, testifying, in character, before a congressional committee, and running for the Republican nomination for the Presidency of the United States. The mirror Stephen Colbert held up to an America that would eventually elect Donald Trump as its President bore a reflection that was more attuned to Colbert holding up an empty frame only to then punch the viewer in the face with its ludicrousness.

And while Stewart and Colbert keep riding strong until their final shows in 2015 and 2014 respectively, there was struggle in the end. With the election of Barack Obama in 2008, there was a strong atmosphere of hope. Perhaps the last eight years of Bush had been one big joke. And in line with the phrase 'one day we will look back and laugh at all of this,' perhaps that day had come and we could rest on the laurels of progress's work done. But sense did not materialise and the asinine culture inculcated during the Bush years had dug in deep, metastasising into hate and anger. Systemic xenophobia saw to a resurgence in racial and ethnic tensions and issues of inequality that had been ignored for too long. Right-wing fanatics and Tea

Partiers were not just comical loons. They were dangerous. Gun Nuts and Fundamentalist Christians were no longer funny characters in the American ensemble. Mass shooting events, school shootings, xenophobic attacks and demonstrations of hate, questionable instances of police brutality were all happening at regular intervals to the backdrop of endless war and looming threats, domestically and abroad, to society, to individuality, to the economy, and to truth. The jokes were not funny anymore. Even the laughing one does to keep themselves from crying was disingenuous. The news had become a parody of itself, competing in absurdity to the warped realities they propagated. Funny men and entertainers had to repeatedly break the fourth wall and cancel their shows to have 'real talk'. Mainstream media and comic entertainers had switched places and, at least for the comics, it was uncomfortable and a taxing burden mentally.

Stewart's interviews became iconic feats of journalism *par excellence*. His criticisms against the War in Iraq, America's imperialistic and Islamophobic foreign policy, police violence against black individuals, and an emboldened stand against mainstream journalists made Stewart a force to be reckoned with. His aim of exposing the absurd so that we may laugh and think shifted drastically towards this exposition that informs and does the work that investigative journalism had not done in a long time. The parody news show in the end become documentary with a humorous tone. And so, this has continued with the successors of Stewart.

The Daily Show under Trevor Noah maintains a very similar style, adding just enough of the fish-out-of-water quality found in a presenter born outside of the US. For a while this revived the parody style as Noah would hold up a mirror to Americans emphasising that the rest of the world looks at the mirror too and sees something completely and utterly ridiculous. In other shows hosted by those whose careers were launched with *The Daily Show* we get more of this notion of humorous documentary. *Full Frontal* with Samantha Bee, *The Nightly Show* with Larry Whitmore, and *The Opposition* with Jordan Keppler did not even attempt to go for the parody style of *The Daily Show*, instead they do straight criticism and inform with various twists and perspectives. John Oliver with *Last Week Tonight* is essentially a column where the columnist occasionally breaks the journalist-subject neutrality principle to take matters into his own hands, mostly trolling wrong doers through a variety of pranks. In a similar vein, Hasan

Minaj's tragically shortly lived *Patriot Act* would dive deep into one issue and propose alternative approaches or solutions to the matters at hand.

Is this then to be the state of the world and the future? The news outlets continue their parade, a toxic joke that lands like one given by an ignorant uncle at a family dinner, out-dated, inappropriate, and gaining no comic utility despite how often it is repeated? Entertainers are weighed down with the burden of conscience and responsibility in democracies corrupted six ways from Sunday? Is this right? It is not hard to see the disheartening weight on those who have risen to the challenge and it is no wonder that this pursuit is not terribly sustainable and the shows come and go with the wind. To see the once glorious Fourth Estate reduced to talking heads screaming back and forth on the television, reality, opinion, and the need for ratings all blended together into a delusion.

Because of this, all sealed in the Presidency of Donald J. Trump, the now overt reality of white supremacy in the US, and the rise of fake news and conspiracy theories, parody is in a moment of existential crisis. While *The Simpsons* is beginning to fade into obscurity under its own legacy and greater buy-in to cheap referential comedy, the other animated sitcom master of parody, *South Park* had a full meltdown. *South Park* prided itself on taking parody beyond the family appropriate bounds *The Simpsons* has mostly maintained in its run. Trey Parker and Matt Stone had no reservations about not only holding a mirror up to America, but one that colours the world in the disgusting vulgar hues of a hyper reality. While the pitfalls of *South Park* reveal the hands of its creators, taking strong stands against organised religions, ideologies, identities, and popular culture, the show ran into the same roadblock of the death of comedy. Comedy was supposed to allow us to laugh at reality, not remind us of how truly messed up the world is. The only way Parker and Stone could seek to parody this reality was by seeking the show's own cancellation with the 2019 season's famed hashtag #CancelSouthPark. It appears Parker and Stone had reached a point of diminishing returns on making reality look any wackier than it already was.

While the Trump Presidency has come to an end, the Covid-19 pandemic has pretty definitively noted that there's no going back. But the seeds of the next step in the evolution of American comedy may just be featured in our social media feeds and message scrolls.

For a Few Memes More

In the noughties, the television station Comedy Central came into its own, transforming from a repository for stand-up comedy and reruns of *Saturday Night Live* and classic comedy films to a major producer of comedy with the success of *South Park* and *The Daily Show*. But there is another Comedy Central great that I have left out and despite its tragedy, only recently redeemed, it may speak to the future of critical comedy. While 2004, a big-time election year, was rounding up to be the biggest year for Comedy Central, a year earlier, comedian producers Dave Chappelle and Neal Brennan began 2003 with their new show, *Chappelle's Show*.

To the untrained eye, *Chappelle's Show* was another sketch comedy show, somewhere between satire and parody (often from sketch to sketch), but upon further examination, something much more interesting was occurring with this experiment. It even began with a familiar structure, where Dave Chappelle, similar to Jerry Seinfeld, would address an audience much like a stand-up comedy special before each sketch. Seinfeld, would deliver a joke that would act as a prologue for a scene for which his sitcom was built upon, which in that case was a parody of New York City life between the 1980s and 1990s. Chappelle on the other hand was more P.T. Barnum than Jerry Seinfeld. Instead of setting up a slice of life, Chappelle invited the audience to explore the strange world we live in through a clever use of satire and parody. But Chappelle's brand of comedy had an aim that set it apart from merely holding the mirror up to the audience. He wanted everyone to be in on the joke and to take the jokes home with them. While other comedy shows provided escape, Chappelle essentially said buckle up because we will take reality for the ride it is.

Chappelle's Show was satire but he cared both about the content and the subject. We see a very sophisticated brand of satire in Chappelle's character Clayton Bigsby, a blind black man raised in the southern US who grew up to become a leader of white supremacists and the KKK, or in his what-would-happen-if sketch where the US government pays out cash for slavery reparations to black Americans and his sketch where a racial draft, similar to a professional sports draft, once and for all settles the status of biracial celebrities. The show also masters parody with Chappelle's portrayal of Samuel L. Jackson, Rick James, Prince, Lil John and others.

Yet in his style, Chappelle takes critical comedy to a new stage. The point is not to make a political statement per say or to criticise one individual or group of individuals, but to point and laugh at normality itself. He throws the spotlight on our culture and our language, and all the norms that, mostly subconsciously, we all live and die by. He has us all laugh at racism, stereotyping, sexism, and a variety of ugly facets of American culture.

Dave Chappelle, who embraced Islam in 2001, maintains that his only goal was to make people smile. For him that was the greatest reward. Many claimed that Chappelle was attempting to educate the public. Whether conscious or not, I believe that Dave Chappelle and the folks behind *Chappelle's Show* were transcending culture. This was done through the creation of memes and before internet memes had become an everyday element of our lives. A meme fundamentally is a unit of information. Memes are these units that take on an image or style or behaviour, a fad, that can move from person to person. Memes are described as having a cultural context, but it is in this context that they have the potential to translate between cultures. Their symbolic value comes in that they bear a meaning which, even if argued as being subjective, is irrelevant. What is relevant is that a meaning is conveyed. Perhaps this extra phenomenon which memes have taken on is an effect of how memes have been adopted by culture. The internet meme, for instance, is usually an image which as a unit, represents the essence of memes in general. What is interesting is that memes have almost become the alphabet for a new language. So much so that memes are made of images from films that many meme users have never seen or even know where they come from. The fact is that the unit image can be used as an expression in anytime. This is how memes transcend cultures, they are almost primally human, and they have a tremendous latent power in invoking opposition.

Internet memes are the language of social media and increasingly a generational bond that could bridge cultures for the Millennials, Gen Z and any other subsequent generations. In fact, Generation X and older generations, knowing the source material which comprise memes can make their own translations and join in on the discourse. While the interpretations of the meme language can be fairly subjective, they can offer an interesting insight to the *Zeitgeist*.

Consider the meme known as Bernie Mittens. This meme arose out of an image captured at the 2021 inauguration of US President Joe Biden. Bernie Sanders, former Democratic Presidential hopeful and Senator from Vermont, was sitting, socially distanced wearing a face mask in a heavy coat with thick mittens on crossed arms. At the moment the image was captured Bernie Sanders happened to be looking down and giving a rather less than content expression. To some this meme represents the champion of progressivism in the US having to play second fiddle to the man who would be President only because he was more palpable for the half of America that wanted Trump to win a second term. To others, Bernie Mittens represents a sentiment of discontent with the Covid-19 pandemic, an exhaustion with facemasks and the global winter of quarantine and despair. And Bernie Mittens can take on countless other interpretations. What is powerful is that such an image can be exchanged from person to person across numerous national, linguistic, and identity borders and garner a few laughs, another pancultural expression of something other than misery.

Memes also take on a political capital most recently seen around a wave of meteorological and policy disasters that rocked Texas in February of 2021. As people were dying throughout the state as a result of this catastrophe, US Senator from Texas, Ted Cruz flew his family off to the safety, and warmth, of Mexico for a holiday. A firestorm of memes called Ted Cruz out for leaving Texas behind, most famous of which depicting the senator as the guy on the Titanic who grabbed a lost child to earn himself a place on one of the few limited lifeboats. Memes have gained incredible power in the political arena. Former President Trump was the star of innumerable memes. And in response to a shamefully low government aid package hand out for those economically rocked by the pandemic, Senate Minority Leader Mitch McConnell had his face grafted onto Marie Antoinette saying 'Let them have $600'. Images have always been powerful throughout history, but memes have the potential to capitalise on this power. And we may be living in a time that will see memes influence elections and potentially overthrow regimes.

Much of *Chappelle's Show* sticks with audiences so well because it is essentially meme content. And in the repetition of Chappelle's memes, the absurdity is not only exposed, but put on trial, made public, and perhaps positioned for change.

But this comes with a very dangerous and delicate balance. Comedy, especially in the last few years, has had a tremendous responsibility thrust upon it. Many comics are resistant to it, but like it or not, this is the pulse of popular culture today. Dave Chappelle put a lot of faith in the audience and expected much more of those who watched his show. In the summer of 2004, while doing a stand-up performance in California, a member of his audience interrupted him with one of his classic lines. For the overworked Chappelle, this was the final straw. The show had been ruling and, according to him, ruining his life. He left the stage in the middle of his set and, after a few minutes, calmed down and returned to the audience. 'You know why my show is good? Because the network officials say you're not smart enough to get what I'm doing, and every day I fight for you. I tell them how smart you are. Turns out, I was wrong.'

The show only lasted two seasons and despite Comedy Central's offering of a historic fifty-million-dollar contract, he walked away. Dave Chappelle took a sick day while filming a third season of the show in 2005 and then suddenly turned up in South Africa on a spiritual retreat. Rumours soared stating it was fame getting to Chappelle or that it was a drug problem, and like rumours tend to go, this was not the truth. While filming a sketch, the wrong laugh made it all fall down. Dave Chappelle had written about these pixies which would appear in racist situations and pressure individuals to live up to various stereotypes, they were the embodiment of racism. When filming the black pixie sketch, a sketch in which Chappelle put on black face and took on the imitation of a Jim Crow black caricature, a white crew member laughed in that way that was less laughing with you and more laughing at you. This sent the comedian on a reflection that killed *Chappelle's Show*.

In various points throughout history artists have been called upon, usually because they are the calmest, or at least the most in touch with the changes we find ourselves living through. Where true talent is a precious commodity, it is quite the moment when an individual can bear the right talent and will push the line a little further. Understandably, the pressure societies put on individuals to navigate change is tremendous. As we can watch US Presidents age decades in years, Jon Stewart looks very different on either end of his seventeen-year career with *The Daily Show*. Dave Chappelle disappeared for almost a decade after *Chappelle's Show*.

We are at an unprecedented moment where reality as seen on the news and in comedy has become almost indistinguishable, the one from the other, where the roles could easily be reversed. For the sake of sanity, I think it is essential that that balance is reinstated. It is interesting to think what a society that calls for communal efforts might look like doing the work we have for far too long waited for individual heroes to take on. I wonder if memes may just bring about the next peak of global human communication and present a real power which can influence change. Maybe, just maybe, one day we will all look back and laugh at this.

MY SARDONIC TWEET

Hussein Kesvani

In November 2018, I caused an international crisis.

It involved a late-night tweet, a number of far-right organisations and influencers, multiple hospitals across London, and a mischievous paediatrician, who had been allegedly whispering Islamic prayers into the ears of new-born children. The incident made it to a number of right-wing blogs and forums, as well as prominent British newspapers. Dozens of people demanded that the doctor be struck off, arrested by both the Metropolitan police and INTERPOL, and 'deported to Pakistan'. Islamophobic influencers from America used the tweet as proof that the UK's medical system, the National Health Service – which they'd already considered to be an evil, communist project – had been taken over by secret Islamists, and that it was only a matter of time before they did the same in other public institutions.

The only problem was that the entire story was fake. There was no mischievous doctor. The hospital that he not only worked at, but was the 'chief doctor' in, had never existed. Even theologically, the claim made no sense. But, since that night, the actions of that doctor have followed me, haunted me, and at times, even defined me.

I had recently moved to Rensselaerville, a small town in Albany, New York, to partake in a writer's workshop. For two freezing cold months, I aimed to finish the manuscript of my first book – a study of young British Muslims and how they used social media – that was already months behind schedule. The town is one of the smallest in the state, with a population of just over 2,000 people, spread across acres of woodland. In the town, there is just one restaurant, a cafe that opened for two hours a day. The nearest city is a three-hour drive, while getting to New York City would require two additional train journeys. Which is to say that the appeal of the writer's workshop was its remoteness and detachment from the world. That, in absence of the hustle and bustle of cities, you could do little more except read and write.

I posted the tweet around 2am, after an unsuccessful late-night writing session, desperately trying to meet my daily word count. As I walked from the writer's studio back to my bedroom, the tweet naturally formed in my head. 'Wouldn't it be funny to see angry right-wing Brexit and Trump supporters get extremely angry about the stupidest thing possible?' I thought to myself. I grinned, pulled out my phone, and tweeted:

> I love being a doctor and whispering verses of the Quran into the ears of white babies, therefore making them Muslim. The hospital I work for knows I have been doing this for years, but can't strike me off because they are scared of being called racist.

I laughed softly at how dumb the post was, put my phone on charge, and fell on my bed, thinking little of it afterwards.

The next morning, I woke up to hundreds of retweets, thousands of likes, and dozens of messages on Facebook, Instagram and Twitter demanding details of where I lived, where I went to medical school, and who had been 'funding me'. At first, I found the responses humorous. For the most part, the people who responded were those familiar with my Twitter posts and writing, which often employs an ironic parlance to magnify the absurdity of subcultural experiences on the internet. Moreover, as someone who had made his living both as a journalist and a comedy writer, posts that created fictional situations to explore the very real oddities and cultural anxieties of British life, were second nature to me. So, I had assumed that in posting the tweet about the Muslim doctor, the vast majority of my online audience would understand that it was both entirely fake, and had been written to satirise the concocted moral panics of 'Islamist' take overs of British institutions like schools and hospitals – a situation that had occurred just a couple of years earlier with Birmingham's 'Trojan Horse' scandal.

The question I return to, then isn't how the Muslim doctor tweet got so out of control, but how did *I* lose control of it? One explanation of the tweet's virility may come from what it actually says. It's no secret that Islamophobic and anti-Muslim sentiment online has consistently and substantially grown, year after year, for well over a decade. In 2019, for example, Tell MAMA, a UK-based organisation that tracks anti-Muslim incidents, suggested that anti-Muslim comments and posts increased by 593 per cent following the Christchurch terrorist attack, while Cardiff University's HateLab, a research unit tracking hate speech online, argued that there was a 'consistent positive association between Twitter hate speech targeting race and religion and offline racially and religiously aggravated offences in London'. Meanwhile, organisations like Hope Not Hate, who also research hate groups and extremist speech online and offline, argue that as social media platforms like Twitter and Facebook become narrower   that is, developing algorithms designed to connect more people together by making their online posts more discoverable – the process of encountering fake news and extremist content makes it far easier to deepen 'an individual's prejudiced politics through content'. In many cases, the group argues, far-right organisations are deeply aware of this, and use the platform's structure to 'actively lead individuals they perceive to be susceptible to far-right ideas into the movement or (encourage) people who are engaged in more mainstream or moderate far-right politics to take up more extreme positions'. So, it would make sense that a tweet about a Muslim doctor posing a supposed 'cultural threat' to a white, presumably non-Muslim baby, that the UK government simply couldn't stop due to 'political correctness' (another, largely fictional moral panic whipped up by tabloids in the early 2000s) would end up being exactly the kind of online content far-right groups needed to advance their cause. It didn't matter if it was true, and it certainly didn't matter if their own followers told them it wasn't true. The fictional tweet aligned with the fictional narrative such groups promote and continually extend to advance their social and political cause. As some of the Muslim critics of my post relayed to me in the months following the tweet, both publicly and in private, the ramifications of such jokes would be long-lasting, and would likely affect entire communities. To them, I hadn't simply posted an 'ill advised' joke that was open to misinterpretation. I had also provided the far-right groups who had already been very successful with spreading Islamophobic rhetoric, a new piece of material that they could readily weaponise as a means of spreading their message and recruit more impressionable, susceptible people.

To understand why my tweet went so viral, and why it is, arguably, the most-read piece of writing I've ever published, you also have to understand the complexities of humour as expressed on the internet. An admission: the format of my tweet wasn't unique. In fact, it followed a tried-and-tested format of political comedy, established by professional, as well as internet comedians, in which the paranoia and suspicions of right-wing ideology are parodied through the mundane, everyday actions of service workers – from police officers and postal workers, to waiters and baristas. In these tweets, comedians, pretending to be low-level service staff, claim online that they are deliberately sabotaging, ordinary, and crucially, *conservative*, people, by inconveniencing them as much as possible – by bagging their groceries incorrectly, short changing them at cash registers, or ensuring they are late to work by obstructing traffic. The most popular format of this tweet came in 2019, when, as *Daily Beast* journalist Kelly Weill reported, former Republican congressman Steve King tweeted:

> A Starbucks manager in North Carolina was firing employees for saying 'Merry Christmas,' a sure sign to him of future persecution against Christians.

The problem, however, was that despite the hundreds of retweets and articles written on right-wing blogs and news sites, the Starbucks manager never existed. In fact, the tweet King was referring to belonged to a user called @MuellerDad69, a comedian and host of the left-wing podcast 'Eat The Rich', a show that combines political analysis and irreverent political comedy. @MuellerDad69's tweet – which had even been featured on Fox News as an example of the 'intolerant left' read:

> I'm the manager of a Starbucks in Charlotte NC. I have informed my employees that they will be fired on the spot if I hear them say 'Merry Christmas' to any customers. I'm doing it because I personally dislike conservative Christians.

@MuellerDad69's tweet had played into an annual hysteria around Starbucks changing its decorative cups in December, when it tends to sell festive-themed hot drinks, which is often used by right-wing media to argue that corporations with socially liberal values are part of a broader plot to undermine conservatism, to 'eradicate' so called 'Christian values' and replace them with nefarious, secular agendas. The aggrieved response to the tweet wasn't the first time this moral hysteria came to fruition either. In 2015, a conservative activist filmed a rant about Starbucks' lack of explicit Christian imagery on its holiday cups, inspiring a wave of right-wing influencers, politicians and media hosts to call for a boycott on the company. In 2016, in the run-up to the US Presidential election, a number of online right-wing personalities filmed themselves going into Starbucks and demanding that the baristas write 'TRUMP' and 'MAGA' on their cups, after the Starbucks Twitter account announced it would release green cups in order to 'celebrate community…during a divisive time in our country.'

To Weill, this hysteria reflects a much broader change in the way that societies are organised   namely, that the decline of publicly accessible spaces like parks, museums and even bathrooms – means that places like Starbucks franchises have become a 'ubiquitous coffee chain that functions as a public space across the country'. In spite of their perceived 'liberal politics', then, places like Starbucks become sites where political and cultural discourse takes place, and, crucially, is centred around. At a time when people don't *feel* empowered and have agency, and where the power to change society seems less likely to occur through democratic political processes, it makes sense that chain coffee shops and restaurants end up becoming one of the few civic spaces upon which political and social anxieties are articulated.

Discussions in recent years around 'freedom of speech' and its application to online platforms such as Facebook and Twitter present a similar conflict between public and private space. While these debates have often been led by right-wing and conservative pundits, decrying big tech platforms for banning and restricting their accounts for spreading false information, or enacting particular hate speech rules that they claim 'suppress' right-wing speech, the reality is more complicated. As privately owned platforms, no technology company has publicly disclosed their rules around speech, and most do not have broad moderation teams, working with clear guidelines over what is and isn't allowed on their networks. As a result, platforms like Facebook have been criticised for allowing the spread of conspiracy propaganda such as QAnon, which led to violent protests and clashes at the US State Capitol in January 2021. Similarly, both Facebook and Twitter have been criticised for either allowing, or acting too slowly on other kinds of extremist content being spread across their platforms, ranging from Islamophobic and antisemitic content, that while not overtly violent in nature, still spreads racial hate and vitriol, as well as online content encouraging local vigilantism from extremist nationalist groups in India, Indonesia, and Brazil.

The ambiguity over these regulations has had a knock-on effect on how language is used on social media, as well as how it's interpreted. Consider, for example, how a term like 'woke' – coined by the revolutionary activist Marcus Garvey in 1923, and popularised by young, African-American women on websites like Tumblr to discuss how structural and economic inequality affected their identity as Black women – has now become an amalgamation of dozens of ambiguous, loosely defined grievances, appropriated in many cases, by older, wealthier and economically secure white men, with newspaper columns and regular TV panel appearances. Or, how once specific terms like 'social justice' or 'intersectionality' – that tended to be seen in academic literature as a way of describing structural inequalities under capitalist modes of production – are now more likely to be used on social media as derogatory terms, describing supposedly 'over sensitive' young people who are 'unable' to face the realities of the world outside of universities and academic institutions. These terms haven't lost their original definitions and meanings. But their continual use and re-use as they circulate through social media, and into mainstream culture, means that their very specific definitions, and their original contexts, have seemingly been forgotten, or in many cases, deliberately ignored, by mainstream outlets wishing to discuss them. While these debates around digital semantics might seem frivolous to some, senior members of the US Congress are publicly demanding big technology companies provide answers to why their tweets and Facebook posts have been deleted. British parliament proposes 'anti-woke' policies that include additional protections for colonial statues and monuments, along with a ban on teaching anti-capitalist literature in state schools – policies that have, in part, come out of social-media-driven moral hysterics. All of this illustrates how the dominance of technology companies has granted social media platforms a unique position as a global civic space for dialogue – only, without any democratic oversight or legislature for its hundreds of millions of users. While the technology platforms we use may run on sophisticated algorithms tailored to our personal desires, the lack of community-centred features means that one of the basic functions of a social media network – to communicate with other people – has become a discursive Wild West, in which words can be easily weaponised, where inane and mundane posts can easily get out of control and be ripped from their context, and where, by the time anything is done by the platform, it's far too late to curb the damage. Much of it can easily flow into the offline world in unexpected, and sometimes even violent ways.

Inevitably, this reorientation of the public, civic space, has had an effect on comedy, particularly for Black and other comedians of colour, as well as women comedians and those who come from the LGBTQ+ community. As Seth Simons, a reporter at *The New Republic* notes, ambiguous rules on free speech on technology platforms, and policies that do not take into account the nuances of language – for example, not being able to identify what is, and isn't satirical or ironic – has ended up punishing and restricting comics from minority, under-represented communities, for whom the internet provided a platform for their work, with an audience that traditional stand-up circuits couldn't offer them. Meanwhile, right-leaning comedians, more often than not white men who stand-up circuits are more willing to embrace, have been able to leverage the fears of 'cancel culture' to their advantage – by building a following not based on the appeal of their humour, but their anxieties about getting 'cancelled' too. 'You empower an audience by giving them what they want,' Simons writes, in his study of right-wing comedy clubs in New York City. 'The power they give you in return is their trust, their loyalty, their willingness to fight for you. The relationship between an entertainer and his audience isn't all that different from the one between a political leader and his movement'. In the age of Twitter, building these kinds of loyal, cult audiences is arguably easier than ever, and comedians who can embrace 'edgy' comedy with a knowingness of how social media metrics work, and what discussions, discourses and communities they need to be a part of to cultivate such an audience, reap huge rewards. Social media hasn't just become a replacement for the stand-up circuit, rather, it is a more powerful, efficient mode of building a long-term personal brand: one that can transform you from a comedian, to a cultural icon.

Does this apply to all social-media-savvy comedians? Not quite. While there aren't any official studies on the impact of social media on Black and other minority ethnic comedians, interviews I conducted for this article with friends and colleagues from the British comedy circuit, suggested an opposite trend – that up-and-coming comedians with limited resources and opportunities to showcase their work, feel they have to employ varying degrees of self-censorship. 'The lack of job security in comedy, and the competitiveness of the circuit, means that you always have to be careful,' one up-and-coming Muslim comedy writer, based in East London told me. 'One spicy joke that gets taken out of context or misinterpreted could end with you getting blacklisted from particular comedy clubs, or make you too much of a liability to places like the BBC, which is one of the places you go to when you're actually pursuing a career in comedy'. Another Muslim comedian, based in Wales, added that the recent 'obsession with cancel culture' by British tabloids, meant that any comedian who wanted to make jokes about racism, Islamophobia or misogyny, would have to prepare themselves for an inevitable backlash, online and offline. 'It's predictable, that even when you make a light hearted joke about your experience as a Muslim…with police, or in a supermarket…that it only takes one person to distort it into an attack on White, English people, post it online, and whip up anger from people who weren't even at the comedy show, or didn't watch or listen to the programme,' she says. 'It's not just about Muslimness either…even when Nish Kumar (a UK-based comedian) made jokes about Brexit, he was subjected to a torrent of online, racist abuse, and recently, Nabil Abdul Rashid (a British Muslim comedian), who made jokes about *himself* as a Muslim on TV, ended up being subjected to the same level of online hate, and received dozens of complaints'. Indeed, that the vast majority of Muslim comedians didn't want to be named for this article suggests that the value of provocative comedy and its intersections in internet culture is far from universal. In fact, for many Muslim comedians and comedy writers, self-censorship is necessary in order to keep themselves, their families and their own mental health as safe as possible.

'I think there are a lot of expectations placed on Muslim comedians – not just by non-Muslims, but also within the community itself…which means that pushing the boundaries of comedy can make a lot of people feel very uncomfortable,' says Sadia Azmat, one of the few British Muslim comedians to have found success both on the comedy circuit, and in mainstream channels like BBC radio. Azmat, whose comedy often explores issues around desire, women's sexuality and how that intersects with multiple facets of her identity as a hijab wearing British-Pakistani woman, has received criticism from Muslim audiences, particularly in relation to her Twitter account, in which she often tweets, in brazen and sometimes outlandish terms, about sexual acts. To Azmat, the challenge Muslim comedians face, both online and offline, is a culture that's become more careful and wary of offence, and where emphasis on representation alone has meant that comedians who aren't white, heterosexual males, are often confined to particular boxes, and expected to 'play' certain roles in order for their careers to progress. 'Comedy is more risk-averse, partly because of the growing concern of public backlash, which is accelerated through the internet,' Azmat says. She adds: 'when you're a comedian that looks different, or has different experiences, you're given opportunities but you're expected to play a particular role…and that role often feeds into what, often White men, think you are. So if you're a Muslim woman comedian who wears a hijab, the expectation is that you are fixated on the hijab, or you're talking about arranged marriages, or misogynist men in your community. So when you don't do that, and when you give the audience jokes that they didn't expect, it's harder to be placed'. And while that can give under-represented comedians more freedom with their material, it also has material knock-on effects. 'It becomes difficult to be given opportunities like being on *Mock The Week*, or *Have I Got News For You*, because the producers of those shows can't 'place' you,' Azmat says. 'So you end up with this reductive view of comedians who don't fit these boxes, and so some comedians end up self-editing, not out of sensitivity or because they don't want to offend, but simply because they want to work…and for female Muslim comedians who generally feel like they don't belong in [comedy] spaces, they have to pay a much, much higher price than a lot of their counterparts'.

For Azmat, then, her use of social media, and the criticism she sometimes gets because of it, is also a reminder of how valuable freedom from these archaic, restrictive expectations is. She's aware that some of her posts might be received poorly by more conservative Muslims who make up her audience, as well as non-Muslims who take issue with the more explicit jokes. But to her, social media platforms still offer one of the few spaces for genuine creativity and experimentation, and, what she suggests is 'the ability to express the truth, which has always guided the way I think about and write comedy'. So, while social media platforms might not be perfect, or even an ideal, way of telling jokes, they are 'more useful ways of telling the truth about the complexities of people as they are, than in a comedy club, or a highly edited TV programme'.

Azmat's framing of social media is not uncommon among young Muslims living in the UK. As I saw when conducting research for my book, *Follow Me Akhi: The Online World of British Muslims,* many young Muslims saw social media as a space where they could be more fluid in how they practised their faith. Outside of the rigid, hierarchised rules employed in Muslim spaces like mosques and madrassas, young Muslims can craft humorous identities online, and would often make jokes about living in the UK as a Muslim. In some cases, that might include the panics that came with accidentally eating pork in a restaurant and enjoying it, or skipping *rakats* in their Salah so they didn't miss watching a football match. In other cases, the Muslim comedy that defined what is known as 'Muslim Twitter' centred around difficult experiences of living in the West – comedic observations about the strange, and leering obsession with hijabs and niqabs, or the 'random checks' Muslim men would face at airports. In most cases, none of the people I interviewed on Muslim Twitter identified themselves as being comedians, or wanting to pursue a future in comedy. Instead, they saw Twitter, and social media, as being a space where they could 'be a different version of themselves', where they weren't solely defined by their religion, or their choice of clothing, or even the decisions they made in their practice of Islam. As one member of 'Muslim Twitter', a London-based secondary school student told me, 'Being funny is how I channel my anger when I'm on the internet… it's better to tell a joke and see people enjoying something I've written, than to complain and cause more anger and sadness'.

My 2018 Muslim doctor tweet has circulated around different parts of the internet with new responses. In 2020, the tweet found itself on the Discord app belonging to the now banned far-right group Britain First, who used it to drum up support through donations, as it faces a declining membership following a number of public scandals. It has been shared on Facebook by Hindu and Sikh nationalists, who warn that as 'Muslims have taken over the UK, they will also take over India'. At the same time, it has also circulated on Instagram and TikTok pages belonging to young, digitally savvy and aware Muslims, who, to my surprise, understand what the tweet was supposed to do: to parody the increasing absurdity of online Islamophobia and mock those who buy into it. However, in most cases, and in spite of messages reminding people that it is fake, and supposed to be a joke, the warning has often fallen on deaf ears.

The doctor tweet has gone well beyond me, and will likely live on in some form after I decide to log off and delete my accounts forever. And while there is a part of me that regrets tweeting it, and being unaware of how much traction it would get, another, is oddly proud of how it achieved what it was set out to do. That the absurdity of the tweet not only showed the scale of Islamophobic hysteria that was rampant online, but also, the double standards that come with discussions on free speech on the internet, and who gets to benefit from it. Indeed, if there's anything I learnt from the doctor tweet it is that some edgy comedy online can get you coveted TV gigs, radio specials and even a book deal. Other kinds, however, will leave you with little more than the threat of an international arrest warrant.

LAUGHING MATTER

Shazia Mirza

Laughter is a beautiful thing. So, why ruin it by talking about it? Like cake and sex, it should never be talked about. The whole point of laughter is to shut people up, so we don't have to hear them talk. It's why couples go to comedy nights together, so they can laugh and have a good time without having to talk about bills, children and why last night they couldn't get a parking space outside their own house. People don't think before they laugh, they just laugh. After I have laughed, I don't analyse why I laughed and try to repeat it. All I know is that I had a good howl, and I feel better. If we discuss laughter too much, we'll kill the joy.

Laughing like mad can be a semi-religious spiritual experience. It can take you right out of your body; forget yourself and your problems. It can be total escapism from the mundane dreary monotony we call life, and more recently, lockdown. Never have I been more desperate for laughter than I have in this past year.

The last time I laughed was last night, by myself sitting on the settee watching the Harry and Meghan interview. It was all very sad and serious, then Meghan announced that the colour of her baby's skin was questioned by someone in the royal family and I laughed out loud at Oprah's response which was mouth wide open and then 'What?' then a pause then 'Who is having that conversation?' I laughed hysterically, shockingly, outrageously and unbelievably. I haven't laughed that much since before the pandemic when I was in a live comedy show of two hundred people where I expected to laugh, that's why everyone was there. That's why laughter can never really be planned. It comes from nowhere. The unpredictability, the surprise, the shock, the relief. That's what laughter is, that's why it is so special and so rare and we will never appreciate it more than now, when we have been deprived of it like never before due to a pandemic coming from nowhere and ripping it from our consciousness.

CRITICAL MUSLIM 38, SPRING 2021

Someone said to me the other day: I can't remember the last time I had
a good laugh. Laughter is like your mother. We don't appreciate it when its
there but when it's not, we really miss it. Before the pandemic I was doing
comedy most nights of the week. I was either at a gig laughing at other
comedians, at home writing material, watching people's shows, or
observing people in the street and then going home to write about them.
Then one day all that stopped. I feel like a part of me had died, I felt
something big missing from my life, a thing that made me feel happy and
human. What happens when the laughter stops, is that we just exist instead
of being alive, a part of us definitely disappears.

I remember being at a gig once, when a woman said to me, 'I don't laugh
at anything. Nothing makes me laugh, I don't laugh at all.' I said, 'Why
not?' She said, 'I don't know, it never happens'. I told her this wasn't true.
As long as you are human you must have a sense of humour. No one lives
a life without laughing. We all know people who we think have no sense
of humour, but even they laugh at some point. There are stereotypes, but
even they aren't based in truth. I've done comedy in Germany, where
people warned me, no one would laugh, they wouldn't understand me,
they wouldn't get me. But I had an amazing show there, where despite us
not even speaking the same language they laughed at almost everything and
I had more rounds of applause there than I have anywhere else in Europe.
Everyone has a sense of humour, the Germans, and even my dad.

I come from an extremely unfunny family. My father was a dictator.
Authoritarian, dictatorial and no Charlie Chaplin. I can't remember him
saying or doing anything funny. Ever. When we, his children, were with
him, it was all so serious all the time. Almost every conversation ended
with the phrase, 'You will go to hell for that'. Yet when he was with his
cousins and friends, there would be constant screams of laughter, really
loud yelling and streams of funny stories being told. I never found the
stories funny but these men as a group used to entertain each other with
anecdotes about day-to-day trips to the shops, people they knew,
conversations they had and silly situations they had encountered. Their
stories never revolved around women, religion, or politics. It really was
everyday observations. I never understood what they were laughing at but
I thought of it as men having a laugh and that was different from women
having a laugh.

When I saw women at family gatherings, standing in the kitchen chatting, they laughed about men, their husbands, their children, clothes, make-up, and all other people. I used to watch my mother in the kitchen talking with other women about other women. Who used to be thin, but was now fat. Who was pregnant now for the fifth time, and whose child had passed their eleven-plus. It was all very domestic, very ordinary but it was their life. I loved hearing my mum laugh, because it was rare. Definitely not an everyday thing because there was so much to do in the day. There was no time for laughter. She had to wash my PE Kit, and make my packed lunch. Who had time to have a laugh in the kitchen with Aunty Nagma putting diesel instead of petrol into her new mini?

Humour and laughter definitely have cultural aspects to them. I know this from doing shows all over the world. I have performed in the US, France, Germany, Norway, Sweden, Denmark, Holland, Switzerland, Italy, India, Pakistan, Kosovo, Dubai, Scotland, Kuala Lumpur, Singapore, Hong Kong, and a year before the pandemic, I toured China. I always spoke in English, in France I did a bit in French. I would adapt my set to the country in which I was performing.

In China, for example, I would walk around during the day, go to shops, try and order food and then at night do jokes to the English-speaking audience, about the difficulties I had during the day. I was starving yet everything seemed to be pork. I was staying in a hotel, where when I looked out of the window there was a shop with pigs hanging from the window. I felt like the pigs had come to get me. Of all the animals in the world, why was I surrounded by pigs? No one spoke English, all the menus were in Chinese, nothing was in English. No one understood me and I wanted to Google vegetable dishes but I couldn't get the pictures to come up on my phone. Google, Facebook, Twitter, and Instagram apps on my phone had all been banned in China. I borrowed someone else's phone to Google aubergine and a pig came up. For the first time ever I felt like I was a total foreigner. I went back to my hotel starving and called a friend. I said: 'everywhere I go and everything I do is a pig. Even the vegetables are pigs'. She couldn't stop laughing. I knew this was going to be in my show that night. It was actually a tragedy. I was starving. I had no one to talk to. I couldn't get the things I wanted and I couldn't get material from conversations with people, because I wasn't having any! But that is what comedy is. There is a famous quote, 'comedy is tragedy plus time'. Every awful thing that happened to me in China was hilarious on stage.

The pinnacle of tragedy in comedy came when I was asked to do a show for the British council in Kosovo. It was very exciting for me. I was being paid to do comedy in a place I couldn't even find on a map. They told me that I had to do an hour of stand up comedy in Pristina and that I would be on with another comedian also doing an hour. That was all fine with me; I do this kind of thing all the time.

I turned up in Pristina at around 3pm in the afternoon. It was pitch black. I couldn't see a thing out of the window as I was transported to my hotel by my driver who couldn't speak English. It was bitterly cold being December, there were sporadic holes in the bumpy road, and bits of concrete were flying everywhere. It was war torn and derelict. There definitely wasn't much to see and I felt that I had to bring the comedy to Pristina rather then me finding the funny whilst I was here.

The show started at 7pm. I entered the venue to find no electricity, no heating, no seats, and people were so cold they huddled close to each other at the bar. People had to stand for two hours. Most of the audience didn't speak English and most were men.

The first comedian went on stage. He was a Swedish man doing an hour of surreal comedy in English to the audience who just stared at him. It was so cold. I don't think they could have laughed even if they'd wanted to. I stood at the back and wondered how on earth I would make these people laugh? They didn't look like me, they didn't speak my language, it wasn't the right temperature let alone the right atmosphere and what could I say that would connect with a hundred cold men in a war torn country who probably haven't laughed for months?

I made it up. On the spot. I decided to ditch my pre-written material and just improvise. I needed us all to speak the same language, find something in common where we all laughed together. I saw a woman in front of the stage, walking to the toilet. She left her handbag behind. I jumped off the stage, grabbed her handbag, took it back onto the stage and started going through it – in public. I pulled out a very small hairbrush, a tennis ball, and some toothpaste. Everyone started laughing. I improvised with all the items in the bag, started a raffle and tried to sell the hairbrush. The woman came back, stood in front of me, and didn't notice that I was in her handbag for about twenty minutes. This made it all the more hilarious. Everyone was laughing, then it dawned on the woman, that it was her handbag and the laughter went through the roof. The look on her face, the shock, the absurdity, the desperation on my part to get some laughs, any laughs out of this situation, all added to the hilarity. I came all this way; I had to do my job.

What I realised in Kosovo is that you do not need to speak the same language, you don't even have to understand each other, but if you can find a connection with someone, physical, mental, emotional, verbal, spiritual, or sexual, then that can be enough to create a spark that can result in a reaction between you and the audience. My result has to be laughter, but in life that result can be anything you want it to be if you can connect in some way.

This has happened to me time and time again, in different countries and different environments. I once did a show in a toilet in Norway. It was a public toilet where I could only fit in eight people; luckily it was a sell out. I stood on top of the toilet seat holding a microphone telling jokes to local people. It was, once again, a right laugh. The situation was not favourable, but laughter was the connection.

Then there is the line I sometimes fear to cross. Will people be offended? How much can I take the piss? Can I say this, can I say that? Race, religion, sex, politics, shall I leave it all out? Should I just talk about men, women, shopping and shoes?

I have been to so many countries where they 'warn me' in advance. When going to Pakistan on tour, I was told, 'Don't talk about sex'. Firstly I have nothing to say on the matter, but secondly I thought why are the organisers making this decision on behalf of the Pakistani people? Surely I should be allowed to do what I think is funny and hope that people also find that funny. But to censor me is really depriving the people of an experience, which they might have loved.

I went on stage in Lahore to a thousand people. Men women and children all flooded into a huge tent. I played it safe, did harmless jokes about my family, marriage, food, travel and the country itself. I mentioned something vaguely sexual and people started shouting, 'Go further, go further!' Men started laughing even louder and everyone started chanting, 'More, more'. I was surprised but relieved and happy. I wanted to do material here, that I did everywhere else. Surely what Westerners find funny about life, Pakistanis could also find funny. And they did, even more. The more I joked about sex, the more they loved it. That doesn't necessarily happen in Europe. In Pakistan all the taboos, all the things that are not spoken about in public, were exactly what they wanted to laugh at. They had a lot of internal repressed laughter that was dying to come out, thankfully I didn't listen to the organisers who wanted to repress it further.

Laughter and humour are so visceral that editing and censoring really has no power over them. You cannot stop someone from laughing. That is like trying to stop me eating cake at four in the morning when I'm locked up in my house in the middle of a pandemic.

I was once at a funeral where people were crying hysterically. All of a sudden amongst the cries of hysteria someone farted, really loudly. It went on a bit. Everyone heard it. No one mentioned it, no one owned up to it, said sorry, or moved. Everyone just carried on crying like nothing had ever happened. I couldn't stop thinking about it afterwards. The audacity of the person to let that happen at such a time of grief. I thought about it for weeks after and as time went on, I found it funnier and funnier. The more I thought about it, the more hilarious it became. Looking back on the funeral, there was pain, grief, sadness and now delayed laughter because someone farted in the wrong place at the wrong time. Is it all the same, sadness and laughter? You can be laughing one minute and crying the next, you can be laughing and crying at the same time like when I was running for a bus in the snow and rolled all the way down a hill only to land on a man putting his bins out at the end of the driveway. I was screaming then I was laughing as I landed on him. He wasn't laughing, which made me laugh even more!

Laughter, like happiness is temporary. It doesn't last. It's just a moment. You can't be laughing, non- stop all day everyday, people will think you're mad and you'd never get anything done. Also you'd wear yourself out and everyone else around you. There is a basic link between laughter and happiness in that we usually laugh or smile when we're happy. It's a by-product of something we feel good about but like all good things, it never lasts and the bursts are short.

I've been at so many comedy shows where people have said to me afterwards, 'I feel better now'. Laughter can be like a shot of heroin. You have it, it feels great, and then you must have it again. It's a good feeling, but the euphoria is short lived. Also, not everyone who is laughing is happy. They might be laughing to mask their unhappiness. And sometimes even though you're happy a smile is all you can muster.

Sometimes I would be on stage and people on the front row would just look miserable. They would come up to me afterwards and say they thought it was hilarious and how they had such a good time. I'd say: 'but you didn't laugh once!' They would say: 'we were laughing on the inside'. I never knew there was such a thing as laughing on the inside. I'd never heard of it. I don't think I've ever done that. How can you laugh on the inside? Laughter is loud, out there, raucous, and fun. It's meant to be out not in. But it is true that some people do laugh on the inside. They don't have the energy to give it some umph. An old woman once said to me, 'I really wanted to laugh, but I just didn't have the energy'. Another woman said to me, 'I really wanted to laugh, but I'm incontinent and I was scared of wetting myself and causing a scene'. Laughter requires a bit of effort then. Some energy, some life inside of you, some will to want to move forward in some way.

Once I crashed into the back of a man's car in a Tesco car park. I just drove straight into him. He was standing at the side of the car, holding eggs, milk and a big cake. He dropped them all. The eggs splattered onto the car next to him and the fresh cream cake went face down into the disabled parking spot next to his car. It was like a children's birthday party had been invaded by terrorists. I couldn't stop laughing. There was victoria sponge on the windscreen, and the man, tall and big, looked helpless and horrified. In comparison, I, a small demure harmless looking Asian woman, had caused catastrophe at 4pm on a Tuesday afternoon. I said, 'I am so, so sorry'. I attempted to pick up the cake from the floor. I picked up the milk carton and gave it back to him. I gave him my insurance details for Direct Line. I also laughed in his face. I didn't mean to, but I did. I thought it was all so funny. I also felt sorry and guilty and didn't know how to cope with it. I felt sorry for the man. I felt sorry for his car. I felt sorry for the cake. Maybe it was a diversion from having to deal with the truth that made me squeal with laughter.

Schadenfreude – laughing at other people's misfortune. I don't like to do it, but sometimes I can't help it. I have laughed at people running for the bus, and then missing it. I have laughed at people falling over in the snow, and someone falling off their bike. It's not a nice thing to do, but my instinct is to laugh. I grew up with my brothers and sister laughing at my misfortune. I got bad exam results, my brother laughed at me. I dyed my hair brown but it went orange, my sister laughed at me. My parents laughed at my misfortunes all the time. My dad used to laugh at me for 'having the worst Birmingham accent in the whole of Birmingham' as he used to call it. He would say, 'we need to get treatment for that accent, it's horrific. No man will want to marry you with that accent'. I never found these accusations remotely funny, but he did.

Laughter is personal, unique, valuable, important, necessary. But most of all I think it's healing. It heals a multitude of tragedies, a mass of pain, and serves as an escape from reality.

This Covid-19 pandemic has shown me what happens when there is a lack of laughter and how much it's needed, and how much I can't wait to have a really good laugh with people, when it all ends. We will look back on this pandemic and laugh again. We will laugh at all the cooking we did, all the Zooms we did, how we lived in our pyjamas for twelve months, and didn't shave our armpits. How I'd only get dressed from the waist up for a meeting and how I'd never run in my life, then tried to run everyday, but the donuts got the better of me on my return. I didn't wear a bra for twelve months, and my breasts had started self-isolating. I shall look back on this and laugh. I sat on the settee for months and months watching documentaries on serial killers. I watched documentaries on all the world's most dangerous men. Fred West, Harold Shipman, Prince Andrew. These documentaries brought me some kind of strange comfort. I kept thinking, 'well I'm alive. I'm doing ok, these programmes are horrific and they're real but I'm sitting in my house eating chips, so my life must be ok.'

I will look back and laugh at all of this, yet while it was happening none of it was funny. The funny can sometimes only happen when we know we've survived. When we're in the thick of it, we don't know if we'll live to tell the tale, so laughter is nowhere to be seen. When we're out of it, we're safe. Then we can laugh.

I said at the beginning that talking about laughter ruins it. And it does. Don't ever dissect a joke. You will kill it and you will look stupid in front of your mates. Don't ever try and work out why something is funny, or how to make something funny, the reverse will happen. The best thing is let the laughter come to you, take it on, feel it, enjoy it, don't judge it, don't be offended by it, don't fight it. Just go with it. And if you think you can laugh a woman into bed, or a man into bed (though this rarely happens and has a low success rate) I'd try other things first. It's a lot of effort and it's ongoing. You might have laughed them into bed once, but then you really have to step up your game for a second, third and fourth time. I'm very busy; I have cleaning, writing, cooking and driving to do. I can't be using my precious energy to laugh a man into bed? That's not how it works anyway according to my mum.

If you get a chance, a minor possibility to squeeze a laugh out of life, go for it. There could be mass misery round the corner; and nothing could make you laugh anymore. Or you could get old and not have the energy to laugh. You want to but you can't. Try and laugh while you still have your teeth, still have your voice, and there is no possibility of passing wind and wetting yourself with a bit of pressure. With laughter there is always a way out. Always an escape from reality. It can get you out of any situation.

But, for God's sake, like cake and sex, let us talk no more about laughter.

ARTS AND LETTERS

QAHERA

Deena Mohamed

It is kind of a funny story, you see! *Qahera* began as a joke. In 2013, then eighteen-year-old Deena Mohamed wanted to talk about a couple of small, less than controversial issues, among them islamophobia and misogyny. Superheroes were all the rage in popular culture and Mohamed had a Tumblr account where she posted her multimedia blogs. So, what was a creative to do? What if, instead of the image that, unfortunately, comes to mind when one thinks of a superhero, one instead imagines a woman? And not just any woman, but a woman in the likeness of a majority of women in contemporary Cairo – a *hijabi* woman. Qahera, the hijab wearing, misogynistic-butt-kicking superhero was born.

Taking the Arabic for Cairo (*al-Qāhirah*) as her namesake, our hero would develop over ten episodes (both in English and Arabic) taking on misinformed teahouse male gossipers, confused French women liberationists (not to mention, exhibitionists), self-absorbed musicians, and would-be agents of the patriarchy, in pursuit of justice. Qahera not only beats the bad guys, but informs the public of wrong doings and strives to broaden the discussion on various issues from the endemic nature of xenophobic sentiment, to equality, and social responsibility (especially in terms of accountability in relation to sexual harassment and violence). In an interview with *Egyptian Streets*, Mohamed said 'I don't really consider Qahera a "superhero" character so much as it [the comic] is an editorial strip – so it's a satirical cartoon that uses the tropes of superheroism to make a point, rather than a superhero comic that addresses political issues.' Similarly, Mohamed's use of Qahera is to bring a face to a community otherwise left faceless and without a voice. Mohamed, herself not a hijbi, said in a behind the scene Qahera blog: 'the women who bear the brunt of Islamophobia are invariably hijabi Muslim women, because they are very visibly Muslim. All of the Islamophobic stereotypes, and many others, are heaped upon their heads. She is a superhero who wears a hijab, not a superhero because she wears a hijab. I'm approaching this from a social perspective, not a religious one.'

'Qahera was created to combat the patriarchy and misogyny I am familiar with,' Mohamed continues. 'Islamophobic logic often means critiquing your own society and will result in others using that as an excuse to claim you are "oppressed" and "backwards" and "a victim of your own culture." Therefore, Qahera combats misogyny and Islamophobia.'

In the following pages are two episodes from the *Qahera* webcomic as a sample of Deena Mohamed's work. To read her entire story thus far and keep an eye out for the next episode, visit https://qaherathesuperhero.com/.

Qahera has gained Mohamed international prestige as an illustrator and designer. Her work has been featured at exhibits all throughout Europe and garnered numerous awards and accolades. Her debut graphic novel, *Shubeik Lubeik*, published in Arabic by Dar El Mahrousa, is an urban fantasy trilogy that takes us to a slightly more magical Cairo and does not disappoint in continuing the social criticism and debate provoking style we have become accustomed to through *Qahera*. *Shubeik Lubeik* won Best Graphic Novel and Grand Prize of the Cairo Comix Festival in 2017. Look out for *Shubeik Lubeik* coming out in its English translation from Granta (in the UK) and Pantheon (in the US) in 2022 (*in sha Allah*).

Mohamed shares a passion not just for art for its own sake, but in working on projects that involve community development, awareness and outreach (particularly editorial illustrations) as well as children's books. She has partnered with Viacom, UN Women, Harrassmap and Mada Masr on her projects. On 20 January 2020, she was the artist behind the Google Doodle commemorating the 106th birthday of Egyptian lawyer Mufidah Abdul Rahman.

While drawing and writing can be lonely and isolating, she loves that her work gives her the opportunity to interact with people, especially those who have read her comics. She loves to hear what other think of her work and the interpretations people take away from it, a grand dialogue of art and spectator that she is happy to be able to contribute to.

Enjoy this selection from *Qahera*. We hopes it inspires more informed and progressive conversations.

Brainstorm

On Femen

HODJA TALES RETOLD

Mevlut Ceylan

Nasreddin Hodja is one of the most important cultural figures in Turkish literature. For generations, Turkish children have grown up listening to the satirical wisdom of this quick-witted hero. Tales starring the Hodja are often absurdist as well as satirical, featuring humorous yet contemplative lessons about life, morals, and society. But the folklore of the Hodja is not limited to Turkey. He is just as widely known in most of the Muslim world, albeit with slightly different variants of his names. In the Middle East he is known as Joha, which is transformed into Guifa, in Sicily and Southern Italy. In the Indian Subcontinent, he often goes under the monocle, Mullah Dopiaza ('two onions'). In China's his name appears in Uyghur translation as Afanti, while in Central Asia he is simply Afandi. The Hodja also has a unique place in Slavic literatures – Russian, Bosnian/Serbian, Bulgarian, and Czech.

The Hodja is a philosopher, a wise man, a fool, Sufi sage and a comic all rolled into one; and, as the title Hodja indicates, a teacher. He is the protagonist of thousands of stories, anecdotes, parables, paradoxes and witty remarks. What is interesting about Hodja stories is not just that they have been adopted by so many cultures, but that his character has been embraced as a transcultural icon who speaks truth to reason and power, across time and space. In some cultures, such as the Swahili and Indonesian cultures, where he is known as Abunuwasi, he is confused – or, should we say, blended – with other historic personalities: in this case, with the eighth/ninth century poet Abu Nawas. And, of course, Hodja's Turkish origins notwithstanding, each culture claims him as their own.

But what are the origins of Nasreddin Hodja? By all scholarly accounts, the Hodja was a real thirteenth century historical figure. Turkish scholars suggest he was born in a village called Hortu in Sivrihisar in the Eskiserhir Proivnce of Turkey. He moved to Aksehir, and later to Konya, where he died around 1275-85. Other scholars suggest that his origins can be located in West Azerbaijan, Iran, that he studied in Khorasan, and eventually ended up in Herat, where he was taught by none other than the great polymath and pioneer of inductive logic, Fakhr al-Din al-Razi (1149-1210). The overall consensus is with Turkish scholars who suggest that he was an Imam of a local mosque, and served as *Qadi*, a judge and ombudsman.

The era of Nasreddin, both man and literary counterpart, was one where his people were suffering constant raids and pillages by the hands of the Mongols. The Seljuk empire was helpless against this constant ransacking and so the people turned to the written word for solace, direction, and comfort. It is during these terrible times that some of Turkey's greatest figures rose to the light: Mawlana Jalaluddin Rumi, the voice of the intellectuals; Yunus Emre, the poet of the people; and finally, Nasreddin Hodja, the folk philosopher.

Much like King Arthur of British legends, Nasreddin Hodja lives in the hearts of many people as a blend of truth and fiction. it is impossible to speak of the historical veracity of all the stories that carry his name. It may very well be the case that the Nasreddin Hodja we know today is a literary creation whose life is as fictional as that of Sherlock Holmes'. But it is equally possible that the legendary wit and droll trickery of the Hodja are based on the exploits and words of a historical imam. What we can say with some certainty is that his stories have a subtle humour and a pedagogic nature. The way to wisdom, Hodja tells us, is in the harmony of mind and heart and the plurality of our beings. Many of his stories force you to think a little bit!

A 'International Nasreddin Hodja Festival' is held annually, between 5-10 July, in Aksehir. In Konya, there is a tomb attributed to him which he is said to have built for himself while he was still alive. It has a single door to mark the entrance, but no walls surrounding it. Even in death, the Hodja has left us with a piece of surreal behaviour that sparks first laughter, and then deeper contemplation. How could one believe that such a striking character was anything but a real person?

Here are a few of my favourite Nasreddin Hodja tales.

The Thief

Thieves stole Nasreddin Hodja's donkey. The Hodja was upset and spoke to his neighbours about this. One of them said: 'Hodja, why didn't you lock the barn?'

Another neighbour shouted at him: 'A thief goes into your barn whilst you are asleep! You love your sleep.'

Another one said: 'Hodja, yes the thieves stole your donkey, but it is your fault because your barn is old and it is not strong.'

Nasreddin Hodja, furious, shouted back: 'Yes I am guilty, but what about the thief?'

The Turban

An Iranian man received a letter from his hometown. He was illiterate, so he gave the letter to Nasreddin Hodja saying: 'Hodja, I cannot read and write. Could you read this letter for me?' The Hodja studied the letter but couldn't read it because it was in Farsi. 'I cannot read it' he said to the man. 'Take it to someone else who can. I don't know Farsi.'

The man got angry and shouted at the Hodja: 'Hodja, I thought you are a learned man. You should be ashamed of the turban you are wearing.'

The Hodja took his turban off and put it on the Iranian man's head, 'Here you are; you wear the turban. You read the letter', he said.

What if?

Nasreddin Hodja wanted to teach a lesson to idle people. He went to Lake Akşehir carrying a large bucket full of yoghurt. He started to spoon yoghurt into the lake. When bystanders saw him, they asked: 'Hodja, what are you doing?' Throwing yoghurt culture into the lake.' They were perplexed: 'Hodja, you cannot be serious, how is it possible for the lake to turn into yoghurt?'

The Hodja replies: 'Just think: what if it happens!'

Where is the Cat?

One day Nasreddin Hodja bought two kilos of meat from the butcher, and taking it to his wife said: 'Prepare the meat, we'll have it for dinner.'
That day his wife's friends came to visit. The Hodja's wife cooked the meat and offered it to her friends.
When the Hodja came home that evening he called his wife 'I could eat an elephant. Let's have our dinner.' His wife prepared the table, but there was only soup. Hodja said to her: 'Where is the meat?' 'The cat ate it', she said. The Hodja did not believe his wife. He asked her: 'Bring the cat here.' His wife brought the cat. The Hodja took the scales and weighed the cat. The cat weighed exactly two kilos. 'If this is how much the cat weighs' said the Hodja, 'where is the meat, and if this is the meat, where is the cat?'

You are Right too

Nasreddin Hodja was a judge in Akşehir. A man came to see him and talked of an incident that had happened to him. As he was leaving, he asked the Hodja: 'I'm right, aren't I?' The Hodja said: 'You're right'. Then another man came and retold the incident as he saw it, and asked the Hodja: 'Hodja, I'm right, aren't I?' The Hodja said: 'You're right,' When the man left, Hodja's wife came and said to the Hodja: 'I heard your talk. You said they are both right. They cannot both be right. Don't you think one of them is wrong?' The Hodja thought a while and said: 'My dear wife, you're right too.'

Hard Cash

Nasreddin Hodja owed some money to his neighbour but couldn't pay him back. The neighbour kept asking the Hodja when he was going to pay the money back. The Hodja was fed up that his neighbour came every day asking for the money.
One evening when the neighbour came to the Hodja for his money the Hodja said: 'Look neighbour, I'm going to pay you back as soon as I can.'
The neighbour looked at the Hodja with questioning eyes: 'How is this going to happen?' The Hodja said: 'In front of that door I have planted shrubs. They will grow this tall by spring'.

'And?'

'All the sheep that pass by will brush against the shrubs and their wool will get caught in the prickly bushes.'

'Yes?'

'Then we will collect the wool from the shrubs and my daughter will spin them into yarn. I will take the yarn to the bazaar and sell it. With the money I get, I will pay you back.'

Presented with this remote and unlikely solution, the neighbour could do nothing but laugh.

'You see!' The Hodja said when he saw the lender laughing. 'Your mood improved when you saw the cash on the nail.'

The Tree

Nasreddin Hodja climbed an apple tree to pick apples. As he stretched out to pluck an apple from a high branch, he slipped and fell. He moaned and groaned with pain. People gathered around him and said to him: 'Hodja, be patient! Stop being a sissy! You are a big man, stop being a cry baby!'

The Hodja got angry. He asked them: 'Have you ever fallen out of a tree?'

They all said: 'No.'

The Hodja quickly replied: 'If that is the case then leave me alone. Let someone whose fallen from a tree come.'

Balanced World

One day people asked the Hodja: 'Why is it that when morning arrives people go in different directions?' The Hodja thought about it and said: 'If people all went in one direction, the world would be thrown off balance.'

The Fur Coat

The Hodja was invited to a wedding. He turned up in his everyday clothes. No one either greeted him nor took notice of him. This made the Hodja upset. He rushed back home, donned his finest fur-coat, and returned to the wedding. When the hosts saw him, they led him to the dinner hall, sat him down and served him many dishes.

The Hodja dipped the lapel of the coat into the soup bowl and said: 'Please have some.' The other guests, perplexed asked him what was he doing. He answered: 'You treated my fur-coat with respect, so, the fur-coat should eat.'

Believe the Donkey

A neighbour knocked on the Hodja's door and asked for his donkey. The Hodja: 'Greetings, neighbour, how are you? I hope everything is alright.' The neighbour answered: 'Thank you, Hodja, I'm fine.' He added: 'Hodja, I want to ask you something. I have to go to town; can you lend me your donkey for two hours?'
The Hodja didn't want to lend the animal. So, he said: 'My dear neighbour, it's not here.' At that very moment the donkey started braying. The neighbour heard the braying and asked the Hodja: 'Well – what is that sound? You said the donkey isn't here, yet I can hear it braying.'
The Hodja replied: 'Shame on you neighbour! You don't believe me, yet you believe the word of a donkey.'

Childhood

One day when Nasreddin Hodja was returning home he met a few children. He sat down to rest and watch the children play. One of them suddenly snatched the Hodja's turban and threw it to the other children. The Hodja ran after them to recover his turban, but got tired and returned home without it. The Hodja's wife was surprised to see him in such a state. 'Hodja, what has happened? Where is your turban?' she asked. The Hodja replied: 'Don't ask, dear wife, my turban missed its childhood; so now it's playing with kids in the street.'

Visiting the Sick

Nasreddin Hodja fell ill and was bedbound. The neighbours who heard about the Hodja's illness came to visit him. But the visitors overstayed and were talking too much. Their talk was making the patient depressed. One of the neighbours said to Hodja:

'Hodja, you look terrible. No one knows when the appointed time with death shall come. Have you prepared your last will and testament?'

'Yes, I have', the Hodja replied. The neighbour asked curiously: 'Well, what is in your will then?'

The Hodja shook his head from right to the left meaningfully and said: 'This is my will: When you visit a sick person, do not stay longer than needed, and do not say depressing things.'

Sound of Money

In the Akşehir marketplace there was a kebab shop. The owner was a penny-pinching and artful man. One day at noon a poor man sat down in front of the shop. The poor man took a deep breath, and sniffed the air for a while. He did not have a penny to buy a kebab. He took out a piece of stale bread and held it against the smoke of the kebab grill and ate it.

The shop owner saw the man and straight away went up to him: 'Pay for your kebab', he said. The poor man was taken aback and said: 'I did not eat kebab. Why should I pay for it?' The owner insisted that the poor man must pay. They had a fight. The neighbours took them to Nasreddin Hodja to sort things out.

The kebab shop owner and the poor man told the Hodja what had happened. The Hodja asked the poor man to give him whatever money he had in his purse.

The poor man was speechless. He gave all his money to the Hodja. The Hodja counted the coins, put them in a purse and shook it.

Nasreddin Hodja asked the kebab shop owner: 'Did you hear the sound of money?'

The owner said: 'Yes, I hear.'

In answer the Hodja said: 'You asked for money for the smoke. The sound of the money is payment enough for your smoke. Now, leave!'

The Last Day

Nasreddin Hodja had a lamb. One day his friends said to him: 'Hodja, tomorrow will be the Last Day. We all shall die. Before we die let's kill your lamb and eat it.' Hodja did not like the idea but he yielded to his friends' insistence. He didn't want to upset them. He said: 'That's fine. Do as you wish.'

The Hodja and his friends went to the forest and lit a fire. They slaughtered the lamb, roasted the meat and ate it. After the meal the Hodja's friends took their clothes off and went to the brook to swim.

The Hodja gathered all their clothes and threw them into the fire. Somewhile later his friends returned. They searched for their clothes but couldn't find them. They said: 'Hodja, we can't find our clothes. Have you seen them?' the Hodja replied: 'I threw them into the fire and burnt them.' His friends were annoyed and shouted: 'Why did you burn them? What are we going to wear now?'

'Calm down, my friends. Tomorrow will be the Last Day! What are you going to do with clothes?' the Hodja said.

The Lost Ring

Nasreddin Hodja lost his ring. He went outside to look for it. When his wife saw him from the window she asked: 'Hodja, what are you looking for?'

The Hodja: 'I'm looking for the ring I lost'. His wife asked: 'Where did you lose your ring?'

'I lost my ring at home'. His wife froze for a moment and then said to the Hodja: 'If that is the case, why don't you look for it in the house instead of the streets?'

The Hodja: 'The streets are bright; the house is dark. How can I find my ring in the darkness?'

The Turkey

One day Nasreddin Hodja went to the marketplace. He saw a parrot for sale. The price tag was twelve gold coins. The Hodja was taken aback by the price, so he asked the people around him: 'Why is that bird so expensive?'

They said: 'This is not an ordinary bird. It is a special bird. She can talk.'

After hearing this the Hodja went straight back to his house; came back to the marketplace with his turkey under his arm.

The folk in the market asked: 'How much is this turkey?' The Hodja: 'Fifteen gold coins' replied. The owner of the parrot was shocked to hear the price. He said: 'Hodja, what are you saying? Fifteen gold coins for a turkey is too much.'

The Hodja: 'But you are selling a small bird for twelve coins.'

'My parrot has got talents, speaks like Man. What does your turkey do? said the owner of the parrot.

The Hodja said: 'Your parrot talks without thinking. But my turkey thinks like Man.'

Donkey Ride

Nasreddin Hodja and his son were riding the donkey on their way to the marketplace. A man saw them and said: 'Hodja, both riding the donkey; shame on you! How can the poor donkey possible carry you both?'

The Hodja let his son off the donkey. When they met another traveller, the traveller came up to them and said: 'Hodja, what kind of father are you? You are riding the donkey while you let your poor child walk.'

What the man said made the Hodja upset. He got off the donkey and put his son on. When another man saw the Hodja walking, he said: 'Children nowadays are bad. The child on the donkey and poor old father walking. Shame!'

The Hodja's son was upset too. He got off the donkey. Thus, the Hodja and his son both were walking. When another man saw them; he came up to them and said: 'What kind of people are you! There is nothing on the donkey and you are walking. Why don't you ride the donkey?'

The Hodja did not know what to do. He said to his son: 'My son, you see - you cannot make everyone happy at the same time!'

Centre of the Earth

The Hodja's neighbours asked him a question: 'Hodja! You are man of knowledge. Tell us, where is the exact centre of the earth?'

The Hodja thought a while and gave a naughty smile: 'The centre is where I am standing', he said.

The men were lost for words: 'Hodja, what kind of answer is this?

The Hodja replied: 'If you don't believe me, you're welcome to measure for yourselves!'

I Keep my Word

One day Nasreddin Hodja was conversing with his friends. The topic of the talk was how quickly the years pass. One of his friends said to him: 'Hodja, how old are you?' Without thinking the Hodja said, 'Forty years old'.
Another friend said: 'No, Hodja, how is this possible? When we asked your age ten years ago you said the same thing.'
The Hodja retorted: 'Friends, I speak true. Whatever I said ten years ago still goes.'

The Loan

Nasreddin Hodja went to the marketplace to sell olives. After a while a woman came to the Hodja's stall and asked him: 'Are your olives of good quality? Are they tasty?'
The Hodja said to the woman: 'Taste one and decide for yourself.'
The woman said: 'I can't eat now because I am fasting.' After hearing the woman, the Hodja weighed a kilo of olives into a bag and said: 'Take these olives to your home. Break your fast with them. You can pay me tomorrow.'
Then Nasreddin Hodja thought to himself 'It is not the month of Ramadan, so why is she fasting?' He asked the woman.
The woman said: 'Three years ago I was ill during Ramadan and couldn't observe my fast. I owe God to make up for it. That's why I am fasting.'
The Hodja changed his mind and decided not to give her the bag of olives.
The woman asked: 'Just now you said I could take them and pay you later - why this sudden change of heart?'
The Hodja replied: 'You compensate for not fasting after three years; who knows when you are going to pay me. That's why I changed my mind.'

Baksheesh

The Hodja went to the Hammam. The workers did not pay any attention to the Hodja. They gave him a tattered bag and small towels. The Hodja said nothing. After finishing his bath, he paid the fee for the bath, plus a generous baksheesh.

A week later the Hodja went to the same Hammam. This time the workers were more attentive. They gave him the best towels, brought him fruits and even offered him coffee.

On his departure he left small amount of baksheesh.

The puzzled workers said: 'Hodja, we served you well, brought you food and drinks, so why did you leave this small amount?'

'What I gave you today is last week's baksheesh. What I gave you last week was for this week's service. Now we are quitting', the Hodja replied.

The Pumpkin

One summer day the Hodja lay under the shade of a walnut tree to take a nap. He saw a host of pumpkins in the field. The Hodja thought: 'these huge pumpkins grow on the ground, yet small nuts grow on this huge tree. What a contrast!'

At that moment a walnut fell on his head. He suddenly got up, extended his hands in token of supplication and said: 'My dear God, please forgive me. I am not going to meddle in your business. You are the Almighty who knows everything. It's good that pumpkins don't grow on the trees. Thanks be to God that a walnut fell on my head and not a pumpkin.'

Selling Pickles

Nasreddin Hodja made pickles in his house. He loaded the donkey with the pickle jars. He went to a neighbourhood. He opened his mouth to shout out: 'Pickles, I sell pickles,' and at that moment his donkey started to bray. The Hodja couldn't make himself heard because of the braying. In another neighbourhood the Hodja again tried to shout: 'Pickles, I sell pickles,' and again his donkey started to bray. The Hodja went from one neighbourhood to another all day long but could not sell his pickles because of the donkey's braying. Finally, the Hodja, furious with his donkey, came up to her and asked: 'Who is selling pickles, you or I?'

The Seasons

One winter day Nasreddin Hodja and his friends came together to have a chitchat. One of them said: 'What kind of weather is this? We are freezing.' Another one said: 'In the summer it's too hot, we burn.' One of them got angry and said: 'These sons of Adam don't know how to thank God, they are ungrateful. They complain about the summer and they complain about the winter.' Then the Hodja said: 'Why are you blaming people? Look at the spring; no one complains about that.'

Poor Donkcy

One day Nasreddin Hodja, mounted on his donkey, arrived at the village square. The Hodja had a sack on his back. When the villagers saw him, they were surprised. They asked him: 'Hodja, you're mounted on the donkey and yet you carry the sack on your back. Why?'

'Poor animal, he works day and night; does all my work. He carries me here and there. I thought it unfair to let him carry the sack as well. He is carrying me, that's fine, but I thought I should carry the sack. That's the least I could do' the Hodja said.

The Pitcher

The Hodja's son was playing in the street with his friends. The Hodja called out to him: 'My son, there's no water left in the house, go to the fountain and fetch some water.'

He handed his son an earthenware water pitcher and slapped him on the face. His son was shocked. When the boy went to fetch the water, the Hodja shouted at him: 'Be careful, don't break the pitcher!'

The Hodja's wife said: 'What are you doing? Why did you slap him? What was the child's fault? He didn't break the pitcher.'

The Hodja: 'I know, but there is no use getting angry with him when he breaks the pitcher. It will be too late. That's why I slapped him before he breaks it.'

The Saddlebag

During a visit to a village, Nasreddin Hodja's saddlebag went missing. 'Either you find my saddlebag or else', he told the villagers.
The villagers were frightened and didn't know what to do. They looked for the saddlebag, and at last they found it and brought it to the Hodja. As Hodja left the villagers asked: 'Hodja, we are wondering, what you would have done if we hadn't found your saddlebag?'
Hodja replied: 'Nothing. I had a kilim. On my return I was going to make a new saddlebag out of it!'

The Fish

Nasreddin Hodja and his friend went to the town. Felling hungry, they went into a restaurant. The waiter welcomed them and asked: 'What would you like to have?' Both of them said: 'We would like to have fish.'
The waiter said to the Hodja: 'I'm sorry but there's only one fish left. I will prepare it so you can share it between yourselves'. The Hodja said to his friend: 'I'm going to have the head of the fish because it is healthy and has rich vitamins. The fish head makes you clever as well.' The Hodja's friend objected and said to the Hodja: 'Why are you going to have the fish's head. I want to have it.' The Hodja: 'Alright. You're my friend. I'm not going to make you upset. You can have the fish's head.'
The Hodja gave the head to his friend and ate the rest of the fish himself. The Hodja was full, but his friend was still hungry. He said to the Hodja: 'You ate the biggest portion; you are full up now. I ate only the head and I'm still hungry.' The Hodja said: 'There you go. The fish's head opened your mind. I told you the head of the fish makes you clever.'

Timur's Elephant

There was an emperor whose name was Timur. He was a tyrant ruler. One day Timur visited Nasreddin Hodja's village. The villagers welcomed Timur with open arms and offered him the best dishes they had. Timur was very pleased with their hospitality. He said to the villagers: 'You have treated me with respect. I like your village. I want to give your village a gift.' He bestowed upon the village the gift of an elephant.

The villagers had a difficult time looking after the elephant. The elephant created havoc in the village: it trampled all the fruits, vegetables and grass. The elephant became a heavy burden on the villagers.

One day all the villagers gathered to discuss the issue: 'We have to find a solution for this problem.' One of the villagers said: 'Let's go and see the Hodja; he is a clever and wise man. He will show us the way'. They all agreed to visit the Hodja and went to talk to him.

'This elephant is destroying our livelihood and our village. Help us to get rid of the elephant.' Nasreddin Hodja thought a while and said: 'Come back tomorrow; we all go to the Timur's Palace. We'll tell him what's happening and give the elephant back to him.'

The next day the Hodja led the villagers to the Timur's Palace. The villagers were afraid of Timur. One by one they all disappeared along the way, and by the time the Hodja arrived at the Palace door no one was left but himself.

Timur asked the Hodja: 'Why did you come here? What do you want from me?' At that moment the Hodja looked back but couldn't see any of the towns' people. Upon this disappointment, the Hodja said to Timer: 'We are very happy with the elephant, but we have a small problem. The elephant is lonesome: he doesn't have a friend. We feel sorry for the poor animal. We want another elephant for our village.'

Embarrassment

One night, Nasreddin Hodja heard noises. He thought burglars must be in the house, and hid himself in a cupboard. There really was a burglar in the house. The man rummaged through the entire house and couldn't find anything valuable, but upon opening the cupboard door he discovered the Hodja.

The burglar was surprised to see him: 'Hodja, what are you doing here?' he asked. The Hodja bowed his head and said: 'Thousand apologies, my friend, there is nothing worth stealing in the house. I was so embarrassed, so I hid myself…'

The Slap

One day as Nasreddin Hodja was walking a young man came up behind and slapped him on his neck. The Hodja was frightened: 'Who are you? Why did you slap me?' The young man apologised to the Hodja, 'I mistook you for my friend. That's why I slapped you', he explained and then laughed. When the Hodja saw the young man laughing, he got upset and took him to court.

The Hodja and the young man both explained what happened to the judge. The judge was a friend of the young man and didn't want to punish him. The judge said to the Hodja: 'Hodja, I understand you well. You have every right to be angry and upset, but he slapped you by mistake and he apologised. Come, you forgive him, let's close the case.'

The Hodja insisted that the judge should 'punish the young man!' At the end, the judge ordered the defendant to pay the plaintiff five lira. The judge told the young man to go home and get the money.

The Hodja waited for the young man until evening but he didn't come back. The judge said to the Hodja, 'I'm going to close the office. It's evening now. Go and come back tomorrow.'

The Hodja was angry. He went up to the judge and slapped him. 'Hodja, how dare you to slap me?' the judge shouted. The Hodja replied: 'Dear Judge Effendi, I cannot wait any longer, you tell the young man tomorrow to give you the five lira.'

Visit

One day the Hodja's friends came to visit him. The Hodja's wife was not in. They said: 'Hodja, your wife never stays in, but wanders from house to house in the neighbourhood.'

The Hodja scratched his head and replied: 'No, that is not true. If, as you all say she keeps going to places, then she would have come to visit me as well.'

The Candle Light

One day Nasreddin Hodja's friends said to him: 'Hodja, you always claim that you are brave and strong. We would like to believe you. Prove to us you are who you said you are. Stay outside all night long and endure the cold. If you can bear the cold night, we will treat you to a feast. If you cannot, you will treat us to a good meal.'

Nasreddin Hodja accepted the challenge. It was a cold night, but he stayed outside until morning. At daybreak his friends came to see him. The Hodja said to his friends: 'Okay, I've waited till morning, I won'. But his friends didn't want to accept that he had won. They said to him: 'No, you lost. There was a candle light shining from a house across the road. You warmed yourself on it. We are not going to give you the feast we promised, but you will give one for us.'

The Hodja was disappointed, yet had no choice but to accept his friends' judgment. He said to his friends: 'I accept the defeat. You all come to my house tomorrow. I will offer you a delicious meal.'

The next evening the Hodja's friends came to his house but found there was no dishes on the table. They said: 'Hodja, we are hungry, where is the meal?' The Hodja asked them to follow him to the kitchen. His friends were puzzled by what they saw. There was a large cauldron on the fireplace, with a single light burning under it.

'Hodja, what's this? How can a candle give enough heat to cook that large cauldron?'

The Hodja smiled and said: 'Why are you surprised? Last night you believed I warmed myself with a candle light, now with that same light I am cooking the food.'

Contentment

The Hodja's neighbour came to see him. 'Hodja, my house is small and difficult to live in', he said. 'Help me find a solution for my troubles.' The Hodja listened to the man carefully and said: 'Now go home, get the goat from the barn and take it inside.' The next day again the man went to the Hodja: 'Hodja, when I took the goat inside the home my distress increased,' he said. The Hodja replied: 'Now go home, put the chickens inside the home.' The next day the man returned once more: 'Hodja, my distress increased even more.' The Hodja calmly said: 'Go and put your cow inside the home.' The next day the man came to see the Hodja again: 'Hodja, Hodja, I had enough. I cannot bear it any longer.' The Hodja said: 'This evening take the goat out of the house'. The man came back to see the Hodja next day and said: 'I'm feeling slightly better.' The Hodja asked the man take the chickens out of the house. The man came back more relaxed. The Hodja said: 'Go home, get the cow out of the house and give the place a good spring clean.'

The man did exactly what the Hodja asked him to do. The following day he came back content in happiness and said: 'Hodja, thank you so much. Because of your advice we are more comfortable. My wife and I are very happy.'

Soup of the Soup

One day a villager brought a rabbit to Nasreddin Hodja. The Hodja welcomed the villager, and compensated him with fine foods. A week later the same man came back to visit the Hodja. He was hospitable to the man. He said: 'I prepared this soup with the rabbit you brought. Enjoy your meal'.

A few days later three villagers knocked on the Hodja's door and told him that they came to see him. The Hodja asked them who they were. They said they were neighbours of the villager who brought the rabbit last week. The Hodja was annoyed but didn't let his feelings be known. He offered them soup as well.

A week later, more people came to the Hodja's house. The Hodja asked them who they were. They said: 'We are the neighbours of the villager who brought the rabbit two weeks ago.' The Hodja was annoyed but said nothing to the guests. He offered a bowl of water as a meal. The visitors were taken aback and said: 'What is this Hodja?' The Hodja replied: 'The rabbit soup of the soup.'

Who will feed the Donkey?

Nasreddin Hodja had to go the forest to collect firewood. It was a hot day; he and the donkey were exhausted. The Hodja unloaded the donkey. His wife was in the garden at the time. The Hodja said to his wife: 'The donkey is tired and hungry. Come on, feed her'.

But the Hodja's wife was also tired. She said: 'all day I've been cleaning, tidying and cooking. I want to rest. Please, feed the donkey yourself.'

The Hodja insisted she should feed the donkey, went straight into the house and to bed.

'No! I'm so tired, I don't have any strength left. I can't feed the donkey', his wife insisted.

Neither the Hodja and nor his wife was prepared to feed the donkey. They started to quarrel.

The Hodja said to his wife: 'let's play a game. Whoever speaks first, let him or her feed the donkey.' The wife accepted the Hodja's offer. For some time neither of them uttered a word. Eventually, the wife got bored and went to see a neighbour, leaving the Hodja alone in the house.

A while later, a burglar entered the house. The Hodja saw the burglar but said nothing because he was afraid of losing the bet. The burglar stole all the furniture.

A few hours later the Hodja's wife returned. When she saw there was no furniture in the house she started screaming: 'Hodja, what happened here? Where is the furniture?'

The Hodja smiled and said: 'Aha, you spoke, and you lost the bet. Go feed the donkey!'

I was in It

One morning Nasreddin Hodja went out to the street. He met his neighbour. He asked the Hodja curiously: 'Hodja, last night I heard a big noise coming from your house. What happened?' The Hodja replied: 'Nothing significant. My wife and I quarrelled. She threw my cloak over the railing'. The neighbour was perplexed to hear this: 'Hodja, how is it possible? How can a cloak make such big noise?' The Hodja replied: 'You don't understand. I was in it!'

DEATH OF A NOBODY

Medina Tenour Whiteman

Jonathon Hanratty was one of those people that nobody ever noticed. I don't mean that figuratively, either. Your vision seemed to flow right past him, like a river around a rock, and rejoin itself on the other side. If you weren't careful you could trip right over him and blame it on a fold in the carpet.

The first time I saw him he was weaving through a crowd of hungry students, trying not to get tripped over. A fortuitous gap between the trustafarians and the armchair anthropologists allowed him to slip through and he darted over to my till, slammed down his tray — meatballs, rice, banana, coke and a forest fruits yoghurt — and said in this tight, wiry little voice, '*I would like to pay for my lunch, please.*'

'Go on then — see if I care,' I retorted. I do like retorting. It's a talent of mine. Most days all I get to say to my customers is a string of numbers, and I'm a creative kind of person. 'Six twenty. But my neck's on the line here, woodlouse.'

He blinked like he'd been freshly extracted from a coal bunker to find that the war has already ended and nobody remembered to tell him.

'Your colleagues didn't even see me,' he said faintly, handing over his cash with trembling hands.

I looked over at Krista and Fran. Both of them were doom scrolling, ringing up the food without even looking at the buttons — that's how long they've been working here, sad twerps — and I was just saying 'I'm not surprised, they don't look at anyone' when I realised he'd disappeared. Faded out into the scenery. I wondered if I'd hallucinated him.

He was back the next day, battered plaice, chips, apple, coke and a forest fruits yoghurt. This time I noticed another peculiar feature of Jonathon Hanratty: his college ID card. Everyone who eats here has to put it on their tray so we'd know if someone from outside was taking the piss and eating on the cheap. The photo on the front of Hanratty's card just had a blue curtain, with the smudged outline of half his face in one corner, grinning for dear life.

'How can you take out library books with a card that doesn't show what you look like?' I asked him. He turned final demand red. 'I had to take the photo myself. They didn't see me standing in the line so I watched how they did it and issued myself a card. The only thing was I couldn't get back to my seat in time for the photo.'

'You do a lot of standing in lines, don't you?'

He shrugged, and then wilted, exhausted by the effort. 'At least the system knew I was there,' he murmured.

'Some consolation,' I replied. 'That'll be six thirty-five. Contactless only – none of your manky coin germs, you lot never wash your hands.'

Hanratty would come in every day for his lunch, from which I deduced that he never skipped a lecture. Poor stupid students, thinking they're getting an education for their money. I learn more than they do sitting here every lunchtime serving them their shonky-looking chicken kievs and unintentionally mushy peas.

I have learned, for example, that most people don't consider what ignominious origins their food might have, or the personal hygiene of the cooks making it. They don't even consider the way it looks, which, at our establishment, is fairly horrific. I've seen prettier endoscopies. They put their trust in the person giving it, the same way they trust any alpha human who's convinced they're right and doesn't give you enough time to ask questions. It's this great life lesson that has enabled me to cultivate an attitude of unshakeable confidence in all things, even ones I don't have a clue about. People just assume you're right, and you save lots of time which can then be wasted on match-three puzzle apps.

A couple of months passed and me and Hanratty would say hello, exchange a few pleasantries over the stodge of the day, nothing more. So when he told me he was going to end it all, I was strangely flattered.

'Why are you telling *me*?' I asked him. Not meaning to be rude or anything. I just wondered. He looked down at his meal – veggie curry, basmati rice, poppadum, banana, coke and a forest fruits yoghurt – and sighed like the world had sat on him by mistake and not even felt a twinge. I suppose he didn't think his last supper looked especially momentous. He was right – I'd already had it, and the poppadums were chewy. Never trust a poppadum that's been fried by white people.

He didn't say anything though, just fingered his serviette distractedly. I could see a couple of thick-necked rugby players loitering behind him with trays of beef cassoulet and cans of Red Bull; I had to hurry him up.

'How are you going to do it?' I whispered.

'I'm going to jump off the roof of the building,' he said firmly. 'I'm going to eat my lunch and go up the stairs and throw myself off the roof. That's what I'm going to do.'

'Where? Onto the front steps? That'll cause a bit of a stir, everyone sits out there to smoke. They don't want disgruntled students whizzing past their faces and splattering onto the concrete at their feet. Really puts a downer on your day. Didn't anyone teach you to have consideration of other people's feelings?'

He gave me the pained look of a card player who's just realized he's bet everything on a pathetically crap hand.

'Where, then?' he whispered. I thought. Then I thought a bit more. The beefcake behind him was pushing his tray along already but I gave him a look that would've brought the bulls of Pamplona to a halt and he went over to Krista's till. Poor thick-necked twerp. Probably doesn't even know where Pamplona is.

'There's a building site on the other side of the building,' I told him, suddenly inspired. 'The builders will all have knocked off for lunch. Do it there.' He mulled my suggestion over. A silent suicide, alone and unseen; or a glorious, sensational mangling on the front steps in full view of his fickle, self-absorbed peers. It was a tricky decision to make in a canteen queue, you have to admit.

'I'll go for the building site, I think,' he said at length.

'Don't think!' I replied sharply, in one of my sagacious moments – they come on from time to time –'You have to *know*. This isn't where you're just going to take a selfie and enjoy the view. You aren't doing it for the 'gram. It's where a lifetime of being ignored is going to flash before your eyes as you plummet to the ground and be compacted to a bloody pulp. This is the biggest decision of the end of your life.'

He gazed down at the cauliflower curry again, deep in thought. The steam was gradually getting thinner. You could almost see it congealing as you watched. Suddenly Hanratty looked at me with resolution in his eyes and said, like he really meant it,

'Thank you, Faiza.'

That gave me a bit of a shock. He even pronounced my name right. Then I remembered that it had been on a badge on my chest all that time. Funny – I hadn't expected him to notice.

It wasn't until I'd finished my shift and started tilling up that my mind wandered back to our conversation. I suddenly remembered I don't believe in suicide. Put a slightly different cast on things. Could I live with the guilt of having influenced this poor, translucent chap in making a terrible decision? Shouldn't I have advised him to be strong, roll with the punches, get a hobby or something? Honestly, though – he'd already made up his mind. I was just suggesting a more civilized way of doing it. Who am I, his unpaid counsellor? Bloody privileged gits.

I did feel a pang, though, that the last thing to go through Hanratty's mind would be some barely digestible, tasteless cauliflower and a rubbery poppadum. That's when it hit me: I'd charged him for a beef cassoulet! I owed him a quid fifty!

Now, I may not be a saint, but I'm no cheat. I honour the role I have been given, feeding these stuck-up cretins their daily bilge, and I wasn't about to overcharge any of them – especially not one who wouldn't be alive to get his refund tomorrow.

So I stuffed my apron and that ridiculous hairnet they make me wear into my locker and I tore up the stairs three at a time, hoping I'd catch him before he'd done the deed. Fourth floor, fifth – the stairwell was empty; everyone had already gone into their classes. So he was skipping a lecture, after all. Good for him.

The fire escape at the top of the stairs had been wrenched open and there was Jonathon Hanratty, standing at the edge of the roof, looking down at the building site below. I was just about to call out to him when the strangest thing happened: *he started to undress.*

I wasn't sure at first that was what he was actually doing. He was right on the other side of the roof with his back turned, and he did have that way of not being entirely visible all at once unless you were close up. But by the time he'd got down to his undies there was no mistaking it. He was getting stark naked, right there on the roof! I couldn't decide whether to admire the boy's guts or look away from them in embarrassment.

Then he started taking out things from his backpack – textbooks, notepads, folders of paper. I wasn't watching him on purpose, honest to God – only out of the corner of my eye. I hate to admit it but I was actually concerned for the chump. He started to pack his books into his shirt, his jacket, trousers, everything, even his skimpy little cotton vest, then – and this was the weirdest bit – *he slung the whole lot over the edge of the roof.*

And then Jonathon Hanratty, one umbilical cord short of his birthday suit, turned around and walked right past me with a grin as wide as freedom on his face. He didn't even realize I was there.

I raced to the edge of the roof and looked over, and a few moments later I saw him walk out the main doors, past the teen anarchists talking revolution and the library ghouls chuffing away on their fags, and strolled right out the gates, calm as you please. Not a single stare. Not the slightest whiff of a stir.

I sat up on the roof for a long time after that, wondering if I had just seen a miracle or if someone had slipped me some acid in my tea.

A couple of weeks later, I heard some of the tutors in the lunch queue chatting about the untimely death of one of their students. He was meant to go to a one o'clock lecture but didn't show up. It was the computer system that showed that he wasn't there. A machine was the only one that registered his absence.

Nobody heard anything more of him until one of the builders found a shoe and a bit of shirt sleeve sticking out of the foundations they'd been laying. The concrete had already set so no body was ever found. But people put two and two together and all of a sudden it was Jonathon Hanratty this, Jonathon Hanratty that. Nice of them to show an interest now he was gone, I thought. 'Model Student's Suicide – Exam Stress Blamed' ran the student paper headline. Someone made up a profile of Hanratty, the well-loved, outstanding member of the student body, the friend to all, the devoted cricketer. They even put up a plaque in his memory with a great song and dance in the local papers. Even the borough MP turned up for the occasion and farted on about this 'tragic loss to the student community, a terrible indictment of how an unhappy youth can slip through the system.' God, that got me angry. It was the system that noticed he'd gone

– nobody else gave a flying monkey's. There were even a couple of dozen girls crying at the memorial service. No parents, no relatives, nobody to mourn him but a few drama queens from his Introductory Accountancy management class.

I've thought a lot about Jonathon Hanratty since then. Lunchtime at the canteen isn't the same without him. Every time someone comes by my till with a forest fruits yoghurt I get a chill. I've got to get out of this godforsaken dungeon, I think, and I look at the Post-It note that's been stuck to the wall by my till for months with the number of a circus school on it, and I think about my childhood dream of being a trapeze artist. Then another customer comes along and I lose my train of thought, and the Post-It note stays stuck there, glaring at me between sales, willing me to ring.

I know Jonathon hasn't forgotten me, either. A few days ago I got a postcard from him. It said 'Great Australian Cuisine' under a picture of a half-eaten meat pie and a can of Toohey's Blue. I was happy he saw some gut-churning crud and thought of me.

I could just see him, lying peacefully on some beach, pootling around street markets, strolling onto flights past all the restless priority bookers, not even bothering to pack a suitcase since he went everywhere in the buff. What a relief it must be for him, making friends with his invisibility at last. Maybe that's all death really is. I wondered what could have given Jonathon Hanratty the guts to die like that, naked, staring his demise straight in the eye without flinching.

Maybe it was because he had nothing to lose.

Maybe it was his alienation from a cruel and selfish world that allowed him to escape it without ever looking back.

Maybe, just maybe, it was the forest fruits yoghurt.

REVIEWS

CARNIVALESQUE UPRISINGS

Shanon Shah

If you haven't seen this already, type 'Egyptian police parade 2020' into YouTube. Don't be surprised if the auto-search function suggests 'topless Egyptian parade 2020'. Hit Enter and, from the results, there should be a cluster of short videos uploaded in early October 2020. The image stills might provoke titillation or disapproval (or both), depending on your disposition. Remind yourself that this is purely for educational purposes. Choose one video and watch. Now, if possible. (The rest of this review can wait.)

If you have found the right videos, you will have witnessed a horde of beefy, bare-chested Egyptian men performing choreographed, Rambo-shaming stunts on tanks, trucks, obstacle courses and goodness knows what else within an Olympic-sized stadium, in the scorching sun. My favourite shot is of a cluster of shirtless hunks standing erect on white police boats with the Egyptian flag fluttering behind them. Mostly because, in this version uploaded by YouTube user Joel Anderson, this image immediately follows a caption calling this spectacle a 'gay circus'. The cheesy rock guitar riff in the background only enhances the scene. These are all police graduates, and this was their (supposedly) Covid-safe graduation ceremony. At the end of the video, these young men – fully clothed by this point and wearing face masks – are congratulated and presented with medals by Egyptian President Abdel Fattah el-Sisi.

Sabine Damir-Geilsdorf and Stephan Milich, editor, *Creative Resistance: Political Humor in the Arab Uprisings*, Bielefeld, by transcript Verlag, 2020

When I first saw the alert for this on Facebook, I could not ignore it the way I usually do with social media notifications. The friend who posted it is a grim and serious academic, but his commentary introducing the video – and comments from some of his friends – was priceless. I was not disappointed. My laughter was not one of mirthful abandon as when, say, I am watching a toddler being playful or the scene with the Killer Rabbit in *Monty Python and the Holy Grail*. Even now, as I recall the Egyptian extravaganza, my jaw is wide open and I am laughing silently and incredulously to myself. At the time, I remember being compelled to share the video with a few friends, introducing it along the lines of 'I have no words' or 'what the f**k?'

How can I effectively describe my reaction? Some of it is clearly context – this is Egypt, after all. Land of non-existent rights for lesbian, gay, bisexual and transgender people and police-led 'virginity tests' for women protesters. Site of systemic and systematic human rights abuses. Home, at the same time, of the historic and prestigious Islamic university, Al Azhar. Scene of an inspiring revolution in 2011 that quickly went wrong, bringing Sisi, yet another military despot, to power again – albeit one whom we hear very little about, since he is a Western ally. This bizarre footage was not intentionally humorous, and I was not alone in laughing – the comments on YouTube testify to this.

Creative Resistance: Political Humor in the Arab Uprisings has greatly helped me to contextualise this episode, among many others. It is easy, in hindsight, for many of us to lament that the outcome of the Arab Uprisings of 2010-12 is too depressing to contemplate. Using humour as a lens to analyse this historic era and its aftermath might strike some people as strange, trivialising or even distasteful. Not according to Sabinen Damir-Geilsdorf, Stephan Milich and the contributors to this collection.

They start by revisiting three dominant theories in academic studies of humour. Superiority theories posit that humour is a means of feeling superior by disparaging or degrading others. Incongruity theories suggest that humour emerges when we experience a discrepancy between what we expect to happen and what actually occurs – for example, the 'transgression of social norms, or the breaking of established social patterns'. Finally, according to relief theories, humour is psychologically and emotionally cathartic, and can have a healing effect.

These theories are not mutually exclusive – humour can serve one or more functions at the same time. Additionally, humour can build social relationships, communities and positive individual identities in some settings whilst creating hostility towards 'others' in other settings. Understanding the role of humour in the Arab Uprisings, however, requires probing deeper with this analysis. This volume proposes that literary critic Mikhail Bakhtin's notion of the 'carnivalesque' is especially relevant in the context of modern Arab political humour. According to Bakhtin, the carnivalesque consists of momentary festivities or festival-like acts that can turn established structures of power upside down, including through 'grotesque realism'. The idea of the carnivalesque could therefore be better suited to analysing political humour in authoritarian societies compared to liberal democracies in which freedom of expression is formally upheld by legal mechanisms.

The video of these virile police graduates oozing Egyptian manhood makes further sense in the light of the grandiose tradition of glorifying and divinising Arab rulers, from Iraq's Saddam Hussein to Libya's Muammar Gaddafi. The current carnivalesque connection for Egypt has roots in the spread of 'Sisimania' in 2013, during the embattled and controversial presidency of the Muslim Brotherhood-affiliated Mohamed Morsi. Back then, even patisseries in Cairo were making chocolates adorned with pictures of soon-to-be President Sisi. Former actress Lubna Abdel Aziz wrote in *Al-Ahram Weekly* in 2013:

> He stands straight and tall, impeccably attired and starched from head to toe. His freshly washed countenance and youthful zeal shield a Herculean strength and nerves of steel. He wears the feathers of a dove but has the piercing eyes of a hawk. During our thousand days of darkness, dozens of potential leaders pranced and boasted, to no avail.... He responded to the 33 million voices clamouring in the streets.

Challenging these sorts of sentiments – which are expressed in all sincerity by the regime's supporters – is not as simple as pointing out that the emperor is wearing no clothes. Yet partially undressing for the emperor seems to be *de rigueur*, but I digress. The point is, dictatorial Arab regimes have a habit of violently silencing dissenters and critics. In these circumstances, resistance can take the subtler form of outdoing the regime's own over-the-top narrative of glorification. Nathaniel Mannone's contribution on Tunisian humour post-Zine El Abidine Ben Ali investigates the notion of *tanfis*, or the 'safety valve' that Arab dictatorships occasionally allow for their citizens to let off steam. Extravagant pomp and ceremony are one way of enabling this. Yet, in the years before the revolution, *tanfis* did not stop the regime from brutalising people who were caught merely telling jokes about Ben Ali. People would shut their curtains and unplug their phones before they even considered telling these jokes in the supposed safety of their own homes.

Change came with the advent of the internet. Suddenly, memes could be produced anonymously with ambiguous messages that made rulers uncomfortable, *tanfis* or no *tanfis*. Tunisia's post-2011 transition has seen this tradition of mock glorification continue to flourish. Even reformist president Moncef Marzouki was not spared – the Tumblr account *Moncef Marzouqui Looking at Things* aggregated a selection of the President's well-staged photo opportunities as he inspected everything from olive bottles, giant chess sets, and 'a scary guy in a funny hat'. Modelled after the photo-blog *Kim Jong-Il Looking at Things*, parodying the late North Korean dictator's penchant for admiration, the Tunisian variant exposes the ridiculousness of political theatre.

This example is probably nearer to the experience of citizens of semi-authoritarian or transitional regimes who enjoy slightly more room for manoeuvring political humour to criticise the ruling regime. They remind me, for example, of the satirical website *The Tapir Times* in Malaysia. But what happens in states where things have gone from worse to unimaginably horrific, such as Syria? Even here, the contributors argue, attention to political humour can provide for enriched analysis. Sabine Damir-Geilsdorf points out in her chapter on Syria that 'black', 'dark' or 'gallows' humour can be a coping strategy *and* a form of political resistance. Many survivors of extreme adversity – including Holocaust survivors – testify that joking about what they endured helped them to maintain group morale and individual dignity within hopeless circumstances. Cartoons of a deadpan Bashar Al-Assad, depicted casually strangling children, are examples of how grotesque humour has evolved as a coping strategy and political resistance in Syria. Stephan Milich's chapter on Egyptian artist Nermine Hammam and her creative chronicling of police brutality from the euphoric beginnings of the country's revolution to its terrifying undoing covers similar analytical territory.

Framing the volume within Bakhtin's idea of the carnivalesque allows the editors and contributors to acknowledge the seriousness of what is happening in regimes such as Syria and Egypt without turning them into exceptions. After all, modern Arab states are no strangers to failed revolutions, or revolutions doomed to perpetual failure due to internal and external sabotage. The two chapters on Palestine, by Chrisoula Lionis and Anna Gabai, contextualise the Arab Uprisings within a wider history of political struggle in the region. In her chapter on museums and other arts infrastructures, Lionis shows that fictional visions of a future, actual Palestinian state share the functions of incongruity and relief in dominant theories of humour. Political humour and visual art thus intersect in nation-building and solidarity-making in ways that challenge the binary stereotype of Palestinians as either permanent victims or permanent terrorists. Gabai's chapter on the comic strip *Zan al-'An*, set in Ramallah, focuses on everyday political analysis from different Palestinian perspectives. The comic strip's humour is 'sarcastic, cynical, ironic and absurd', teasing out the 'discord between ideological narratives and the blank reality of everyday life'. Furthermore, the strip contextualises the significance of the Uprisings for Palestine, which has been in 'a constant state of uprising due to the Arab-Israeli conflict that has been going on for more than 60 years'. The chapter by Sébastien Boulay and Mohamed Dahmi on Western Sahara also explores the role of humour in situations of perpetual uprising – in this case, by Sahrawi activists against the Moroccan regime and the Sahrawi political leadership. Taken together, these chapters emphasise that any analysis of political humour in the Arab Uprisings must acknowledge that these protests and the crackdowns against them are but part of a longer revolution-in-progress. Some of these regimes, for example, have experienced their pre-Uprising 'dress rehearsals', such as Syria's Damascus Spring (2000-01). Others, such as Sudan and Algeria, saw the successful ouster of their dictators – Omar al-Bashir and Abd al-Aziz Bouteflika – only later, in 2019. It is to the editors' credit that this volume includes an illuminating chapter on Sudan by Larissa-Diana Fuhrmann. Sudan is particularly interesting for its own history of successful uprisings against dictatorial regimes in 1964 and 1985. This chapter provides much-needed context for Sudan's most recent democratic transition by looking at the use of humour by the student-led, pro-democracy, and non-violent *Girifna* movement, founded in 2009.

For balance, the volume also includes perspectives from contexts where there has been ostensibly no revolution – not overtly anyway – in this case, Lebanon and Kuwait. Fatema Hubail's chapter on *Sheno Ya3ni*, Kuwaiti comedians who launched their YouTube channel in 2012, shows that resistance is not only political but cultural, too. The group's skits are set in the fictional 'Great Republic of *Tolaytila* (Toledo)' – 'a city-state with cupcakes as its main currency'. *Tolaytila*'s citizens appear happy and serene, but each episode reveals a world of social restrictions, hypocrisy, and pervasive monitoring by an 'all seeing' state. Although *Sheno Ya3ni* do not have a particular regime as their target, their comedy is not any less political. Take the sketch *A'raf makbuta* ('Confined/Hidden Norms'), which exposes what really goes on in the bridegroom's experience of a typical Khaleeji (Gulf Arab) wedding. An innocent-looking groom prepares for a group photograph and is ogled at lasciviously by other men. They eventually start 'fingering' him (Hubail's term, not mine), in a re-enactment of the actual harassment, molestation and inappropriate touching that men face at the hands of other men on their wedding day. The exposure of these practices by *Sheno Ya3ni* occurs against a backdrop of toxic masculinity that goes hand in hand with political hypocrisy in patriarchal, authoritarian regimes.

The final chapter on Lebanese rap, by Fernanda Fischione, addresses the question of the role of religion in the Uprisings. It is indeed surprising that religion does not figure more prominently in any of the chapters recounted so far. Even the two chapters on Egypt – by Fabian Heerbaart (on street art, comics, stand-up comedy and internet memes) and Liza Franke (on popular poetry) – do not touch on religion. In Lebanon, however, rap music as cultural resistance – or 'conscious rap' – explicitly explores themes of religious hypocrisy and sectarianism. Lebanese rappers adopt Sufi themes and metaphors to put themselves in the shoes of the Prophet Muhammad, seen through their eyes as a social justice reformer. They justify these creative choices by drawing links between rap's affinity with poetry and the orality of the Qur'an.

Initially, this chapter's focus on the aesthetics of rap and poetry in relation to Islam and political activism made it seem disconnected from the theme of humour. What helped its argument come alive to me, however, was my own enjoyment of the work of the Syrian-American poet and rap musician, Mona Haydar. Released in 2017, Haydar's first single, 'Hijabi (Wrap My Hijab)', went viral and was named by *Billboard* magazine as one of the 20 Best Protest Songs of the year. Her next single, 'Dog', also went viral. A feminist take-down of hypocritical Muslim sheikh-bros, the track is earnest, politically savvy, and utterly hilarious. This balance of humour and righteous anger is on display from Haydar's deadpan opening line: 'If you think this song is about you / I don't know what to tell you'. She then breaks into the first refrain: 'Sheikhs on the DL / Sheikhs in my DM / Begging me to shake it on my cam in the PM / Sheikhs on the DL / Sheikhs in my DM / Ridin' in that Audi like a Saudi Arabian'. Haydar raps in English, but there is definitely resonance here with the Arab-language track 'Innocence', for example, by the Lebanese rapper Naserdayn al Touffar: 'God has neither parties nor Salafist wings / God is innocent of all religion in which women have no rights / When you pray to your Lord, don't orient yourself towards the *Ka'ba* / God is sick of Saudis, in front of them he wears a bulletproof vest'.

Creative Resistance makes no apologies for focusing on political humour as resistance in the Arab Middle East and North Africa. Even the editors of *Critical Muslim* used a bit of humour to frame our analysis of the Arab Uprisings – our first ever issue, published in January 2012, carried the tongue-in-cheek title 'The Arabs are Alive'. But, as with the editors and contributors of *Creative Resistance*, this was no cheap tit-for-tat against Orientalists and Islamophobic ideologues who harp on whether Muslims can even have a sense of humour or political acumen. I am, of course, personally embittered by the imbecilic public rhetoric on Islam and humour – by both anti-Muslim and Islamist-apologist ideologues – that has been dominated by the *Jyllands-Posten* or *Charlie Hebdo* 'Muhammad cartoon' controversies. The contributions to *Creative Resistance* show that humour in Muslim contexts is about so much more than whether Muslims can laugh, or whether they are capable of intellectual criticism and political protest. What this volume provides is a range of genres (visual art, online videos and memes, comic strips, political jokes, satire, street art, and rap music), a range of political regimes (monarchies, military regimes, republics, and occupied territories), and a range of outcomes (revolutionary successes, failures, and 'wait-and-sees') showing that political humour is a form of creativity, justice-seeking, and intellectual analysis. If the contributions sometimes feel slightly exploratory or not entirely focused on 'humour', this is because humour is generally neglected in more 'serious' scholarly studies of social change. The contributors also highlight the difficulty in measuring the depth, breadth and impact of the *reception* of political humour amongst the wider public. Again, this is a challenge shared by scholars of political humour more generally, especially regarding authoritarian or transitional contexts.

The more pertinent question is whether, in addition to providing political capital for resistance or relief, humour can have 'positive' potential to cultivate 'new forms of egalitarian sociality' that emerged during the Uprisings. In other words, can humour not just be a political weapon, but a vehicle for creating a better and more just society? This does not mean we are forbidden to laugh about surreal video montages of topless Egyptian police graduates. But perhaps we should reflect further on *why* we are laughing and what we are going to do with our laughter.

CLASSIC DRINK

Samia Rahman

Growing up in an environment as sober as you could get, I was terrified of drunk people. Perhaps because consuming alcohol is one of those taboos in some Muslim communities that seems to cause the faithful of all degrees to become overly vexed. It had been drummed into me that the spiral of decay that started with just one small sip was the most catastrophic act of self-harm I could inflict upon myself, my family, my extended family, not to mention dishonouring my forefathers and destroying any future prospect of 'marrying well', the sole purpose of my existence, obviously. A sin second only to promiscuity, I grew up with nightmare visions of what intoxication could lead to and steered well clear.

In hindsight, this was a very effective tactic employed by my parents who, as first-generation immigrants in the late twentieth century were typically preoccupied with preserving in their children the values they themselves had been brought up with. It wasn't until I moved out of home to go to university that I was exposed, in any significant way, to people who drank alcohol to excess, and finally managed to overcome my abject fear. The haram-ness of all the drunkenness surrounding me seemed worlds away from the wholesome, halal, home environment I had left behind. Many years later I would come to realise this dichotomy was, perhaps, not as clear cut as it seemed.

To label the drinking of alcohol as a travesty utterly anathema to Muslim traditions is a misnomer, as illuminated by Alex Rowell in his enthralling and meticulously researched *khamriyyat*, or collection of droll Islamic wine poetry, by Abu Nuwas. In *Vintage Humour: The Islamic Wine Poetry of Abu Nuwas*, Rowell provides an enchanting translation in English rhyme from Arabic in the hope that Abu Nuwas may finally become as well-known outside the Arabic-speaking world as the likes of Rumi and Hafez. The bard, immortalised, albeit inaccurately, in the celebrated collection of folk tales originally compiled in Arabic, *One Thousand and One Nights*, is a legendary figure in the Arab world and considered one the greatest poets and champions of wine-drinking to have lived. Rowell does not preoccupy himself with the theological arguments for and against the permissibility of drinking alcohol in Islam as such. Instead, by capturing the life and work of the gifted and notorious Nuwas, whose poems Rowell has given titles such as 'We Turned Not to Fire, But to Wine', 'The Hangover's Thrust', 'The Wine in Heaven', and 'Pour Me the Haram Before the Halal' among others, we come to understand the erroneous rigidity with which we view the separateness and labelling of so-called halal and haram in Islamic practice. Nuwas implores:

> Will you not pour your brother aged wine?
>> For life is in aged wine addiction
> And if the reproachers reproach, I'm not
>> One who shuns pleasure fearing theologians
> It's *haram*, though its start was *halal*
>> So let permission replace proscription

Ambiguity on this issue, I would argue, is laid out in the Qur'an itself. In 4.43 of M A S Abdel Haleem's translation, the warning is clearly sounded: 'You who believe, do not approach prayer while you are intoxicated, until you know what you are saying.' This has been argued to forbid drunkenness only when performing the ritual prayer, although such an assumption is contested by those who cite later rather more strongly worded verses, such as 5: 90: 'O you who have believed, indeed, intoxicants, gambling, [sacrificing on] stone altars [to other than Allah], and divining arrows are but defilement from the work of Satan, so avoid it that you may be successful'. The implication is that a drunkard, and a lascivious one at that, who flirts outrageously with irreverence, bordering on blasphemy, surely has no place in circles of piety, even if he is a brilliant poet who continues to be lauded some 1300 years after his death.

Alex Rowell, *Vintage Humour: The Islamic Wine Poetry of Abu Nuwas*, Hurst, London, 2017

So, who is this extraordinarily acid-tongued wordsmith who both delighted and scandalised eighth-century Abbasid courts in equal measure? Rowell offers a fascinating and comprehensive biography in his introduction and we learn Abu Nuwas was born Al-Hasan ibn Hani' in 757 or 758, near Ahwaz in modern-day Iran, to an Arab father and Persian mother. His father died when he was young, by which time the family had moved to Basra, which was a dynamic intellectual hub of creativity and learning; a pivotal centre of what came to be known as the Islamic Golden Age. The adolescent quickly gained a reputation for his astonishingly good looks and brilliant mind. His mother sent him, as was the custom, to a traditional *madrasah* where he memorised the Qur'an, flawlessly uttering his recitations to mesmerised audiences and in the same breath delivering spontaneous quick-witted and acerbic ditties that earned him great infamy, not to mention more than one or two enemies who did not take kindly to being the target of his ridicule.

Nuwas formed part of the literati crowd who made the most of Basra's louche nightlife, before coming to the attention of the Persian poet Abu Usama Waliba ibn al-Hubab. Dazzled by the young, beautiful and gifted young man, al-Hubab invited him to stay with him in the nearby city of Kufa, another fulcrum of dynamic intellectual activity, and mentored him in the fundamentals of poetic craftsmanship while also introducing him to hardcore drinking and the salacious delights Kufa had to offer well into the small hours. It was as a result of this eclectic schooling that Nuwas learned the joy of getting utterly wasted in a manner conducive to creativity that ensured he was still able to compose exquisite poetry upon waking the next morning, despite nursing a hangover from hell. Astounded by the unique talent possessed by the adolescent, al-Hubab arranged for him to spend a year in the desert to immerse himself in the oral traditional culture of the Bedouin.

Upon his return, and with his already impeccable skills sharply polished, Nuwas settled once again in Basra, picking up his decadent lifestyle where he had left off, but this time mentored by the more sober and strict literary scholar and poet Khalaf al-Ahmar, who is the one who named his disciple Abu Nuwas and is credited by Rowell for adding a 'depth and sophistication' to his poetry that no doubt resulted in its enduring legacy. It is also at this time that Abu Nuwas is thought to have experienced profound heartbreak at the hands of a slave girl named Janan with whom he fell hopelessly in love. His attempts to woo her were all-consuming and included the rather obsessive act of following her on a pilgrimage to Mecca and theatrically positioning his face alongside hers as she went to kiss the black stone of the Ka'aba, thereby orchestrating their only physical encounter – the chaste and innocent accidental touching of cheeks:

> We stayed, concealed by our hands
> > Placed at the sides of our faces
> Doing, in the Mosque, that which
> > The pious don't do in such places

Sadly for Nuwas, his infatuation would never come to fruition, and, devastated, it is speculated by some commentators that the young man never loved again, throwing himself instead into a life that by today's standards would be considered one of unbridled iniquity. His devotion to the pursuit of pleasure until his death was without limits and his mockery was directed at anyone who attempted to detract from his whim. He was resolutely anti-war, ridiculing the zeal for martyrdom when life was there to be lived if only one surrendered to indulgence and hedonism.

His satire of religion was certainly provocative; on performing Hajj for reasons other than stalking the woman he was crazy for, his response at the idea was: 'Why would I go on Hajj as long as/I'm plunged in a wine house, or a pimp's pad?' But he refrained from ever identifying as anything other than a believing Muslim. Unlike other famous poets of the day who declared they had become atheist, he did not metaphorically step outside the realms of the faith. Instead he embraced his contradictions and quirks, regarding them as harmonious elements jostling within his being, onto which he incessantly poured wine, the ultimate soothing balm for his soul: 'How often we've cured with the glass/ Worries more bitter than death's stress.' Wine became, to him, more than a drink, it was a symbol of the mysticism that is as much at the heart of Islam as are scriptures, while intoxication is a door to the unseen in the same way that dreams and visions are.

With this is mind, one wonders whether perhaps our understanding of Islam is coloured by a modern pietistic approach that emphasises legal rulings and diminishes the pluralistic and diverse way in which pre-modern Islam was characterised. In her talk on gender variance and sexual diversity in Islam at the 2018 Inclusive Mosque Initiative's 'Raise Your Gaze' conference in London, anthropologist Leyla Jagiella revealed that Abu Nuwas was a teacher of *hadith*, alongside spending his evenings in taverns and his nights indulging in all manner of sensual delights offered by the alluring men and women his poetry extols. The multitudinous expressions of his passions – Islamic scholarship, poetry, wine and sex – do not appear to negate one another in the society in which he lived. Can you imagine the scandal if a high-profile scholar of Islam today wrote unapologetically of lustful desires and the joy of alcoholic intoxication? The frenzy of the right-wing press picking over the carcass of their devoured prey would know no bounds.

It is important, however, to emphasise that Abu Nuwas did indeed face consequences for what many in eighth-century Iraq, Persia and the Middle East, considered to be his immoral behaviour. The Abbasids had only just won power at the expense of the Umayyads, the Shi'i were beginning to emerge and organise, while the puritanical Kharawij were agitating on the fringes. Abu Nuwas was living in politically charged times, and although he was celebrated by members of the court of Harun al-Rashid, the fifth Abbasid Caliph, when he eventually established himself in the illustrious and awe-inspiring city of Baghdad, his inebriated wordplay would often land him in trouble. More than once he found himself sanctioned by the Caliph who did not appreciate his lampooning of royal aides and courtiers. When Harun al-Rashid died and his son al-Amin succeeded to the throne, Nuwas found as near to a kindred spirit as he could have hoped and gained greater prominence in the Abbasid court through the patronage of his dear friend. The poet's notoriety was at fever-pitch, however, and Al-Amin's close friendship with Abu Nuwas was maliciously used against him by political opponents, particularly his half-brother al-Mamun, who would one day brutally depose him. Al-Amin even imprisoned Abu Nuwas for a while, in an attempt to assuage his detractors, and Abu Nuwas himself made a great show of repentance amid accusations of degeneracy. This has been seized upon by contemporary conservative Muslim scholars who claim that Abu Nuwas sincerely repented for his erstwhile deviancy, when in fact his rueful reams of verse were likely tokens of expedience and intended merely to mollify.

As late distinguished Muslim scholar, Shahab Ahmed, argues in *What Is Islam?* contemporary approaches to the Muslim faith are mired in the legislation of observance and a narrow definition of what constitutes a believer. Anyone who does not fit neatly within these specific margins is cast adrift and dismissed as 'secular', or adhering to a mystical form of

Islam that transgresses Islamic norms. Abu Nuwas belongs instead to what Ahmed describes as a pluralistic pre-modern Islam that emerged from the 'Balkans to Bengal' with its rich array of manifestations entirely comfortable with contradictions and complexity. This cosmopolitan Islam was held together not by inflexible laws but by a common way of life and collective consensus of constantly evolving thought driven by scholarship committed to expanding the idea of what Islam is. Jagiella too bemoans the unyielding harshness of the halal/haram dichotomy, reminding us that knowledge can be gained from beyond the scriptures, as it exists everywhere in Muslim history whether that be the wine poetry and biting satire of the work of Abu Nuwas, or the hadith that he teaches.

I am reminded of another brilliant contemporary mind who departed our world far too soon, my dear friend, colleague and mentor, the late Merryl Wyn Davies who also vehemently believed in the need for Muslims to be critical and introspective, similar to Ahmed's encouragement of a hermeneutical engagement with Revelation, a conglomerate he terms 'Pre-text, Text and Context'. The contradictions laid bare in the life of Abu Nuwas are nothing new, in fact they represent the messy and complex lived realities of ordinary Muslims across the world as they navigate composite existences. Plurality of thought, debate, discussion and division is inherent to Muslim traditions since the time of the Prophet, something which Ahmed feels has been marginalised by contemporary scholarship that posits the separation of idealised outward public piety and private internal inconsistency as an acceptable, even desirable, way to exist. All this does is perpetuate a misrepresentation that Davies articulated perfectly when she would frequently talk about the immense vibrancy of thinking and ideas in Muslim communities, saying that it is so important these conversations that many of us hold in private are made visible, because if you have a seemingly unchanging stereotype, you won't see signs of change.

Abu Nuwas is part of the conversation, and, as Jagiella also argues, is vital to any understanding of Muslim tradition. When an assertion is made that we need to differentiate between 'Islam' and 'culture', as if the two are exclusive and immutable, we should remember that Islam was revealed into a pre-existing culture and the notion of there ever having been a pure Islam is a fallacy. Just as Ahmed does, Jagiella questions the narrow prism through which we currently ascribe faith and suggests we ask ourselves who has created the knowledge that dominates our narrative, and which voices have been drowned out. Abu Nuwas was a seeker of pleasure, whether that takes the form of drinking wine or sexual activity with men and women. Even now when we speak of gender and sexuality as being fluid, we are actually speaking theoretically. In practice, the rise of Western non-binary identity is, Jagiella says, 'tied to the way in which we have constructed gender in the West, constrained by social norms in the absence of any existing framework'.

Muslims must make space for Abu Nawas in our traditions. He is an integral part of the fabric of Islamic tradition and what it means to be a Muslim.

SHARED VALUES

Giles Goddard

In March of this year, I had a conversation with a Sierra Leonian member of the church where I am vicar. He lives with his wife and children in London and sends financial support to the village in Sierra Leone where he grew up. 'Giles', he said, 'I want to help rebuild the church. But I am paying for the rebuilding of the mosque, first. It was in a terrible state, all falling down. Look.' He pulled out his smartphone and showed me a video. In a dusty clearing in the forest, surrounded by houses, a piece of corrugated iron roofing was being formally presented to the elders sitting grandly in armchairs. With delight they received the gift and added it to the pile nearby, soon to be used for the completion of the mosque.

> 'When I have finished the mosque, I will pay for the church. That's OK, isn't it?'
> 'Yes, of course,' I said. 'It's good that you're helping to get the mosque rebuilt.'
> 'Thank you. I thought you would say that but I wanted to get your advice.'
> 'I think relations between Christian and Muslim are good, in Sierra Leone?'
> 'Oh yes. We all intermarry. It's all fine.'

In St John's there is also a Ugandan family, of which the husband is of Muslim heritage and keeps Ramadan while the wife is Christian. Their daughter observes both Lent and Ramadan and was very pleased when she discovered that I also keep both fasts.

The many positive stories of Christian-Muslim relations are rarely heard. Historically, too, the periods of good interfaith relations are often cast into the shadows. The period of *convivencia* in southern Spain under the Umayyads is probably the best-known example – but there are others, barely registering in the historical narrative. Sicily was conquered by

Muslims between 827 and 900 and was ruled by three Muslim dynasties until 1071. The monk Theodosius wrote in 883 that Palermo was

> full of citizens and strangers, so that there seems to be collected there all the Saracen folk from East to West and from North to South . . . Blended with the Sicilians, the Greeks, the Lombards and the Jews, there are Arabs, Berbers, Persians, Tartars, Negroes, some wrapped in long robes and turbans, some clad in skins and some half naked; faces oval, square, or round, of every complexion and profile, beards and hair of every variety of colour or cut.

In the eleventh century Norman mercenaries were brought in to support one of the dynasties and, as is the way of these things, ended up taking over – but under King Roger II (1130-1154) the island was a ferment of intellectual endeavour by Jews, Muslims and Christians. King Roger is said to have spoken Arabic fluently, and one of the seminal works of geography, the Book of Roger – *kitab rudjdjar* – was written by Muhammad Al-Idrisi at his court.

It hardly needs repeating that the history of Christian-Muslim relations is also studded with flashpoints of hostility, from the Crusades to the Siege of Vienna to 9/11. And judging by public perception, relations between the two faiths appear to be at an historic low. *Fine Differences: The Al-Alwani Muslim-Christian Lectures 2010 – 17* is an attempt to rediscover the positive, tolerant relationships which have existed in the past: it is seeking to chart a way towards a renovation of deep mutual respect.

Richard. J. Jones. Editor, *Fine Differences: The Al-Alwani Muslim-Christian Lectures 2010 – 17*, International Institute of Islamic Thought, Washington, 2018

Taha J. al-Alwani was an internationally recognised and respected expert in the fields of Islamic legal theory, jurisprudence (*fiqh*) and a former president of the International Institute of Islamic Thought. *Fine Differences* brings together lectures delivered between 2010 and 2017 as part of a series sponsored by the Washington Theological Consortium and named in his honour. The first lecture, by al-Alwani's daughter Zainab (founding Director of Islamic Studies at Harvard), recounts how his sermons in a mosque in Baghdad attracted many people from different faiths, and how their Christian neighbour, Uncle John, came often to discuss religious, political and philosophical issues with him. 'My father pursued natural interactions with other people throughout his life. This example … demonstrates his *ta'āruf* – his precious ability to relate to others bearing the diverse faces of humanity'.

The lectures mainly predate the presidency of Donald Trump, with all that that dark time entailed for many Muslims. But when the lecture series began, the memory of 9/11 was still fresh and controversy was never far away. In 2007, a conversation opened up between John W. Crossin, a priest and member of the Washington Theological Consortium, and Ahmed Alwani, son of Taha, seeking an institutional home for his father's project of relating Islamic scholarship to Western social sciences. These lectures are one outcome of those conversations: they ask questions germane to Christian-Muslim relationships in the melting pot and political cauldron which is Washington D.C:

> Must religious emotions and ideas fuel social conflict?
> Who pays the cost of mediating conflict?
> What is the right way to value human labour?
> What part may Islamic family law play in American civil law?
> Is the term 'People of the Book' (the phrase which is often used to translate *ahl al-kitāb* in the Qur'an, referring to Jews and Christians) honorific or pejorative?

Questions of power lie very close to the surface in this book. Washington is the seat of power, the capital city of a 200-year-old nation of immigrants, including migrants from war zones and poverty, professionals and scholars, as well as converts to Islam. It is the focus for struggles of religious and national identity, the place where disagreements and controversies over federal and international law are played out, and where decisions are taken which affect the daily lives of millions around the world. The Protestant Christian hegemony based in Washington inhabits its own fears: even before the Trump years the sense of threat expressed by white evangelical Christians was palpable, to say nothing of the complexities of the USA's relationship with Israel and the millenarian connections between the 'restoration' of the Jewish nation and the return of Christ.

Therefore, behind the stated themes of the book – economics, mediation, law, the question of violence in religion – lies a deeper question about the balance of power in these interfaith conversations. It seems clear who holds most of the cards. The history of the USA is, by and large, a history of the dominance of white Christians. Muslims have too often been cast as enemies of the USA – the axis of evil – and Islam has often, despite its deep roots in America, (some scholars estimate that twenty percent of enslaved people brought to the US from Africa were Muslim) been portrayed as inimical to the American way of life, liberty and the pursuit of happiness. This book sets out to disrupt that narrative, by asking how and where common ground can be found.

The subtext seems to demand that the burden of proof is laid upon the Muslim contributors, to demonstrate that the negative preconceptions about Islam are ill-founded and that an alternative narrative is both necessary and possible. The contributors rise to the challenge without denying the complexity of the issues at stake. But the discourse between these two faith traditions is not only troubled by questions of power. The history of conflict demonstrates the consequences of the belief that Islam and Christianity are essentially irreconcilable: that the Qur'an and the Incarnation represent inimical understandings of how God acts in the world.

At the heart of Christianity is the belief that God became flesh and dwelt among us: the incarnation of Christ as one of the three coequal and integral parts of the Trinity which is also the Unity of God. Christianity is grounded in the revelatory event of the personhood of Jesus Christ as described in the Bible, which bears witness to the Christ event. The Bible bears witness to the revelation rather than being the revelation itself: so, there are strong parallels between what the Qur'an represents for Muslims and what Christ represents for Christians. Anthony Quainton, in the chapter on 'Violence in the name of religion' reminds us that

> both religions deeply believe in their own righteousness: and in the obligation to engage in what Christians call evangelisation ... that leaves us very little room to compromise, and where there is no compromise, violence is often the result.

Perhaps wisely, *Fine Differences* does not delve deeply into the divergent understandings of the Divine expressed in the person of Jesus Christ and the words of the Qur'an. Rather, it draws upon the strong traditions of openness and welcome between the traditions, exemplified by the centuries of Arabian intellectual ferment and the tolerance (albeit conditional) of the Ottoman empire towards non-Muslims and by individuals such as Taha al-Alwani, to ask: what is there within Islam and Christianity which might enable a better way of cohabiting? Is a generous pluralism possible? Or is the best we can hope for, as Daniel Madigan says, 'to set up boundaries that we think of as make our religions more or less impervious to one another, thinking that that will somehow enable a peaceful coexistence?

By focusing on the contested interpretations of controversial passages or by reminding readers of little-known events in the history of Islam and Christianity an alternative approach is presented which both finds common ground and suggests ways of working through areas of difference. Abdulaziz Sachedina's chapter, 'The Qu'ranic Foundation of Interreligious Tolerance', quotes from a letter from the Fourth Caliph, Ali, written as he dispatched Malik bin Ashtar to exercise minority rule over Christian Egypt:

> Infuse your heart with mercy, loving kindness with your subjects. For they are of two kinds, either they are your brethren in religion or your equal in creation. You cannot treat them as inhuman, because they have been created like you... errors catch them unaware, deficiencies overcome them, so grant them your pardon ... to the same extent that you hope God will grant pardon and His forgiveness.

Sachedina grounds a pluralist vision of interfaith relations in the Qur'an:

> When you look at the Qur'anic vision of the human community, it strikes us that the Qur'an is engaged in formulating religious space for each faith community. 'Say, O disbelievers, I do not worship what you worship. Nor are you worshippers of what I worship. For you is your religion, and for me is my religion.

In an extended reflection on the phrase *ahl al-kitāb*, Seyed Amir Akrami argues that a more appropriate translation of 'the People of the Book' is 'the People of Scripture', reflecting a more inclusive approach to the communities of which the Qur'an speaks – an approach which is supported by commentaries such as that of Tabataba'i. Speaking of 5.69:

> Surely, they that believe, and those of Jewry, and the Sabaeans, and those Christians, whosoever believes in God and the Last Day, and works righteousness – no fear shall be on them, neither shall they sorrow.

Akrami argues that 'the pluralistic and general tenor of this verse is so obvious that, I think, it leaves no room for any claim to exclusivity in the name of the Qur'an'.

So, the depths of both traditions are mined for evidence that such generosity is not only possible but required. A series of closely argued jurisprudential lectures from Muslim thinkers, rooted in the concepts of *ta'āruf* – getting to know each other, *tawhid* – affirming God's oneness, *taqwā* – God consciousness, and *fiqh al-ta'ayyush* – understanding of living together harmoniously, are responded to with a series of lectures from Christians which focus on the two great commandments, to love God and love your neighbour. Who is my neighbour? It is, in this case, my Muslim brother or sister.

In a powerful article on the place of mediation within interreligious dialogue, Richard Jones, the al-Alwani Chair of Christian-Muslim Studies at the Washington Theological Consortium and the editor of *Fine Differences*, cites the famous encounter between St Francis of Assisi and Sultan Malik al-Kamil, an attempt to bring peace before the Fifth Crusade. They, as well as the Prophet Muhammad and former UN Secretary General Dag Hammersköld, are offered as 'God-given mediators (who) have understood in their own ways that their work is sacred'.

Fine Differences is notable for the breadth of disciplines reflected in the lectures. For example, in the contributions on the relationship between Islamic *shar'iah* and the law of the land, and between Christian and Muslim legal processes, Richard Jones acknowledges that 'we may have to continue our study of the law of God in our separate workshops. But our parallel work to extract first principles from our respective bodies of law may possibly make a shared contribution to the way the law of the land operates'.

The final chapter, by Daniel Madigan, *Religious Faiths in a Pluralist Society*, draws together the strands of the conversation. Too often, he argues, interreligious conversations have worked on the basis of a 'patchwork pluralism' where the boundaries between faith traditions are impassable. But this vision of the possibility of peaceful coexistence is a mirage 'because we share one ecosystem. What one person believes about race or slavery or gender or ethnicity or war or peace or health or well-being has its effect on all of society. We do not live isolated human lives'. Which is not to say that the things about which we differ are marginal. They are at the heart of what it means to be human, because our understanding of God is intimately entwined with what constitutes human flourishing.

How, then, are we to live alongside one another? By, suggests Madigan, engaging humbly in working together. Bringing two kinds of humility to the conversation – first, epistemological humility: 'we need to have a certain humility about what we can know, and the possibility for human language fully to express the truth about God'. And, second, moral humility: 'Could we find the honesty and courage to acknowledge to one another not only that we ourselves have sinned but that we are entangled together in webs of oppression that stretch across centuries – and this not just in our conflicts with one another, but in our failure to do justice in the world?'.

A particularly welcome pair of lectures in *A Fine Difference* consider the effect of African nationalism and governance on interreligious relations. Both Sulayman Nyang and his respondent, Kwasi Kwakye-Nuako, call for a rediscovery of the traditions which inform and underpin the lived experience of Christian-Muslim relations in Africa. Says Nyang:

> Human beings have to recognise that if they do not go back to their old texts and study their texts and see the history of their texts, then they will not be able to engage with any meaningful dialogue with other human beings.

To which Kwakye-Nuako responds by tracing the history of Christian missionary activity in Africa:

> If we are committed to interfaith dialogue in Africa, we must resurrect the intrinsic nature of Africans that saw the sacredness of life and the wholistic worldview of tolerance.

None of the authors in *Fine Differences* denies that there are fundamental differences between Islam and Christianity which may never be reconciled. And the absence of the shared ancestor of both traditions, Judaism, is notable. But it is, in the end, a work of hope. It tries to reach below the storm-tossed surface to find a shared stillness beneath, where currents meet and mingle and life is nourished. I think the people of the village in Sierra Leone would recognise and applaud the book: it is a manifestation of the conviction that a better world is possible.

THREE AFRICAN GIRLS

Hodan Yusuf

The film is beautiful in so many different ways, and it is quite challenging to contain my enthusiasm for it. It opens with children's voices cascading from a school playground. Three girls in their late teens are talking with each other in the courtyard of a high school and three boys are behind them having a separate conversation among themselves. The conversations between the students are in a mix of mainly Somali and French, and the multilingual youngsters switch from one language to another with consummate ease. This is the opening scene from *Dhalinyaro*, the first full length feature film from Djibouti.

Dhalinyaro, meaning youth in Somali, was also released under its French name *Jeunesse*. Although released in 2017, the film emerged into the spotlight in 2020 after it won several awards at international film festivals – including Festival International des Films de la Diaspora Africaine 2019, Afrika Film Festival – Cologne 2019, Urusaro International Women Film Festival – Rwanda 2019, and Arabisches Film Festival – Tubingen 2019. In April 2020, it was screened for free on a digital platform promoting African cinema and when people heard about it via Twitter, it proved to be so popular it received nearly thirty times more views than all the other film screenings combined. It continued to be screened free for a while, which meant it reached audiences who may not have otherwise been able to access it.

The film is the brain child of Lula Ali Ismail, a Djibouti-Canadian filmmaker, actor and director, who co-wrote and directed *Dhalinyaro*. Djibouti does not have a film industry, so Ismail is a pioneer who has earned the nickname 'the first lady of Djibouti cinema'. Half of the budget for the film was fundraised in one and half years from the Djiboutian government and prominent businesses. Ismail was overwhelmed with the level of support she received for the production. She impressed that she wanted to make a film that was not focussed on people who were undergoing hardship, such as migrating refugees, or victims of conflict. She wanted to show African people living their day to day lives. Her aim was to allow for this space to create with freedom. She didn't want to replicate fetishised stories of Africa that depict problems and pain all of the time. Ismail set out to create a story that speaks to young people across the world, and her premise is one that anyone who has navigated friendships, parent-child relationships and intimacy, can identify with.

Dhalinyaro is a coming-of-age story that follows the lives of three high school students, Deka, Asma and Hibo, during the year of their baccalaureate, which is equivalent to A-levels in the UK. This is a time of transition when these girls become young women, and the film is consciously centred within the context of contemporary Djibouti, honouring the cultures, and most importantly the voices of its youth. Indeed, Djibouti city itself is the fourth main character in the film – its harbour, its cityscape, and the day to day lives of its citizens. Djibouti, a former French colony on the Horn of Africa, was previously known as *French Somaliland* and then as *French* Territory of the Afars and Issas before the country won its sovereignty from France as recently as 1977. That was when it officially became the Republic of Djibouti. French is very widely spoken and interspersed within conversations in the Somali and Afar languages.

We first meet Deka on Eid. Deka and her mother are from a middle-class family and are getting ready to attend the communal Eid Prayer in their local masjid. They go *inside* the masjid – not under or behind or barred from, but inside and not from the back door but from the *front* door, using the same entrance as everyone else. Many Muslims around the world will find this unusual but it is the norm in Djibouti. No doubt, many Muslim women will find it refreshing to see these women and girls on screen in their brightly coloured Eid clothes confidently entering the mosque courtyard from the main entrance, praying and listening to the *khutbah* in the main hall, without being shooed away to a side entrance and herded into an improvised and less than ideal space. Welcome to Djibouti.

The length of the salah is shortened for the purposes of filming, but unlike in many films and TV shows depicting Muslim characters in prayer, this is not a contrived scene. Expression of piety through congregational prayer is an integral part of everyday life and is shown without judgement or comment. It is simply a part of tradition. It is small but significant things like this scattered throughout the film, which add to its enchantment. There is value in seeing yourself reflected back at you, in people who look, sound, dress, eat, love, pray and live like you. This is why *Dhalinyaro* received such a positive response by Djiboutians, who could relate to the characters depicted and saw themselves in the film. Authenticity is crucial for the integrity of any art that is being produced, and is so often ignored by filmmakers who self-appoint themselves the storytellers of cultures and communities with which they have only a superficial connection, instead of elevating the voices they have appropriated. That is not to say artists can only make work from their own communities, but at the very least they should allow the local communities to speak for themselves.

Dhalinyaro, directed by Lula Ali Ismail, screenplay by Lula Ali Ismail, Alexandra Ramniceanu, and Marc Wels, produced by Lula Ali Ismail, Alexandra Ramniceanu, Jean-Frédéric Samie and Gilles Sandoz. Samawada Films, Djibouti, 2017. 86 Minutes. Available on Amazon Prime.

Offering a never-before-seen picture of Djibouti society, the film illustrates the joys and challenges these young friends face. We see the girls filling out their university applications and considering whether or not to study abroad, prompting one of the characters to say: 'Imagine the freedom [of] no one looking at you to say you're so and so's daughter.' This no doubt will resonate with many women and girls who are made to carry the burden of responsibilities and being attached to the men of their families in a way young men are not always beholden to. The lure of leaving their close-knit communities for the promise of freedom of anonymity is one way in which Ismail explores the frisson between tradition and modernity.

The three friends represent the social strands that comprise Djiboutian society's hierarchies. We peek into Asma's family life; studious and sensible, she is the eldest of her siblings. Her family is from a rather more working-class background, particularly when contrasted with the wealthy family of the third lead character Hibo, who even has her own chauffeur to drop her to and from school. In one such car ride, the popular song *Djibouti My Home* by Don DeltFa featuring Houssein Ali Hayle, comes on the radio and she asks her driver to 'turn this song up, I love it'. This is what Ismail does so well throughout the film. Through the smallest details she manages to convey how immersed within and familiar to this world she is, and we cannot help but feel fortunate that she is welcoming us to observe alongside her. Often the film feels like someone placed a documentary film crew in a regular neighbourhood high school and then magically made that crew invisible. It vocalises the thoughts and hopes of the youth and it very much feels like it is their own work. Ismail presents the information and the messaging without it feeling laboured or making you feel as if you are being lectured. You truly feel and see Djibouti through the eyes and lives of these young people. As there are no casting agencies in the country, Ismail visited schools in Djibouti, interviewing around 300 girls before settling on our three protagonists who evidently possess raw natural talent.

Djibouti has three main ethnic groups, Somali, Afar and Arab peoples. All of these ethnic groups live side by side with each other; attending the same schools, forming mixed friendship groups. The ethnic backgrounds of the three lead actresses reflects this very well. Deka is Somali, Asma is Afar and Hibo is mixed with an Arab father and Somali mother. It is surprising to learn that this diversity was not something Ismail set out deliberately to portray. She explains it was a coincidence. She did not have to force the representation because it was already present. Arguably, it was already present because she was so attuned to co-existing demographics that not having a representative mix of ethnicities would have been glaringly amiss to her. This is what it looks like when someone embodies the idea of representation without it being a performative exercise. It is not tokenistic, rather it becomes a holistic practice. Not to include each of those groups would have meant to exclude them consciously. So if 'unconscious bias' is a thing instilled by years of conscious discrimination, then I would argue unconscious inclusion comes from the depth and practice of conscious deliberation.

Socio-economic disparities are also teased out in the film. In one scene, a small boy, under ten years old, approaches a man sitting in a coffee shop to polish his shoes. The inequalities of the haves and the have-nots is contrasted with the very comfortable middle and upper classes sipping coffees in old colonial buildings of downtown Djibouti city. These are all important and subtle snapshots touching on nuances, bursting with historic symbolism without spelling it out for the audience in any blunt kind of way. In a world dominated by white supremacy and its tentacles of colourism and anti-blackness, it is not insignificant to me to see that two out of the three lead characters are played by darker-skinned Black girls. One girl wears hijab and abaya and interestingly, there isn't any demarcation of a 'hijabi' or a non-hijab-wearer couched in judgement or dis/approval. There doesn't appear to be the rigidity often projected onto Muslim women and girls in the UK and other places on what constitutes visible and pious Muslim women. The hijab-wearing character is not shamed on the occasions she chooses not to wear a hijab and the non-hijab wearer is not praised when she wears one to the masjid. Hijab is not exceptionalised or sensationalised as a motif for freedom or lack of, as is so often the case.

Deka has a beautiful friendship with an elderly neighbour who lives across the road. She regularly takes him a thermos of tea that her mother has prepared for him. Her mother often gives out buttered bread and tea to disadvantaged children in the neighbourhood and we feel the warmth and solidarity of this group of families. After one such day of helping her mother in their courtyard, Deka goes across the road with the tea. It is worth noting the kindness and respect with which Deka and her mother treat those who live around them. It is a supremely touching moment that ensures the dignity of those on the receiving end of charity remains fully intact. This is a demonstration of how mutual aid was and is done in our communities. It is a familiar scene to me.

When Deka speaks to the older gentleman, she asks if he ever left Djibouti. He says he went to France in 1944 and fought in World War II. He narrates a detailed account of his postings and deployments as part of the French army. Like much of Western Europe at the time, armies were comprised of various troops of people conscripted or recruited from the lands they were colonising. The French recruited their armies from Africa, inspired by the racist views that Black people could withstand more pain, using this to justify putting Black soldiers on the front lines of battle as dispensable cannon fodder. Many families, including my own, have heard the harrowing stories of relatives who endured such brutal experiences.

Even though Somali culture can at times be 'shame' heavy or defensive, Ismail knew that a film about youth had to talk about certain things if it was to be taken seriously — namely, intimate relationships and sex. She deals with this delicate subject by being considerate of the audience's sensitivities because it was important to her that the film was shown in Djibouti and she wanted Djiboutians to enjoy it and not feel it was an affront. So she alluded to things without showing any sexual activity or being explicit or gratuitous. Ismail asked the questions that Somali youth are asking themselves and made the film in a way that was like opening a window onto the lives of young people. She also has a cameo appearance in the film as a professor advising students on their university applications, such is the intimacy of the lens through which she invites us in.

Before writing *Dhalinyaro*, Ismail came back to Djibouti to spend time at the high school where the film was eventually shot. She did this because she wanted to be sure she was writing with authenticity. Although she is a Djiboutian woman of Somali heritage, born and raised there, steeped in the culture, city, with an in-depth knowledge of the various ethnic groups, religious communities, and the complexities of society. She was no longer a high school student. So, she insisted that she spend time listening to this age group because although she had once been eighteen years old, she felt she shouldn't speak over these young people as they were now. So, she spent three months, an entire school term, at the high school, sitting at the back of the class. She listened, and she learned. She spoke with the students who would approach her, asking questions. And even though she did not set out to cast three girls, her time in the class rooms at the high school lead to the birth of the three lead characters. So the script evolved; and the lead actors – Amina Mohamed Ali who plays Deka, Tousmo Mouhoumed Mohamed who plays Asma, and Bilan Samir Moubus who plays Hibo – emerged naturally from the process.

I have deliberately avoided saying anything about the plot so not to spoil the film for anyone. Perhaps, it would suffice to say that Deka is caught between her mother's hopes for her to go abroad to study and her own wish to remain in a Djiboutian local university. Highlighting the motivations of young Africans who wish to remain in Africa, develop their own countries, and make their lives prosperous by their own efforts. That is the overall message of *Dhalinyaro*.

Watch it. Go and see young Black Africans living, loving and being. See the parents who have loved and sacrificed for them and those who have chosen to be absent. Go and see them make complex and life-changing decisions as they emerge into adulthood and challenge their leadership about creating opportunities for them at home while being seduced by opportunities to take their lives abroad. Watch the socio-economic commentary which takes the viewer through the lens of young people's experiences. Go see these young women navigate their relationships, their friendship and their youth.

ET CETERA

ON PIGEONS AND PRAYER

Ziauddin Sardar

I don't have to tell you that 2020 was an *annus horribilis*. In May, a few weeks or so after the first lockdown in the UK, I was sitting in my garden, contemplating the suffering that the year had inflicted on me, and anticipating the torments to come. I had just finished a year of gruelling treatments for my prostate cancer. The hormone treatment and radiotherapy were accepted with abounding good cheer but the indignity of colonoscopy – or what my nurse described as 'camera up your back passage' – was too much. During my first examination, the surgeon, who turned out to be Turkish, repeatedly urged me to 'relax, relax'. After his umpteenth exhortation, I couldn't help exclaim: 'how can I relax? You have got an iron rod up my arse!'. He managed to control his laughter so as not to disturb the procedure. 'If you put it that way', he said, 'then don't relax'. At the beginning of the year, I was diagnosed with Type 2 diabetes. It was in my genes I discovered. And if this wasn't enough, I have, as a Robbie Williams song has it, bags under my eyes and am getting on a bit. As we know, Coronaviruses are ageist. As such, our pestiferous government classified me as 'vulnerable' and decreed that I should be 'shielding'.

So, there I was, 'shielding' in my garden, self-flagellating myself, even though I am not Shia, self-isolating from the rest of humanity, when a flock of pigeons landed right in front of me. It was much, much larger than the usual number that grace my patch. They jumped, they flapped, and flew around the garden in circular formations. A feeding frenzy occurred when I threw a handful of seeds; it triggered a couple of memories. My memory, a source of pride for me in my heyday, is not what it used to be. Nowadays, it is prompted by certain observations or events. But before I could begin my reminiscence, my elder son scolded me. 'Stop feeding the pigeons, Dad', he shouted. 'They are vermin. Like rats and cockroaches. They will leave their droppings all over the place'. I said nothing and quietly returned to my swing seat.

It is, I think, a calumny to describe pigeons as vermin. Woody Allen's *Stardust Memories* branded them 'rats with wings'. A colossal injustice. Vermin, by definition, spread diseases, cause harm to crops and livestock, and can actually kill people. Who has ever heard of death by pigeon? Pigeons are in fact delightful creatures. As John McEwen points out in *The Oldie*, a rag I am devoted to, pigeons 'can be radiantly plumaged and are wonderful flyers. They clean the streets of takeaway scraps and are a perpetual amusement: in London they travel by tube and stop the traffic by using the zebra crossing in Regent's Park. For many of us they are our closet bird and we take comfort from their crooning companionship'. There are around 300 varieties and hybrids, including fantail, tumblers and carrier and racing pigeons, and the one we are most familiar in our urban conurbations, the feral, wild or city pigeon. They are our earliest companions and were domesticated before cats and dogs. Indeed, our most ancient and abiding relationships are with pigeons, going back to the Sumerians, who flourished between c. 4100-1750 BCE, and who first house-trained them. Pigeons provided our original postal service, which even played an important part during the two world wars – well illustrated by the permanent exhibition at Bletchley Park's *Pigeons at War* display. How many rats and cockroaches can do *that*?

Our dislike of pigeons is a modern, urban fetish. Yes, they do disfigure our roofs, and their droppings block our gutters. I had to have my gutters cleaned twice last year. But rewind the time tape a few hundred years and you will see that pigeon guano was a highly prized fertiliser. In England, pigeon guano had to be guarded from thieves. In Iran, dovecotes were established as a source of regular fertilisers for melon crops. In *The Fihirst of Al-Nadim*, the catalogue of books by the tenth century bookseller, we find an entry, adjacent to 'The Names of Books Composed about Sexual Intercourse – Persian, Indian, Greek, and Arab – in the Form of the Story of Passionate Love', for *The Book of Bird Droppings*, a manual, I suspect, for putting pigeon guano to good use!

The proficiencies of pigeons are a wonder to behold. They are simply amongst the most intelligent birds on the planet. I suspect that Farid ud-Din Attar knew this when he wrote *The Conference of the Birds* in the twelfth century. The birds of the world gather for a convention to select their ideal king, the Simorgh bird, guided by their leader, the hoopoe. But to find the king they have to go on an onerous journey, which most of them are not keen on. One bird after another comes up with an excuse; which are all answered with calm, eloquence and insight by the hoopoe, tighter with anecdotes, stories and allegories. It is worth noting that all the birds that are reluctant and express concerns about the journey are identified: the nightingale, the hawk, the peacock, the duck, the heron, the owl, and the rest. But the pigeons are not identified; they appear as generic common o' garden 'bird', often seeking advice on such topics as audacity, and the length of the spiritual journey. 'A bird who burns with aspiration' expresses just how I feel:

'O hoopoe', cried another of the birds,
'What lofty ardour blazes from your words!
Although I seem despondent, weak and lame,
I burn with aspiration's noble flame –
And though I'm not obedient I feel
My soul devoured by an insatiate zeal.'

I must admit I do feel 'weak and lame' when compared to lofty pigeons roaming my garden.

While I can't differentiate between different species, let alone different birds of the same species, pigeons can recognise different people, and distinguish between two different persons in a photograph. While I find it difficult to recognise my own face as it withers away, pigeons have no problem in recognising their own reflection in the mirror. While I am finding it more and more difficult to read my own handwriting – creeping dotage has brought dysgraphia with it – pigeons can recognise all twenty-six letters of the English language. While I am finding it difficult to tell my left from my right, let alone find my way around urban sprawls, the navigating abilities of pigeons are truly astounding. They can return to their own loft from a place they have never been before thousands of miles away. While my olfactory pathways are deteriorating, despite a large hooter, pigeons can, as

John Day tells us in *Homing*, smell the wind, and use it, along with magnetic fields and the sun as a compass to navigate. They have not one but a number of GPS trackers built-in! Not surprisingly, I have come to the conclusion that pigeons are more useful and valuable then my good self.

The denizens of Abbasid Baghdad would agree. Pigeons were an intrinsic part of the economy of the city and the Baghdadis were infatuated with them. An entire market, known as *suq al-tuyur*, was devoted to the buying and selling of pigeons and their eggs. They were loved and adored, cared for and trained, raced and watched, and their pedigrees were carefully recorded. Sophisticated methods were developed for training homing pigeons. As they are monogamous, they were mated early, and their love was then used to intensify their homing instincts. Rich and poor, as well as Caliphs – Harun al-Rahsid, Mahdi, Wathiq and Nasir being the most notable – enjoyed racing pigeons. And, of course, some gambled, which, naturally, led for calls to ban them. In *Social Life of the Abbasids*, Manazir Ahsan says that 'the populace became so infatuated with pigeon racing that it became a social problem. The government sometimes had to take repressive measures against it, ordering the demolition of dove-cotes (*abraj haradi*) on the grounds that the privacy of the women dwelling nearby might be endangered and that the clamour of pigeon trainers, and their hurling of stones at pigeons sitting on roof-tops, were a cause of public disturbance'. The *ulama*, however, refused to ban them citing their use as an essential tool of communication; and got one of the few things right! It is the ninth-century philosopher, writer, all-round intellectual, and amongst the first evolutionary theorist, Al-Jahiz, who reveals the real worth of a pigeon. 'Pigeons have such a high intrinsic value and such superiority that a single bird may be sold for 500 dinars', Jahiz wrote. 'No other animal can command such a price, neither the goshawk, the peregrine falcon, the saker, the eagle, the pheasant, the cock, the camel, the ass or the mule...A pair of pigeons is as productive as a landed estate; indeed, it will cover the living expenses of a family and bring in enough to allow it to pay off its debts, build fine houses and buy highly profitable shops. At the same time, it is a wonderful hobby, a pleasing sight, an education for thinking men and a clue for those given to looking at things'.

So, there I was, swinging gently in my swing chair in the garden, looking at the pleasing sight of a flock of pigeons flapping and flying around me.

They conjured up an image of my mother. She just loved feeding pigeons. When she developed Alzheimer's, and could still walk around the house, she would go in the garden and feed the pigeons. Then she would forget. And go in the garden and feed the pigeons. Dementia is not just about memory loss. It is also about issues with language; and my mother simply forgot how to speak. She would say, '*Jalla jata hai*' (it's gone) repeatedly. If I said, 'Mumsey, you have already fed the pigeons!'. She would reply: '*Jalla jata hai*'. Dementia also leads to the loss of the ability to judge distance, direction, or place. If unattended, she would wander off – well, anywhere. But she never lost the ability to go straight to the garden first thing in the morning, finding the bag of seeds, and sprinkle them all over the garden – right up to the days when she became bed bound and had to be moved to a care home. She would throw the seeds in the air and watch the birds fly and flap around her with excitement. As she began to lose one faculty and ability after another, I realised that I was losing her not just as a mother but also as a go-ahead, assertively independent person. Alzheimer's is an exceptionally cruel disease: it takes everything, but everything, away from an individual that makes them a whole person. Then, of course, I lost her altogether right in the middle of the pandemic. But the memories of the sheer delight on her face, the beaming smile, the shrieks of laughter, as she played with the pigeons, will always stay with me.

The other memory takes me back to a scourging May in 1976, during the days I worked for the Hajj Research Centre of the King Abdul Aziz University. I was in the Haram, the Sacred Mosque in Mecca, with my colleague Saleem Tabligh, counting the pilgrims in the Haram, and measuring the flow of pilgrims performing the tawaf, which requires pilgrims to walk around the Kaaba seven times. In those days, the Haram was much smaller than it is today; and we were trying to estimate how difficult it was for pilgrims to perform their rituals at any given time. At what point does the throng become so vast that old and frail pilgrims are in danger of being crushed? It was low season, on an intensely hot afternoon – when most of the sensible people in the Kingdom have their *qylula*, or, as the Spanish call it, siesta - so the Haram was relatively quiet and our task was much easier. We were taking a break, sitting not too far from the Kaaba, leaning on a carved marble Ottoman column, which has since been demolished and replaced with an ugly substitute. Suddenly,

Saleem Tabligh became agitated. '*Aoozo billaahi minahs-Shaytaanir-rajeem*', he uttered loudly and repeatedly. 'I seek refuge from Satan, the outcast'.

At this point, I should say that Saleem Tabligh was a statistician, and a good one at that. But he was also, shall we say, a few beads short of a full *tasbih*. His real name was Saleem ul-Hassan. He was a devout member of the Tablighi Jamaat, and believed that there was a special prayer for every human act – getting up, sitting down, blowing your nose, going to the toilet, having a bath. And, of course, he knew all of them by heart. He believed that all images are forbidden in Islam; and television was a complete and utter taboo. That's why, in his apartment, he kept his own device hidden inside a cupboard; it came out at night when he and his wife secretly watched 'the continuing story of Payton Place' and an Egyptian soap opera which continued even longer. There was also a large stock of VHS videos, bought from the street markets of Jeddah and carefully hidden – including a selection of Bollywood films and compilations of songs (which were also forbidden). Of course, Saleem did not know that we knew.

Initially, I paid no heed to Saleem's Tablighi idiosyncrasies. Then, his father came for hajj. He was a slim, fragile man in his late seventies, with a long Tablighi beard and thick glasses. On the day of his arrival, Saleem was busy with research duties so he asked me if I could take his father to perform the tawaf. I thought that would be a pious thing to do and uttered an enthusiastic yes.

It did not take me long to realise he was a couple of steps ahead of his son on the Tablighi ladder; and a complete *majnoon*. He carried an Urdu pamphlet with him, *How To Perform the Hajj*, a special Tablighi Jamaat issue, which he constantly held in his left hand close to his eyes. It wasn't enough to chant *Allah-o- Akbar* (God is Great) and *Labik Allahumma Labbaik* ('Here I am at your service, O God here I am'). It was also necessary to say a special prayer at every step you take inside the Haram the book instructed, and he said it as loudly as he could. It took us hours to get to the tawaf area. Once there, I put my arms around him, held him tightly, and moved gently to join the circumnutating crowd. 'What are you doing?', he exclaimed. 'I am going to help you perform the tawaf', I said. 'No, No', he shouted. 'You are going in the wrong direction'. I could not believe my ears. 'The book says you must start the tawaf from Sang-e-Aswad' (Black Stone). 'We will', I said. 'We will follow the flow and you can start counting when we reach Sang-e-Aswad'. 'No, no, no', he screamed. 'I must start at Sang-e-Aswad'. He turned around, and as I was holding him, I too was forced to turn around – both of us now faced a tsunami of pilgrims, in full religious ecstasy, moving past us with tremendous force. I held him tightly – for I knew if he fell he would never get up again – and with all my might I turned him around, and then allowed the wave of 80,000 or so pilgrims performing the tawaf that day to carry us. That is the closest to death I have ever been.

Somehow, I managed to take Saleem's father around the Kaaba – anti-clockwise as it should be – seven times. He was fuming with anger when I took him back to his son. 'I must sacrifice a camel', he kept saying. 'I have committed a great sin. I did not perform the tawaf correctly. The penalty requires me to sacrifice a camel'. He also held me responsible for losing his precious guide book, which meant he could not perform the hajj exactly as he should. 'My hajj is ruined', he declared. 'I must sacrifice many camels'.

It was at that point that I realised the Saleem was not just a Tablighi. He was a generational Tablighi. I awarded him the moniker Tabligh. Since that day, he is known as Saleem Tabligh. Hardly anyone knows his surname.

Back in the Haram, Saleem Tabligh was now frantic. 'O my Lord', he prayed, 'I seek refuge in Thee from the evil suggestions of the Satans' (*Rabbi aaoozubika min hamazaatish shayaateeni*). 'What is wrong?', I asked. 'Look over there'. He pointed to a far corner of the Haram, adjacent to the *Sai* area, where the pilgrims run between the hills of Safa and Marwah. I looked but did not notice anything particular. 'In that niche', Saleem Tabligh said, now highly distressed, 'that couple under the blanket. They are copulating'. He paused then loudly uttered the rest of the prayer: ' I seek refuge in Thee O my Lord , lest they come near unto me'. (*wa aAAoozubika rabbi an yahzuroon*).

The Haram is, of course, the Sacred Sanctuary. But it is also the abode of all human life. It is rare, but hardly surprising for pious couples to try to conceive a much wanted child in the most holy of all places! The child would be blessed. My research in the Haram had taught me that something was definitely afoot when the following verse of the Qur'an was repeatedly, reverently and, I should say, passionately murmured: 'O my Lord! Grant me from You, a good offspring. You are indeed the All-Hearer of invocation' (3:38). I had also noticed that the *Mutawa*, the religious police who guard the morality of the Haram, and kept an eager eye on women who dare reveal their arms, often turned a blind eye towards those trying to increase the piety quotient of the Muslim population.

It is when Saleem Tabligh went to report his observation to the Mutawa that I realised I was surrounded by pigeons. Someone had left a bag of seeds just where we were sitting. The pigeons were gorging on a feast. I looked at them; and carried on looking. The more I looked the more I was hypnotised by the precision with which each pigeon picked a seed, then rapidly moved on to the next, and the next, and the next; the whole flock moving in unison, coordinated and synchronised. Then, suddenly, the flock flew off only to return moments later to engage in the same ritual. I looked up to the Kaaba; then lowered my gaze to the pigeons. Then again. The pilgrims performing the tawaf turned into a stream revolving around a centrifugal force. But the pigeons remained solid, discrete, yet an organic collective. I was suspended between the stillness of the Kaaba and the rapid movements of the pigeons; caught between the material world of the pigeons and the spiritual realm of the Kaaba. It was a moment of eternity. A tick of synchronicity. I started weeping. And realised that I knew. I knew that the Kaaba was a symbol of our direction but God has no direction. He is everywhere. I knew that my encounter with Saleem Tabligh's father, and the brush with death, was no accident. I knew that it was no coincidence that the pigeons were eating frantically by my feet; they were there to provide me with, as Al-Jahiz said, 'an education for thinking men and a clue for those given to looking at things'. I looked and saw God revealing Himself yet remaining Unknown. I knew I knew the truth but was incapable of knowing the Truth. Sobbing, I burst into prayer: 'Say, O Lord! Let my entry be, By the gate of Truth, And let my exit be, By the Gate of Truth, And grant me from Thy Presence, A helping power' (17:80).

So, I can say, with some pride, that my firm belief in God, and the limited attended spirituality, was ushered by the collective unconscious of pigeons!

Of course, I am not the only one to have received such generosity from pigeons. They have played an important part in Islamic history and tradition. The 'flock of birds' sent against 'the army of the elephant', led by Abraha, the ruler of Yemen, who wanted to destroy Mecca, were probably pigeons, who bombarded 'them with pellets of hard-backed clay' and turned them to 'cropped stubble' (105:3-4). Tradition has it that two pigeons mated at the entrance of Cave Hira, where the Prophet and his companion Abu Bakr were hiding during the migration to Medina. Thus, pigeons played their part in fooling the enemy Quraish. Then, there is the tradition of Prophet Noah which states that he released a pair of pigeons from his ship after the flood. They returned with an olive branch to indicate that the earth was ready to mark a new beginning.

Muslims have also been dreaming about pigeons for centuries. Otherwise, how does one explain the literature on interpretation of dreams about pigeons? I am reliably told that a white pigeon in a dream means spirituality, a green one piety. A frightened one means divorce; an adequate punishment, I think, for those who go around alarming the innocent birds. Eating pigeon in a dream means you are a thief. Rightly so; pigeon meat is forbidden in Islam. If you see a flock of pigeon landing on your roof then expect the arrival of a long awaited loved one. But I just can't fathom why slaughtering a pigeon in a dream would lead to marriage. Surely, there are other routes to dream about conjugal bliss!

Nowadays, you won't find pigeons inside the Haram. Arrangements have been made to keep them out. But you will be greeted by flock after flock when you come out of the Haram. Indeed, pigeons are everywhere in Mecca; and pilgrims feed them generously. The Meccan birds are known as pigeons of Al-Hema, or the Pigeons of the Household. They belong to the ménage of the Sacred City and are thus looked upon with grace and favour. The local government has built special towers in the Al Hujun area for these birds to nest, rest and relax. Indeed, providing roosting places for pigeons is a well-established tradition in Muslim cities. Look closely, for example, at the walls of the old city of Fez. You will notice niches and alcoves built into the wall for the birds to lay their eggs and rear their squabs. You will find stone pigeon lofts in many old mosques throughout the Muslim world, some mosques set aside grain specifically to feed pigeons. One of the pleasures in visiting the Blue Mosque in Istanbul is to come out to the Sultanahmet Square to feed the pigeons.

So you, who look down on pigeons, look up to them. They are not just a pleasing sight, but they also provide an education. Do not demean or disparage God's creations because you cannot see their value or utility on the surface. Cherish them for what they are. Pigeon lives matter! For me:

they are my aid memoire. A diplomatic reminder of my personal history, engagements with family and friends, as well as the meaning and purpose of my life. I owe them a debt of gratitude for the arrival of meaning in my heart, which by the way is said to be the definition of true spiritual knowledge.

THE LIST

BOLLYWOOD COMEDY AWARDS

Rachel Dwyer

Welcome to my personal lockdown awards ceremony for comedy in Hindi film. I don't think this is the place for me to be funny and sometimes now it's hard to think of what comic potential there is in lockdown. So, I hope I won't make you feel even more miserable as there's nothing so unfunny as something that's meant to be funny which isn't, unless it's having something funny explained, or, even worse, having it theorised. I hope these 'awards' will serve as a reminder of comic moments, perhaps to make you look them up online, perhaps to see the films if you haven't seen them, and when we can all look forward to finding life funny again.

1. Best comic film: 'Amar Akbar Antony' (dir. Manmohan Desai, 1977)

The blockbuster features two of my all-time favourite comic actors, Amitabh Bachchan and Rishi Kapoor. The film has a mad plot, flamboyant costumes, memorable characters and, above all, perfectly placed songs that expand and tie together the narrative knots of this outrageous excess.

2. Best comic scene: The performance of the Mahabharata in 'Jaane bhi do yaaro' (dir. Kundan Shah, 1983)

The film mixes satire on the building trade with farce, knowing references to European cinema, its greatest moment being a farcical staging of the Mahabharata, where the story has to be adjusted to conceal a corpse as Draupadi. The disrobing cannot take place. Dhritarashtra, the blind king, might well ask, '*Yeh kya ho raha hai* / What's going on?'

3. Best comic director: Hrishikesh Mukherjee

The master of light comedy, of complicated plots, and chaos which has to be resolved. My favourite scene is Dharmendra giving a brilliant performance as the *shuddh* Hindi-speaking driver (*vahan-chalak*) of *Chupke chupke* (1975). Mukherjee is also an expert at sad films such as *Anand* (1971) and *Abhimaan* (1973), covering a range of human emotions.

4. Best comedian (M): Salman Khan

My students always complained that I liked Salman Khan and demanded to know why. Salman is a fighting hero for many but for me his genius lies in his comedy and his own send-up of his shirt-removing. From *Andaz apna apna* (1994) to *Dabangg* (2010) and *Bajrangi Bhaijan* (2015), this innocent fool is pitch perfect.

5. Best comedian (senior/late): Rishi Kapoor

Rishi Kapoor, though seen as the romantic hero in colourful sweaters was funny right up to the end. Who can forget him in *Student of the Year* (2012), when the young men stomp around, their muscles performing better than their feet, Rishi picks up his *dafli* (drum), which he uses as a *cakra* (discus) to knock out his rival? He shows that age and weight are irrelevant when you are a light-footed star dancer.

6. Best comedian (Female): Sri Devi

One of India's biggest stars across the country, Sri Devi's talents were extraordinary. My favourite is when she goes undercover to give a dance performance as Miss Hawa Hawaii in *Mr India* (1987) where she shows she can do the sexy and funny together.

7. Best comedian to use comedy to raise social issues: Ayushmann Khurrana

Ayushmann Khurrana takes roles in comedy films that seem unlikely choices for a hero. A sperm donor (*Vicky Donor*, 2012), a useless husband who despises his more talented wife for being fat (*Dum laga ke haisha*, 2015), the grown-up son whose mother gets pregnant (*Badhai ho*, 2018), a female voice impersonator (*Dream Girl*, 2019), a police officer fighting caste discrimination (*Article 15*, 2019), a gay man (*Shubh mangal zyada saavdhan*, 2020) as well as acting in Hindi films like *Andhadhun* (2018).

8. Best film for dark humour: 'Gangs of Wasseypur 1 and 2' (2012)

I'm a bit sick of men with guns who find extraordinarily beautiful and chic women in the Badlands of North India, but GoW charms with style, outrageously good actors (Manoj Bajpai and Nawazuddin Siddiqui), and some hilarious moments. Nawaz at the wedding? Guns that explode? Goats?

9. Best satire: 'Peepli Live!' (2010)

When I saw *Peepli Live!* without subtitles, I couldn't understand any of the villagers' Hindi. Mortified, I told a Bombay-based film critic. She said 'same'. Hmm. The story of a farmer who decides the compensation his family will get if he kills himself is a staple of cunning villagers against the supposedly smart metropolitans. It joins other media satires such as *PK,* and the recent funny OTT series *Panchayat.*

10. Best comic character: Munna Bhai ('MBBS', 2003; Lage raho Munna Bhai, 2006)

Sanjay Dutt, now the subject of a biopic, was born to film royalty, Nargis and Sunil Dutt. His career seemed to be derailed by his personal issues but Munna Bhai, the street gangster who is redeemed by falling for educated women – doctors and Gandhian VJs – is a great character, and he shows that the heart comes before the brain. He and his sidekick, Circuit (Arshad

Warsi), perform all kinds of comedy but their mastery of language is outstanding.

11. Best comic song: Kishore Kumar's 'Mere saamne wali khidki mein' (In the window across from me)

I just have to see Kishore Kumar to start laughing. The man who sang so many of the most beautiful songs of Hindi cinema could do full body comedy, especially to music. There are too many songs to choose from but perhaps *'Mere saamne wali khidki mein'* (*Padosan*, 1968), where he dresses as a music master doing playback for Sunil Dutt or 'Panch rupaiya' (*Chalti ka naam gaadi*, 1958).

12. Most memorable comic dialogue circulated outside Hindi films: Written by Ajit

Ajit (Hamid Ali Khan) was associated with crazy dialogues and catchphrases ('Come on Lily, don't be silly'). These circulate more widely than the films themselves ever did as they also send up the craziness of some Hindi film dialogues themselves: *'Ise Hamlet poison khila do... 'To be or not to be'!* (Give him the Hamlet poison – 'To be or not to be'!)' and ' *Isko liquid oxygen mein daal do...Liquid isko jeene nahin dega aur oxygen isko marne nahin degi* (Put him in liquid oxygen. The liquid won't let him live and the oxygen won't let him die)'

So, I had to leave out way more than I could put in, all of whom are essential to history of comedy in Bollywood. Raj Kapoor for his Chaplin slapstick, Bhagwan for comedy and song, Johnny Walker whose walk alone is funny (and the immortal 'Sarjo tera chakraye' from *Pyaasa, 1957*), Mehmood, loved for silly accents in Gumnaam and Padosan, Shammi whose look of surprise and general silliness is seen well in 'Suku Suku', Govinda for getting into terrible scrapes and dancing like a dream, Akshay Kumar – for innocence and simplicity, Shahrukh Khan for clowning, Ranbir Kapoor, who inherits so much of the family talent, Ranveer, for his winks to the audience.

All of the above are major stars but who add a certain empathy and innocent mixed with wit and comic timing. There aren't enough women in my list perhaps because they haven't been given enough scope. Madhubala could stand up to Kishore in *Chalti ka naam gaadi* and Radhika Apte would be my best bet for the future.

CITATIONS

Introduction: We Have No Humour
by Hassan Mahamdallie

For the rules of writing comedy, see John Vorhaus, The Comic Toolbox (Silman-James Press, Los Angles, 1994). The quote from Khalid Kishtainy is from his *Arab Political Humour* (Quartet Books, London, 1985, p20). On Ashab the Greedy ad other Muslim humourists, see Franz Rosenthall, *Humour in Early Islam* (reprint of 1976 edition, Brill, Leiden, 2011). See also: Georges Tamer, editor, *Humor in Arabic Culture* (De Gruyter, Berlin, 2009), and Haris Mubeen, 'Humour and Comedy in Arabic Literature', *Al-Hikmat* 28 13-30 (2008).

Al-Jahiz's *The Book of Misers* has been translated by R B Serjeant (Garnet, London, 1998). For a flavour of the content of Abu al-Faraj al-Isfahani's *Kitab Al-Ghani*'s, see *Erotica, Love and Humor in Arabia: Spicy Stories from The Book of Songs by al-Isfahani*, translated by George Dimitri Sawa (McFarland & Co, Jefferson, New Carolina, 2016).

Humouring the Humourless by Hussein Abdulsater

The following works are mentioned in this article:
Ghazzī, Badr al-Dīn Muḥammad b. Muḥammad. *al-Marāḥ fī al-muzāḥ*. Edited by Bassaām al-Jābī. Beirut: Dār Ibn Ḥazm, 1977; Ibn Abī ʿAwn, Ibrāhīm b. Muḥammad. *al-Ajwiba al-muskita*. Edited by Mayy Aḥmad Yūsuf. Cairo: ʿAyn, 1996; Ibn al-Jawzī, Abū al-Faraj ʿAbd al-Raḥmān. *Akhbār al-ḥamqā wa-l-mughaffalīn*. Beirut: Dār al-Qalam, 1403 h.; Ibn Qutayba, ʿAbdullāh b. Muslim. *Tāwīl mukhtalif al-ḥadīth*. Edited by Muḥammad Muḥyī al-Dīn al-Aṣfar. Beirut: al-Maktab al-Islāmī, 1999; Ibn Qutayba, ʿAbdullāh b. Muslim. *ʿUyūn al-akhbār*. Cairo: Dār al-Kutub al-Miṣriyya, 1925; Jāḥiẓ, Abū ʿUthmān ʿAmr b. Baḥr. *Kitāb al-Bukhalāʾ*. Edited by Ṭāhā al-Ḥājirī. Cairo: Dār al-Maʿārif, n.d; Jāḥiẓ, Abū ʿUthmān ʿAmr b. Baḥr. *Kitāb al-Ḥayawān*.

Edited by ʿAbd al-Salām Hārūn. Cairo: ʿĪsā al-Bābī al-Ḥalabī, 1965; Jāḥiẓ, Abū ʿUthmān ʿAmr b. Baḥr. *Rasāʾil al-Jāḥiẓ.* Edited by ʿAbd al-Salām Hārūn. Beirut: Dār al-Jīl, 1991; Muqātil b. Sulaymān. *Tafsīr Muqātil b. Sulaymān.* Beirut: Dār al-Kutub al-ʿIlmiyya, 2003; Rosenthal, Franz. *Humour in Early Islam.* Netherlands: Brill, 2011; Ṭabarī, Muḥammad b. Jarīr. *Tafsīr Jāmiʿ al-bayān ʿan tāwīl āy al-Qurʾān.* Edited by ʿAbdullāh b. ʿAbd al-Muḥsin al-Turkī. Cairo: Dār Hajar, 2001; and van Gelder, Geert Jan. 'Mixtures of Jeſt and Earneſt in Classical Arabic Literature: Part I.' *Journal of Arabic Literature,* Vol. 23, No. 2 (Jul., 1992), pp. 83-108.

Sufi Satire by Bruce B Lawrence

The definition of satire by David Mamet can be found at Masterclass.com, 20 November 2020. The depiction of Shaykh Nizam ad-dinin's *khanqah* is set forth in K.A. Nizami, Introduction to *Nizam ad-din Awliya: Morals for the Heart (Conversations of Shaykh Nizam ad-din Recorded by Amir Hasan Sijzi).* Translated and annotated by Bruce B. Lawrence. New York: Paulist Press, 1992. Reissued with a new foreword by Zia Inayat-Khan. Manchester, UK: Beacon Books, 2017. All the subsequent citations are from this rendition of *Morals for the Heart.* They are, in sequence: 82-83, 135, 108-09, 354-55, 125, 168, 90-91, 162, 228-29, 309-10. For the Rumi reference, see *Signs of the Unseen: The Discourses of Jalalad-din Rumi,* Translated and introduced by W.M. Thackston, Jr. (Putney, Vermont: Threshold Books, 1996). For general information about Sufi orders and some of the saints mentioned in *Morals for the Heart,* there is no better source than the classic, Annemarie Schimmel, *Mystical Dimensions of Islam* (Chapel Hill, NC; University of North Carolina Press, 1975, reissued 2011 with a new foreword by Carl W. Ernst.) And for a sustained inquiry on *adab* as both literature and moral deportment, see the lucid, broad gauged analysis of Irfan Ahmad, *Religion as Critique: Islamic Critical Thinking from Mecca to the Marketplace* (Chapel Hill, NC; University of North Carolina Press, 2017), especially 67-70.

How Islamists Became Laughable
by Gilbert Ramsay and Moutaz Alkheder

For the rare video of Abdel Nasser, See "The Supreme Guide of the Muslim Brotherhood isn't able to get his daughter to wear a headscarf, and he wants me to get ten million people to wear it"', *Al Watan Voice,* 27 Dec.

2011, https://www.alwatanvoice.com/arabic/news/2011/12/27/232
261.html (accessed 17 Nov. 2019).

For more on the use of the term 'Islamism', an excellent review of various
disciplinary perspectives on the subject is to be found in Frederic Volpi's
Political Islam Observed, London: Hurst, 2010.

For more on early Islamist comedy, See S. Al-Qaranshawi, 'Actor Adel
Imam sentenced to imprisonment for three months on charges of "insulting
religion"', *Al-Masry Al-Youm* [Arabic], 1 Feb. 2012, http://www.
almasryalyoum.com/news/details/148570; Sky News Arabic, 'Rejection
of "insulting religion" charges against Adel Imam', https://www.
skynewsarabia.com/varieties/; Sky News Arabic, 'Adel Imam faces prison
on charges of "insulting religion"', 5 Feb. 2012, https://www.
skynewsarabia.com/varieties; A. Rowell, 'Introduction' in *Vintage Humour:
The Islamic Wine Poetry of Abu Nuwas*, trans. A. Rowell, London: Hurst, 2018;
S. Stroumsa, *Freethinkers of Medieval Islam*, Leiden: Brill, 2016, p. 16;
Observers, 'Jihadists behead statue of Syrian poet Abul Ala al-Maari', http://
observers.france24.com/en/20130214-jihadists-behead-statue-syrian-
poet-abul-ala-al-maari; A.L. Al-Sayyid Marsot, *Egypt in the Reign of
Muhammad Ali*, Cambridge: Cambridge University Press, 1984.

For more on Ibn Daniyal, See Yusuf Idris's play *Farafir* based on the second
shadow play in Ibn Daniyal's trilogy, *The Amazing Preacher and the Strange*.
See M.M. Badawi, 'The Plays of Yusuf Idris' in *Critical Perspectives on Yusuf
Idris*, ed. R. Allen, Washington, D.C.: Three Continents Press, 1992; M.
Al-Faruque, 'The Mongol Conquest of Baghdad: Medieval Accounts and
their Modern Assessments', *Islamic Quarterly*, Vol. 32, No. 4, pp. 194–206;
S. Mahfouz and M. Carlson, 'Introduction' in *Theater from Medieval Cairo:
The Ibn Daniyal Trilogy*, New York: Martin E. Segal Theater Center, 2013;
R. Amitai-Preiss, *Mongols and Mamluks: The Mamluk-Ilkhanid War*,
Cambridge: Cambridge University Press, p. 47; L. Guo, 'Paradise Lost: Ibn
Daniyal's Response to Baybars' Campaign against Vice in Cairo', *Journal of
the American Oriental Society*, Vol. 121, No.2, 2001, pp. 219–235; M.M.
Badawi, 'Medieval Arabic drama: Ibn Daniyal', *Journal of Arabic Literature*,
Vol. 13, pp. 83–107; L. Guo, 'The Devil's Advocate: Ibn Daniyal's Art of

Parody in His Qasidah No. 71', 2003, *Mamluk Studies Review*; M. Carlson, 'The Arab Aristophanes', *Comparative Drama*, vol. 47, no. 2, 2013, pp. 151–66.

For more on the evolution of comedy in early Arab states, See L. El-Ramly, 'The Comedy of the East, or, The Art of Cunning: A Testimony', trans. Hazem Azmy, *Ecumenica: Journal of Theater and Performance*, vol. 1.2. Autumn, 2008, pp. 75–86; K. Kishtainy, *Arab Political Humour*, London: Quartet Books, 1985, p. 123; E. Kedourie, *Afghani and Abduh: An Essay on Religious Unbelief and Political Activism in Modern Islam*, London: Cass, 1966; P. C. Sadgrove, *The Egyptian Theatre in the Nineteenth Century*, New York: Ithaca Press, 2007, p. 96; Amal Fu'ad, *Censorship: The Expressive Dilemma Between Writer and Producer* [Arabic], Cairo: Arab Press Agency (Nashiroon), 2018, pp. 52–57; R. Sami, 'Art after the 23rd of July, by direct command', [Arabic], *Fakartany*, 24 July 2017, http://fakartany. com/a/44142332125343dd8e5b4072f0754baf; I. Hamam, 'Disarticulating Arab Popular Culture: The Case of Egyptian Comedies', in *Arab Cultural Studies: Mapping the Field*, ed. T. Sabry, London: IB Tauris, 2012.

See D. Boyd, 'Egyptian Radio: Tool of Political and National Development', *Journalism Monographs*, No. 48, Association for Education in Journalism, February 1977, http://files.eric.ed.gov/fulltext/ED137821.pdf

For more on Arab comedy in the age of television and the early internet, See M. Kraidy and Khalil, J. *Arab Television Industries*, London: British Film Institute, 2009, p. 2; N. Sakr, *Satellite Realms: Globalisation, Transnational Television and the Middle East*, London: I.B. Tauris, 2002; R.M. Abdulla, *The Internet in the Arab World: Egypt and Beyond*, Oxford: Peter Lang, 2007; A. Hammond, 'Maintaining Saudi Arabia's *Cordon Sanitaire* in the Arab Media' in R. Rasheed, *Kingdom Without Borders: Saudi Arabia's Political, Religious and Media Frontiers*, London: Hurst, 2008; See A. Nasr, 'An Historical Perspective on Fundamentalist Media: The Case of Al Manar Television', *Global Media Journal*, vol. 6, no. 11, 2007.

For more on Arab comedy and terrorism, See L. Abu Lughod, *Dramas of Nationhood: The Politics of Television in Egypt*, Chicago: University of Chicago

Press, 2004; W. Armbrust, 'Islamically Marked Bodies and Urban Space in Two Egyptian Films' in *Islamism and Cultural Expression in the Arab World*, eds A. Hamdar and L. Moore, London: Routledge, 2015; H. Darwish, 'Egyptian Cinema and Terrorism', [Arabic] in *Terrorism and Cinema: Controversies of the Relationship and Possibilities for Employment*, eds Rima al-Mismar and Ahmad Zu'bi [Arabic], Beirut: Madarek, 2010, pp. 27–105; A. Salem, *The Image of Islamists on the Screen*, [Arabic] Beirut: Nama Centre for Research, 2014.

For more on modern Egyptian cinema and representation, See L. Abu Lughod, 'Movie Stars and Islamic Morality in Egypt', *Social Text* No. 42, Spring 1995, pp. 53–67; S. Gauch, 'Egypt's Media Target Islam', *Christian Science Monitor* 2 Sept. 1992, https://www.csmonitor. com/1992/0902/02141.html; W. Armbrust, 'Islamists in Egyptian Cinema', *American Anthropologist*, Vol. 104, No. 3, 2002, pp. 922–931.
V. Shafik, *Popular Egyptian Cinema: Gender, Class and Nation*, Cairo: American University in Cairo Press, 2007; L. Khatib, 'Arab film and Islamic fundamentalism' in *Media and Society*, ed. J.L. Curran, London: Bloomsbury, 2010; A. Hammond, *Pop Culture in North Africa and the Middle East*, Santa Barbara, Ca: ABC-Clio, 2017, p. 92; R. Baker, 'Combative Cultural Politics: Film Art and Political Spaces in Egypt', *Alif: Journal of Comparative Poetics*, No. 15, Arab Cinematics: Toward the New and the Alternative, 1995, pp. 6–38; I. Allagui and A. Najjar, 'Framing Political Islam in Popular Egyptian Cinema', *Middle East Journal of Culture and Communication*, Vol. 4, No. 2, 2011, pp. 203–224; O. Leaman, ed., *Companion Encyclopedia of Middle Eastern and North African Film*; U. Lindsey, 'The Egyptian comic convicted of "insulting Islam",' *National*, 5 May 2012, https://www.thenational.ae/arts-culture/the-egyptian-comic-convicted-of-insulting-islam-1.361908; C. Hedges, 'Cairo Journal: Battling the Religious Right: The Celluloid Front', *The New York Times*, 18 Apr. 1994, https://www.nytimes.com/1994/04/18/world/cairo-journal-battling-the-religious-right-the-celluloid-front.html (accessed 29 Dec. 2018);02; A. Hammond, *Popular Culture in the Arab World*, Cairo: American University of Cairo Press, 2007, p. 124; N. Galal, *Hello America*, Cairo, Al-Nasr Films, 2000; A. Arafa, *The Embassy in the Building*, Cairo, Essam-Imam Productions, 2005; M. Yassine, *The Gazelle's Blood*, Cairo, El Arabia, 2005;

M. Hamed, *The Yacoubian Building*, Cairo, Good News, 2006; A. Idris, *Al Thalatha Yashtaghalonaha [Three Men Deceive Her]*, Cairo, Arabica Movies, 2010.

For more details on jihadism and Saudi Arabia, See Y. Trofimov, *The Siege of Mecca: The Forgotten Uprising in Islam's Holiest Shrine*, London: Penguin, 2008. S. Lacroix, *Awakening Islam: Religious Dissent in Contemporary Saudi Arabia*, Cambridge, MA: Harvard University Press, 2011; T. Hegghammer, *Jihad in Saudi Arabia: Violence and Pan-Islamism since 1979*, Cambridge: Cambridge University Press, 2011; See T. Hegghammer, *Jihad in Saudi Arabia*, 2010; See J. Braude, *Broadcasting Change: Arabic Media as a Catalyst for Liberalism*, Lanham: Rowman and Littlefield, 2017.

For more on general Arab comedy post 9/11, See L. Wedeen, *Ambiguities of Domination: Politics, Rhetoric and Symbols in Contemporary Syria*, Chicago: University of Chicago Press, 2015, p. 89; S. Haugbolle, 'That Joke isn't Funny Anymore: Bass Mat Watan's Nasrallah Skit and the limits of laughter in Lebanon', *Arab Culture and Society*, 1 Oct. 2008, https://www.arabmediasociety.com/that-joke-isnt-funny-anymore-bass-mat-watans-nasrallah-skit-and-the-limits-of-laughter-in-lebanon/ (accessed 12 Nov. 2019); J. Tarabay, 'Popular Iraqi TV Comedian Killed; Ministers Attacked', National Public Radio, 20 Nov. 2006, https://www.npr.org/templates/story/story.php?storyId=6515072; U. Lindsey, '.V Versus Terrorism: Why This Year's Ramadan Shows Tackled One "Controversial" Subject, But Were Barred From Broaching Others', *Arab Media and Society*, 1 Sept. 2005, https://www.arabmediasociety.com/tv-versus-terrorism-why-this-years-ramadan-shows-tackled-one-controversial-subject-but-were-barred-from-broaching-others/

War of Words by Boyd Tonkin

I have quoted from the 2015 two-part paperback edition of *Leg Over Leg* by Ahmad Faris Al-Shidyaq, translated by Humphrey Davies with a foreword by Rebecca C Johnson, in the Library of Arabic Literature series of New York University Press, and have used its numbering of volume, chapter and paragraph (eg, 1.1.6). For al-Shidyaq's literary background, see Kamran

Rastegar, *Literary Modernity Between the Middle East and Europe* (Routledge, 2007), Sabry Hafez, *Genesis of Arabic Narrative Discourse: A Study in the Sociology of Modern Arabic Literature* (Saqi Books, 2001) and, for the broader context, Roger Allen's *An Introduction to Arabic Literature* (Cambridge University Press, 2000). Christopher De Bellaigue's *The Islamic Enlightenment* (Bodley Head, 2017) discusses the Ottoman intellectual life of the period, while *The Arab Renaissance*, edited by Tarek El-Ariss, gathers key documents from the progressive culture of the *Nahdah* (MLA Texts & Translations, 2018). Jens Hanssen and Max Weiss's *Arabic Thought Beyond the Liberal Age* (Cambridge University Press, 2016) supplies a wide-ranging survey of the intellectual landscape that al-Shidyaq helped to shape. The Russian theorist Mikhail Bakhtin's conceptualisation of comedy and carnival in literature fits al-Shidyaq's art supremely well: see MM Bakhtin, *The Dialogic Imagination: Four Essays* (University of Texas Press, 1982). For the other great "total book" of the early 1850s, see Herman Melville, *Moby-Dick, or, The Whale* (Penguin Classics, 2003). For the classic antithesis of the Fariyaq and Fariyaqiyyah's volubly intimate marriage, see Adam Thorpe's outstanding recent translation of Gustave Flaubert, *Madame Bovary* (Chatto & Windus, 2011). And, for an edition of al-Shidyaq's closest English (or rather, Anglo-Irish) cousin that illuminates the later impact of that work, consult the Norton Critical Edition of Laurence Sterne, *The Life and Opinions of Tristram Shandy* (WW Norton, 2018).

Old Arab Jokes by Robert Irwin

On Arab humour in general, see Charles Pellat, Seriousness and Humour in Early Islam', *Islamic Studies*, vol.2 (1963) pp.353-62); Franz Rosenthal, *Humor in Early Islam* 2nd ed. (Leiden, 2011); Ulrich Marzolph *Arabia Ridens* 2 vols. (Frankfurt am Main, 1992). The one with the Frank in bed, Usama ibn Munqidh, *The Book of Contemplation: Islam and the Crusades*, tr. Paul M. Cobb (London, 2008) p.148. On Jahiz, *The Life and Works of Jahiz*, ed. Charles Pellat, tr. D.M. Hawke (Berkeley and Los Angeles, 1969). For Nuwayri on the relaxing effects of humour, Shihab al-Din al-Nuwayri, *The Ultimate Ambition in the Arts of Erudition: A Compendium of Knowledge from the Classical Islamic World*, ed. and tr. Elias Muhanna (New York, 2016). The one about a prophet as mind-reader, the one about Ash'ab and the estimable

Prophetic tradition, and the one about 'or what', Bernard Lewis, *Islam from the Prophet Muhammad to the Capture of Constantinople*, vol.2, *Religion and Society* (New York, 1974). Michael Cooperson has translated al-Hariri's *Maqamat* as *Impostures*, with a foreword by Abdelfattah Kilito (New York, 2020). The one about Ash'ab chasing the children, Pellat 'Seriousness'. The other Ash'ab jokes are in Rosenthal, *Humor*. The one about Juha and the door, in Ul;rich Marzolph, *101 Middle Eastern Tales and Their Impact on the Western Oral Tradition* (Detroit, 2020). Other Juha stories in Salma Khadra Jayyusi tr, *Classical Arabic Stories: An Anthology* (New York, 2010). The ones about gate- crashing, in al-Khatib al-Baghdadi, *Selections from the Art of Party-Crashing in Medieval Iraq*, tr. Emily Selove (New York, 2012). Shadow plat scripts inb Ibn Daniyal, *Theatre from Medieval Cairo: The Ibn Daniyal Trilogy*, ed. and tr. by Safi Mahfouz and Marvin Carlson. For Ibn Sudun's marvellous recipe, Geert Van Gelder, *Of Dishes and Discourse: Classical Arabic Literary Representations of Food*, (Richmond, Surrey, 2000). For everything else about Ibn Sudun, Arnoud Vrolijk, *Bringing a Laugh to a Scowling Face: A Study and Critical Edition of the Nuzhat al-Nufus wa-Mudhik al-'Abus by 'Ali Ibn Sudun* (Leiden, 1998). The one about the one-legged goose, 'Abd al-Wahhab Azzam, *Majalis al-Sultan al-Ghawri*, (Cairo, 1941).

Comedy and Islam in America by Eric Walberg

Paul Theroux's *Deep South: Four Season on Back Roads* is published by Hamish Hamilton (London, 2015). The quote from E Fuller Torrey is from *Freudian Fraud: The malignant effect of Freud's Theory on American thought and culture* (HarperCollins, 1992, p 235.). On 'The Problem with Apu', see Vikas Bajaj, 'A Reckoning for Apu, "The Simpsons" and Brownface', *New York Times* 29 April 2018.

All the comedians and films mentioned in the article can be easily found on the internet and YouTube.

The Other Humours by Leyla Jagiella

To read more about the medical theory of the Ancient Greeks see Robert Lane Fox, *The Invention of Medicine: From Homer to Hippocrates* (Penguin 2020), and to learn about the life of Paracelsus see *Paracelsus: The Man who*

Defied Medicine by Hugh Crone (Albarello Press, 2004). The most accessible translation of ibn Sina's *The Canon of Medicine*, completed in 1025, is by Lleh Bakthtiar (Kazi Publications, Chicago, 1999). See also: Mones Abu-Asab et al, *Avicenna's Medicine: A New Translation of the 11th-Centiury Canon with Practical Applications for Integrative Health Care* (Healing Arts Press, London, 2013) and Hooman Keshavarzi, *Applying Islamic Principles to Clinical Mental Health Care* (Routledge, London, 2020). *Jahangirnama: Memoirs of Jahangir, Emperor of India* is translated by W M Thackston and published by Oxford University Press (Delhi 1999).

Other works mentioned: Rachel Laudan's *Cuisine and Empire: Cooking in World History* is published by University of California Press (Berkeley 2013), Noah Gordon's *The Physician* is published by Sphere (London 2015), and Iftikhar Malik essay, 'Montagu and Ottoman Inoculation', appeared in *CM37:Virus* (Hurst, London, 2021)

For more on the history of Islamic medicine, see Manfred Ullmann, *Islamic Medicine* (Edinburgh University Press, 1997) and Ahamad Rajab, *The Medieval Islamic Hospital: Medicine, Religion and Charity* (Cambridge University Press, 2018).

My Sardonic Tweet by Hussein Kesvani

The sources mention in the article are: Sam Bright, 'Far-right groups spread fake news about Muslim doctor', *Scram News,* October 4th 2019. (https://scramnews.com/far-right-groups-spread-fake-photoshopped-tweet-journalist/); Samira Shackle, 'Trojan horse: the real story behind the fake "Islamic plot" to take over schools', *The Guardian,* September 1st 2017. (https://www.theguardian.com/world/2017/sep/01/trojan-horse-the-real-story-behind-the-fake-islamic-plot-to-take-over-schools); Lizzie Dearden, Islamophobic incidents rocket by 600% in UK during week after New Zealand terror attack', *The Independent,* 23 March 2019. (https://www.independent.co.uk/news/uk/crime/new-zealand-shooting-attack-muslim-hate-crime-rise-uk-a8836511.html); 'Increase in online hate speech leads to more crimes against minorities', *Cardiff University News,* 15th October 2019 (https://www.cardiff.ac.uk/news/view/1702622-

increase-in-online-hate-speech-leads-to-more-crimes-against-minorities); Nick Lowles, 'State of Hate 2020: The Far Right Goes Global', *Hope Not Hate,* November 2020. (https://www.hopenothate.org.uk/wp-content/ uploads/2020/02/state-of-hate-2020-final.pdf); Kelly Weill, 'Why Does Starbucks Melt Conservative Brains?'. *The Daily Beast,* 21st December 2019; (https://www.thedailybeast.com/why-does-starbucks-melt-conservative-brains)Aja Romano, 'A History of Wokeness', *Vox,* 9th October 2020. (https://www.vox.com/culture/21437879/stay-woke-wokeness-history-origin-evolution-controversy); Sheera Frenkel and Tiffany Tsu, 'Facebook Tried to Limit QAnon. It Failed', *The New York Times,* 18th September 2020. (https://www.nytimes.com/2020/09/18/ technology/facebook-tried-to-limit-qanon-it-failed.html) Seth Simons, 'The Comedy Industry Has a Big Alt-Right Problem', *The New Republic,* February 9th 2021. (https://newrepublic.com/article/161200/ alt-right-comedy-gavin-mcinnes-problem); and Hussein Kesvani, *Follow Me Akhi: The Online World of British Muslims* (Hurst, London, 2019)

Classic Drink by Samia Rahman

Shahab Ahmed's *What is Islam? The Importance of Being Islamic* is published by Princeton University Press (2016). To watch Leyla Jagiella's talk on 'Gender Variance and Sexual Diversity in Islam', at Inclusive Mosque Initiative's 2018 conference in London, 'Raise Your Gaze', visit https:// www.youtube.com/watch?v=WDozaBdXLDQ

Last Word: On Pigeons and Prayer by Ziauddin Sardar

The Jahiz quote is from Justin Marozzi, *Baghdad: City of Peace, City of Blood* (Da Capo Press, Boston, 2014), p103; and M M Ahsan quote is from *Social Life of the Abbasids* (Longman, London, 1979), p250. John McEwen's article, 'Feral Pigeon' appears in *The Oldie* June 2018, p103. Farid ud-Din Attar's *The Conference of the Birds*, translated and with an introduction by Afkham Darbandi and Dick Davis, is available as Penguin Classic, the most recent edition published in 2011; quote from p144. See also: John Day, *Homing: On Pigeons, Dwellings and Why We Return* (John Murray, London, 2020).

CONTRIBUTORS

Hussein Abdulsater is Assistant Professor in the Department of Classics, University of Notre Dame ● **Moutaz Alkheder** is a PhD candidate at the University of St Andrews Centre for the Study of Terrorism and Political Violence ● **Mevlut Ceylan**, poet and translator, is Associate Professor of Cultural Studies at Çanakkale Onsekiz Mart University, Çanakkale, Turkey ● **Rachel Dwyer** is the first professor of Bollywood in the UK ● **Giles Goddard** is a Fellow of the Muslim Institute and Vicar of St John's Church, Waterloo, London ● **Robert Irwin**, a regular contributor to *Critical Muslim* also writes intellectual tomes and novels ● **Leyla Jagiella** is a cultural anthropologist exploring orthodoxy and heterodoxy in South Asian Islam ● **C Scott Jordan** is Executive Assistant Director, Centre for Postnormal Policy and Futures Studies ● **Hussein Kesvani** is a journalist and co-host of the comedy podcast Trashfuture ● **Bruce B Lawrence** is Marcus Family Professor of Islamic Studies Emeritus, Duke University ● **Shazia Mirza** is a comedian ● **Deena Mohamed**, Egyptian illustrator and designer, won the Grand Prize of the Cairo Comix Festival in 2017 ● **Samia Rahman** is still the Director of the Muslim Institute ● **Gilbert Ramsay** is a lecturer at the University of St Andrews Centre for the Study of Terrorism and Political Violence ● **Shanon Shah** once had an alter ego, Kak Nora, an agony aunt who dispensed absurd yet creative political advice in the now-defunct Malaysian website *The Nut Graph* ● **Boyd Tonkin**, writer and literary critic, is a regular contributor to *Critical Muslim* ● **Eric Walberg** is a Toronto based journalist and writer ● **Medina Tenour Whiteman** is a writer and musician, among many other talents ● **Hodan Yusuf** is a poet, actress and playwright.